Learning

SIMULINK® 6

MATLAB®
& SIMULINK®
STUDENT VERSION

The MathWorks

How to Contact The MathWorks:

www.mathworks.com	Web
comp.soft-sys.matlab	Newsgroup

suggest@mathworks.com	Product enhancement suggestions
bugs@mathworks.com	Bug reports
doc@mathworks.com	Documentation error reports

ISBN 0-9755787-190000

Learning Simulink

Printing History:	August 1999	First printing	New manual
	January 2001	Second printing	Revised for Simulink 4.0 (Release 12)
	November 2002	Third printing	Revised for Simulink 5.0 (Release 13)
	July 2004	Fourth printing	Revised for Simulink 6.0 (Release 14)

Contents

**Introducing the
MATLAB & Simulink Student Version**

1

Getting Started

2

How Simulink Works

3

Simulink Basics

4

Creating a Model

5

Working with Blocks

6

Working with Signals

7

Running Simulations

8

Exploring, Searching, and Browsing Models

9

Creating Masked Subsystems

10

Simulink Debugger

11

Block Libraries

A

Index

Introducing the MATLAB & Simulink Student Version

This chapter introduces the MATLAB & Simulink Student Version and provides resources for using it.

About the Student Version (p. 1-2)	Describes the MATLAB & Simulink Student Version.
Obtaining Additional MathWorks Products (p. 1-4)	How to acquire other products that work with the MATLAB & Simulink Student Version.
Getting Started with Simulink (p. 1-5)	Basic steps for using Simulink.
Finding Reference Information (p. 1-6)	Techniques for learning more about Simulink.
Troubleshooting (p. 1-7)	Getting information and reporting problems.
Other Resources (p. 1-8)	Additional sources of information for the MATLAB & Simulink Student Version.
Differences Between the Student and Professional Versions (p. 1-10)	Product differences.

About the Student Version

MATLAB® and Simulink® are the premier software packages for technical computing in education and industry. The MATLAB & Simulink Student Version provides all of the features of professional MATLAB, with no limitations, and the full functionality of professional Simulink, with model sizes up to 1000 blocks. The Student Version gives you immediate access to high-performance numeric computing, modeling, and simulation power.

MATLAB allows you to focus on your course work and applications rather than on programming details. It enables you to solve many numerical problems in a fraction of the time it would take you to write a program in a lower-level language such as C, C++, or Fortran. MATLAB helps you better understand and apply concepts in applications ranging from engineering and mathematics to chemistry, biology, and economics.

Simulink is an interactive tool for modeling, simulating, and analyzing dynamic systems, including controls, signal processing, communications, and other complex systems.

The Symbolic Math Toolbox, also included with the Student Version, is based on the Maple® 8 symbolic math engine and lets you perform symbolic computations and variable-precision arithmetic.

MATLAB products are used in a broad range of industries, including automotive, aerospace, electronics, environmental, telecommunications, computer peripherals, finance, and medicine. More than one million technical professionals at the world's most innovative technology companies, government research labs, financial institutions, and at more than 3,500 universities, rely on MATLAB and Simulink as the fundamental tools for their engineering and scientific work.

Student Use Policy

This MATLAB & Simulink Student Version License is for use in conjunction with courses offered at degree-granting institutions. The MathWorks offers this license as a special service to the student community and asks your help in seeing that its terms are not abused.

To use this Student License, you must be a student either enrolled in a degree-granting institution or participating in a continuing education program at a degree-granting educational university.

You may not use this Student License at a company or government lab. Also, you may not use it for commercial or industrial purposes. In these cases, you can acquire the appropriate professional version of the software by contacting The MathWorks.

Obtaining Additional MathWorks Products

Many college courses recommend MATLAB as standard instructional software. In some cases, the courses may require particular toolboxes, blocksets, or other products. Toolboxes and blocksets are add-on products that extend MATLAB and Simulink with domain-specific capabilities. Many of these products are available for student use. You may purchase and download these additional products at special student prices from the MathWorks Store at www.mathworks.com/store.

Some of the products you can purchase include

- Bioinformatics Toolbox
- Communications Blockset
- Control System Toolbox
- Fixed-Point Toolbox
- Fuzzy Logic Toolbox
- Image Processing Toolbox
- Neural Network Toolbox
- Optimization Toolbox
- Signal Processing Toolbox
- Statistics Toolbox
- Stateflow® (A demo version of Stateflow is included with your MATLAB & Simulink Student Version.)

For an up-to-date list of available products and their product dependencies, visit the MathWorks Store.

Note The toolboxes and blocksets that are available for the MATLAB & Simulink Student Version have the same functionality as the professional versions. The only restrictions are those described in "Differences Between the Student and Professional Versions" on page 1-10. Also, the student versions of the toolboxes and blocksets will work only with the Student Version. Likewise, the professional versions of the toolboxes and blocksets will not work with the Student Version.

Getting Started with Simulink

What I Want	What I Should Do
I need to install Simulink.	See Chapter 2, "Installing MATLAB Student Version," in the Learning MATLAB book.
I want to start Simulink.	On all operating systems, your MATLAB & Simulink Student Version CD must be in your CD-ROM drive to start MATLAB.
	(Microsoft Windows) Double-click the MATLAB icon on your desktop. Click the Simulink icon on the toolbar to start Simulink.
	(Macintosh OS X) Double-click the MATLAB icon on your desktop. Click the Simulink icon on the toolbar to start Simulink.
	(Linux) Enter the matlab command at the command prompt. Click the Simulink icon on the toolbar to start Simulink.
I'm new to Simulink and want to learn it quickly.	Start by reading Learning Simulink. You'll learn how to model, simulate, and analyze dynamic systems. Since Simulink is graphical and interactive, this book encourages you to use it quickly. You can access the rest of the Simulink documentation through the online help facility (Help).
I want to look at some samples of what you can do with Simulink.	There are numerous demonstrations included with Simulink. You can see the demos by clicking **Demos** in the Help browser or selecting **Demos** from the **Help** menu. There are Simulink demos for simple models, complex models, and other related products. You also will find a large selection of demos at www.mathworks.com/demos.

Finding Reference Information

What I Want	What I Should Do
I want to know how to use a specific Simulink block.	Use the online help facility (Help). The Simulink blocks are described under Simulink (**Simulink -> Blocks — Categorical List** or **Simulink -> Blocks — Alphabetical List**).
I want to find a block for a specific purpose, but I don't know the block name.	There are several choices: • From Help, browse **Blocks — Alphabetical List** or **Blocks — Categorical List** under **Simulink**. • Use **Index** or **Search** from Help.
I want to know what blocks are available in a general area.	Use Help to view **Blocks — Categorical List** under **Simulink**. Help provides access to the reference pages for the blocks included with Simulink.

Troubleshooting

What I Want	What I Should Do
I have a specific Simulink problem I want help with.	From Help, select **Support and Web Services** and then choose **Technical Support**.
I want to report a bug or make a suggestion.	Use Help or send e-mail to bugs@mathworks.com or suggest@mathworks.com.

Other Resources

Documentation

When you install the MATLAB & Simulink Student Version on your computer, you automatically install the complete online documentation for these products. Access this documentation set from Help.

Note References to UNIX in the documentation include both Linux and Mac OS X.

Web-Based Documentation

Documentation for all MathWorks products is online and available from the Support area of the MathWorks Web site. In addition to tutorials and function reference pages, you can find PDF versions of all the manuals.

MathWorks Web Site

At www.mathworks.com, you'll find information about MathWorks products and how they are used in education and industry, product demos, and MATLAB and Simulink based books.

MathWorks Academia Web Site

At www.mathworks.com/academia, you'll find resources for various branches of engineering, mathematics, and science.

MATLAB and Simulink Based Books

At www.mathworks.com/support/books, you'll find an up-to-date list of MATLAB and Simulink based books.

MathWorks Store

At www.mathworks.com/store, you can purchase add-on products and documentation.

MATLAB Central — File Exchange/Newsgroup Access

At www.mathworks.com/matlabcentral, you can access the MATLAB Usenet newsgroup (comp.soft-sys.matlab) as well as an extensive library of user-contributed files called the MATLAB Central File Exchange. MATLAB Central is also home to the Link Exchange where you can share your favorite links to various educational, personal, and commercial MATLAB Web sites.

The comp.soft-sys.matlab newsgroup is for professionals and students who use MATLAB and have questions or comments about it and its associated software. This is an important resource for posing questions and answering those of others. MathWorks staff also participates actively in this newsgroup.

Technical Support

At www.mathworks.com/support, you can get technical support.

Telephone and e-mail access to our technical support staff is not available for students running the MATLAB & Simulink Student Version unless you are experiencing difficulty installing or downloading MATLAB or related products. There are numerous other vehicles of technical support that you can use. The "Additional Sources of Information" section in the CD holder identifies the ways to obtain support.

After checking the available MathWorks sources for help, if you still cannot resolve your problem, please contact your instructor. Your instructor should be able to help you, but if not, there is telephone and e-mail technical support for registered instructors who have adopted the MATLAB & Simulink Student Version in their courses.

Product Registration

At www.mathworks.com/academia/student_version/register.html, you can register your MATLAB & Simulink Student Version.

Differences Between the Student and Professional Versions

MATLAB

The Student Version provides full support for all MATLAB language features as well as graphics, external interface and Application Program Interface (API) support, and access to every other feature of the professional version of MATLAB.

MATLAB Differences

There are a few small differences between the Student Version and the professional version of MATLAB:

- The MATLAB prompt in the Student Version is

  EDU>>

- The window title bars include the words

  <Student Version>

- All printouts contain the footer

  Student Version of MATLAB

  This footer will always appear in your printouts.

- The **Check for Updates** menu option on the desktop tools is not available in the Student Version.
- The MATLAB & Simulink Student Version CD must be in your CD-ROM drive to start MATLAB. Once MATLAB starts, you can remove the CD.

Simulink

The Student Version contains the complete Simulink product, which is used with MATLAB to model, simulate, and analyze dynamic systems.

Simulink Differences

- Models are limited to 1000 blocks.

Note You may encounter some demos that use more than 1000 blocks. In these cases, a dialog will display stating that the block limit has been exceeded and the demo will not run.

- The window title bars include the words
  <Student Version>

- All printouts contain the footer

  Student Version of MATLAB

  This footer will always appear in your printouts.

Note The Using Simulink documentation, which is accessible from the Help browser, contains all of the information in the Learning Simulink book plus additional advanced information.

Symbolic Math Toolbox

The Symbolic Math Toolbox included with this Student Version lets you access all of the functions in the professional version of the Symbolic Math Toolbox except maple, mapleinit, mfun, mfunlist, and mhelp. For more information about the Symbolic Math Toolbox, see its documentation.

Getting Started

The following sections use examples to give you a quick introduction to using Simulink® to model and simulate dynamic systems.

What Is Simulink?

Simulink® is a software package for modeling, simulating, and analyzing dynamic systems. It supports linear and nonlinear systems, modeled in continuous time, sampled time, or a hybrid of the two. Systems can also be multirate, i.e., have different parts that are sampled or updated at different rates.

Tool for Interactive Simulation

Simulink encourages you to try things out. You can easily build models from scratch, or take an existing model and add to it. Simulations are interactive, so you can change parameters on the fly and immediately see what happens. You have instant access to all the analysis tools in MATLAB®, so you can take the results and analyze and visualize them. A goal of Simulink is to give you a sense of the *fun* of modeling and simulation, through an environment that encourages you to pose a question, model it, and see what happens.

Simulink is also practical. With thousands of engineers around the world using it to model and solve real problems, knowledge of this tool will serve you well throughout your professional career.

Tool for Model-Based Design

With Simulink, you can move beyond idealized linear models to explore more realistic nonlinear models, factoring in friction, air resistance, gear slippage, hard stops, and the other things that describe real-world phenomena. Simulink turns your computer into a lab for modeling and analyzing systems that simply wouldn't be possible or practical otherwise, whether the behavior of an automotive clutch system, the flutter of an airplane wing, the dynamics of a predator-prey model, or the effect of the monetary supply on the economy.

For modeling, Simulink provides a graphical user interface (GUI) for building models as block diagrams, using click-and-drag mouse operations. With this interface, you can draw the models just as you would with pencil and paper (or as most textbooks depict them). This is a far cry from previous simulation packages that require you to formulate differential equations and difference equations in a language or program. Simulink includes a comprehensive block library of sinks, sources, linear and nonlinear components, and connectors. You can also customize and create your own blocks. For information on creating your own blocks, see the separate *Writing S-Functions* guide.

Models are hierarchical, so you can build models using both top-down and bottom-up approaches. You can view the system at a high level, then double-click blocks to go down through the levels to see increasing levels of model detail. This approach provides insight into how a model is organized and how its parts interact.

After you define a model, you can simulate it, using a choice of integration methods, either from the Simulink menus or by entering commands in the MATLAB Command Window. The menus are particularly convenient for interactive work, while the command-line approach is very useful for running a batch of simulations (for example, if you are doing Monte Carlo simulations or want to sweep a parameter across a range of values). Using scopes and other display blocks, you can see the simulation results while the simulation is running. In addition, you can change parameters and immediately see what happens, for "what if" exploration. The simulation results can be put in the MATLAB workspace for postprocessing and visualization.

Model analysis tools include linearization and trimming tools, which can be accessed from the MATLAB command line, plus the many tools in MATLAB and its application toolboxes. And because MATLAB and Simulink are integrated, you can simulate, analyze, and revise your models in either environment at any point.

Related Products

The MathWorks provides several products that are especially relevant to the kinds of tasks you can perform with Simulink and that extend the capabilities of Simulink. For information about these related products, see
http://www.mathworks.com/products/simulink/related.html.

Running a Demo Model

An interesting demo program provided with Simulink models the thermodynamics of a house. To run this demo, follow these steps:

1 Start MATLAB. See your MATLAB documentation if you're not sure how to do this.

2 Run the demo model by typing `thermo` in the MATLAB Command Window. This command starts up Simulink and creates a model window that contains this model.

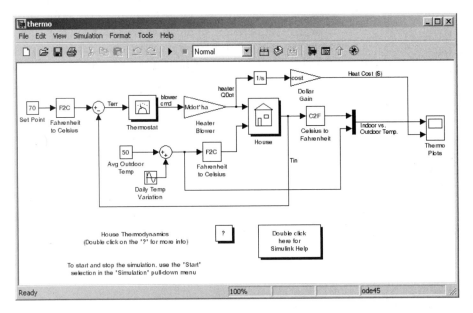

3 Double-click the Scope block labeled Thermo Plots.

The Scope block displays two plots labeled Indoor vs. Outdoor Temp and Heat Cost ($), respectively.

4 To start the simulation, pull down the **Simulation** menu and choose the **Start** command (or, on Microsoft Windows, click the **Start** button on the Simulink toolbar). As the simulation runs, the indoor and outdoor temperatures appear in the Indoor vs. Outdoor Temp plot and the cumulative heating cost appears in the Heat Cost ($) plot.

5 To stop the simulation, choose the **Stop** command from the **Simulation** menu (or click the **Pause** button on the toolbar). If you want to explore other parts of the model, look over the suggestions in "Some Things to Try" on page 2-6.

6 When you're finished running the simulation, close the model by choosing **Close** from the **File** menu.

Description of the Demo

The demo models the thermodynamics of a house. The thermostat is set to 70 degrees Fahrenheit and is affected by the outside temperature, which varies by applying a sine wave with amplitude of 15 degrees to a base temperature of 50 degrees. This simulates daily temperature fluctuations.

The model uses subsystems to simplify the model diagram and create reusable systems. A subsystem is a group of blocks that is represented by a Subsystem block. This model contains five subsystems: one named Thermostat, one named House, and three Temp Convert subsystems (two convert Fahrenheit to Celsius, one converts Celsius to Fahrenheit).

The internal and external temperatures are fed into the House subsystem, which updates the internal temperature. Double-click the House block to see the underlying blocks in that subsystem.

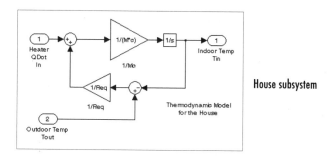

House subsystem

The Thermostat subsystem models the operation of a thermostat, determining when the heating system is turned on and off. Double-click the block to see the underlying blocks in that subsystem.

 Thermostat subsystem

Both the outside and inside temperatures are converted from Fahrenheit to Celsius by identical subsystems.

 Fahrenheit to Celsius conversion (F2C)

When the heat is on, the heating costs are computed and displayed on the Heat Cost ($) plot on the Thermo Plots Scope. The internal temperature is displayed on the Indoor Temp Scope.

Some Things to Try

Here are several things to try to see how the model responds to different parameters:

- Each Scope block contains one or more signal display areas and controls that enable you to select the range of the signal displayed, zoom in on a portion of the signal, and perform other useful tasks. The horizontal axis represents time and the vertical axis represents the signal value.

- The Constant block labeled Set Point (at the top left of the model) sets the desired internal temperature. Open this block and reset the value to 80 degrees. See how the indoor temperature and heating costs change. Also, adjust the outside temperature (the Avg Outdoor Temp block) and see how it affects the simulation.

- Adjust the daily temperature variation by opening the Sine Wave block labeled Daily Temp Variation and changing the **Amplitude** parameter.

What This Demo Illustrates

This demo illustrates several tasks commonly used when you are building models:

- Running the simulation involves specifying parameters and starting the simulation with the **Start** command, described in "Diagnosing Simulation Errors" on page 8-68.
- You can encapsulate complex groups of related blocks in a single block, called a subsystem. See "Creating Subsystems" on page 5-20 for more information.
- You can customize the appearance of and design a dialog box for a block by using the masking feature, described in detail in Chapter 10, "Creating Masked Subsystems." The thermo model uses the masking feature to customize the appearance of all the Subsystem blocks that it contains.
- Scope blocks display graphic output much as an actual oscilloscope does.

Other Useful Demos

Other demos illustrate useful modeling concepts. You can access these demos from the MATLAB Command Window:

1 Click the **Start** button on the bottom left corner of the MATLAB Command Window.

The **Start** menu appears.

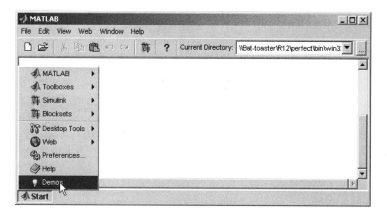

2 Select **Demos** from the menu.

The MATLAB Help browser appears with the **Demos** pane selected.

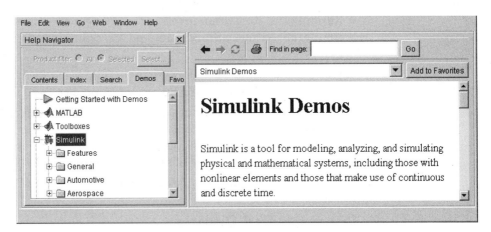

3 Click the **Simulink** entry in the **Demos** pane.

The entry expands to show groups of Simulink demos. Use the browser to navigate to demos of interest. The browser displays explanations of each demo and includes a link to the demo itself. Click on a demo link to start the demo.

Building a Model

This example shows you how to build a model using many of the model-building commands and actions you will use to build your own models. The instructions for building this model in this section are brief. All the tasks are described in more detail in the next chapter.

The model integrates a sine wave and displays the result along with the sine wave. The block diagram of the model looks like this.

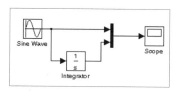

To create the model, first enter simulink in the MATLAB Command Window. On Microsoft Windows, the Simulink Library Browser appears.

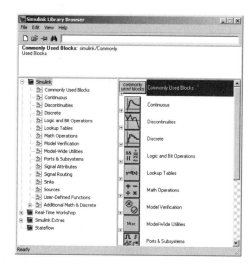

On the Macintosh or Linux, the Simulink library window appears.

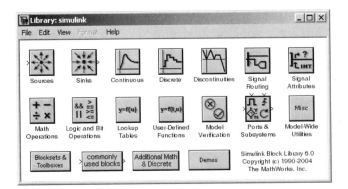

To create a new model on the Macintosh or Linux, select **Model** from the **New** submenu of the Simulink library window's **File** menu. To create a new model on Windows, click the New Model button on the Library Browser's toolbar.

New model button

Simulink opens a new model window.

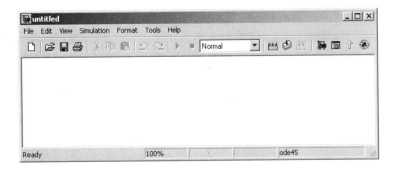

To create this model, you need to copy blocks into the model from the following Simulink block libraries:

- Sources library (the Sine Wave block)
- Sinks library (the Scope block)
- Continuous library (the Integrator block)
- Signal Routing library (the Mux block)

You can copy a Sine Wave block from the Sources library, using the Library Browser (Windows only) or the Sources library window (the Macintosh and Linux and Windows).

To copy the Sine Wave block from the Library Browser, first expand the Library Browser tree to display the blocks in the Sources library. Do this by clicking the Sources node to display the Sources library blocks. Finally, click the Sine Wave node to select the Sine Wave block.

Here is how the Library Browser should look after you have done this.

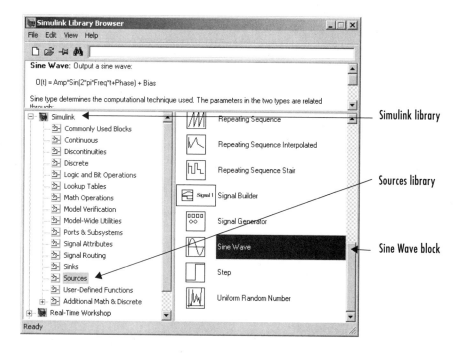

Now drag a copy of the Sine Wave block from the browser and drop it in the model window.

To copy the Sine Wave block from the Sources library window, open the Sources window by double-clicking the Sources icon in the Simulink library window. (On Windows, you can open the Simulink library window by right-clicking the Simulink node in the Library Browser and then clicking the resulting **Open Library** button.)

Simulink displays the Sources library window.

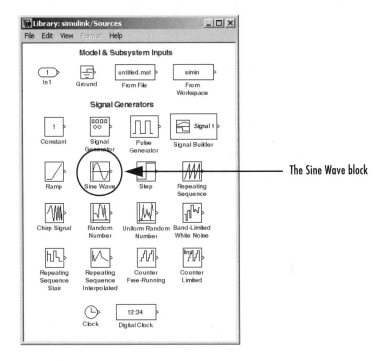

The Sine Wave block

Now drag the Sine Wave block from the Sources window to your model window.

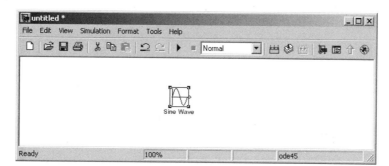

Copy the rest of the blocks in a similar manner from their respective libraries into the model window. You can move a block from one place in the model window to another by dragging the block. You can move a block a short distance by selecting the block, then pressing the arrow keys.

With all the blocks copied into the model window, the model should look something like this.

If you examine the blocks, you see an angle bracket on the right of the Sine Wave block and two on the left of the Mux block. The > symbol pointing out of a block is an *output port*; if the symbol points to a block, it is an *input port*. A signal travels out of an output port and into an input port of another block through a connecting line. When the blocks are connected, the port symbols disappear.

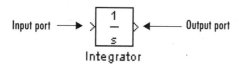

Now it's time to connect the blocks. Connect the Sine Wave block to the top input port of the Mux block. Position the pointer over the output port on the right side of the Sine Wave block. Notice that the cursor shape changes to crosshairs.

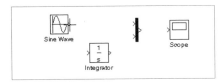

Hold down the mouse button and move the cursor to the top input port of the Mux block.

Notice that the line is dashed while the mouse button is down and that the cursor shape changes to double-lined crosshairs as it approaches the Mux block.

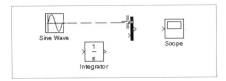

Now release the mouse button. The blocks are connected. You can also connect the line to the block by releasing the mouse button while the pointer is over the block. If you do, the line is connected to the input port closest to the cursor's position.

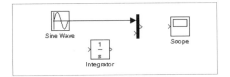

If you look again at the model at the beginning of this section (see "Building a Model" on page 2-9), you'll notice that most of the lines connect output ports of blocks to input ports of other blocks. However, one line connects a *line* to the input port of another block. This line, called a *branch line*, connects the Sine Wave output to the Integrator block, and carries the same signal that passes from the Sine Wave block to the Mux block.

Drawing a branch line is slightly different from drawing the line you just drew. To weld a connection to an existing line, follow these steps:

1 First, position the pointer *on the line* between the Sine Wave and the Mux block.

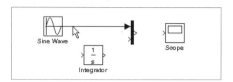

2 Press and hold down the **Ctrl** key (or click the right mouse button). Press the mouse button, then drag the pointer to the Integrator block's input port or over the Integrator block itself.

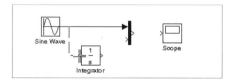

3 Release the mouse button. Simulink draws a line between the starting point and the Integrator block's input port.

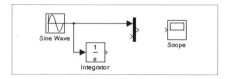

Finish making block connections. When you're done, your model should look something like this.

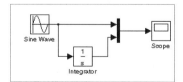

Now set up Simulink to run the simulation for 10 seconds. First, open the **Configuration Parameters** dialog box by choosing **Configuration Parameters** from the **Simulation** menu. On the dialog box that appears, notice that the **Stop time** is set to 10.0 (its default value).

Stop time parameter

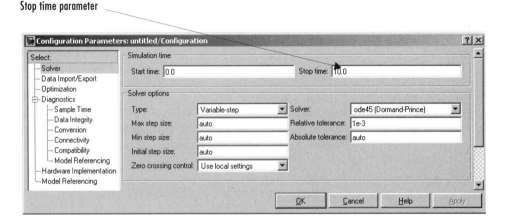

Close the **Configuration Parameters** dialog box by clicking the **OK** button. Simulink applies the parameters and closes the dialog box.

Now double-click the Scope block to open its display window. Finally, choose **Start** from the **Simulation** menu and watch the simulation output on the Scope.

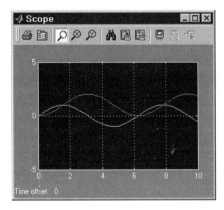

The simulation stops when it reaches the stop time specified in the **Configuration Parameters** dialog box or when you choose **Stop** from the **Simulation** menu or click the **Stop** button on the model window's toolbar (Windows only).

To save this model, choose **Save** from the **File** menu and enter a filename and location. That file contains the description of the model.

To terminate Simulink and MATLAB, choose **Exit MATLAB** (on a Microsoft Windows system) or **Quit MATLAB** (on a Macintosh or Linux system). You can also enter quit in the MATLAB Command Window. If you want to leave Simulink but not terminate MATLAB, just close all Simulink windows.

This exercise shows you how to perform some commonly used model-building tasks. These and other tasks are described in more detail in Chapter 5, "Creating a Model."

Setting Simulink Preferences

The MATLAB **Preferences** dialog box allows you to specify default settings for some Simulink options. To display the **Preferences** dialog box, select **Preferences** from the Simulink **File** menu.

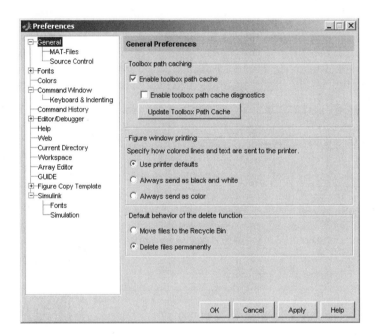

Miscellaneous Preferences

Selecting Simulink in the left hand pane of the preferences dialog box displays a **Simulink Preferences** pane on the right side of the dialog box.

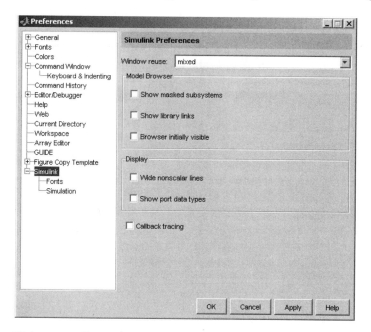

This pane allows you to specify the following Simulink preferences.

Window reuse

Specifies whether Simulink uses existing windows or opens new windows to display a model's subsystems (see "Window Reuse" on page 5-23).

Model Browser

Specifies whether Simulink displays the browser when you open a model and whether the browser shows blocks imported from subsystems and the contents of masked subsystems (see "The Model Browser" on page 9-22).

Display

Specifies whether to use thick lines to display nonscalar connections between blocks and whether to display port data types on the block diagram

Callback tracing

Specifies whether to display the model callbacks that Simulink invokes when simulating a model (see "Using Callback Routines" on page 5-38).

Font Preferences

Selecting the Fonts subnode of the Simulink node in the left side of the dialog box displays a stack of tabbed panes on the right side of the dialog box.

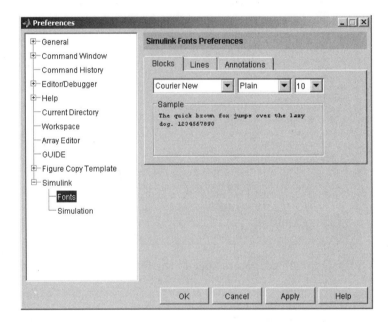

The panes allow you to specify your preferred fonts for block and line labels and model annotations, respectively.

Simulation Preferences

Selecting the Simulation node beneath the Simulink node in the left side of the dialog box displays a button to start the Model Explorer (see "The Model Explorer" on page 9-2).

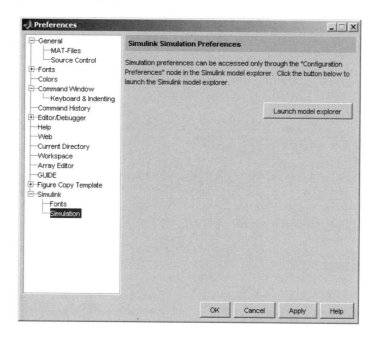

Use the Model Explorer to set your simulation preferences.

How Simulink Works

The following sections explain how Simulink models and simulates dynamic systems. This information can be helpful in creating models and interpreting simulation results.

Introduction

Simulink is a software package that enables you to model, simulate, and analyze systems whose outputs change over time. Such systems are often referred to as dynamic systems. Simulink can be used to explore the behavior of a wide range of real-world dynamic systems, including electrical circuits, shock absorbers, braking systems, and many other electrical, mechanical, and thermodynamic systems. This section explains how Simulink works.

Simulating a dynamic system is a two-step process with Simulink. First, a user creates a block diagram, using the Simulink model editor, that graphically depicts time-dependent mathematical relationships among the system's inputs, states, and outputs. The user then commands Simulink to simulate the system represented by the model from a specified start time to a specified stop time.

Modeling Dynamic Systems

A Simulink block diagram model is a graphical representation of a mathematical model of a dynamic system. A mathematical model of a dynamic system is described by a set of equations. The mathematical equations described by a block diagram model are known as algebraic, differential, and/or difference equations.

Block Diagram Semantics

A classic block diagram model of a dynamic system graphically consists of blocks and lines (signals). The history of these block diagram model is derived from engineering areas such as Feedback Control Theory and Signal Processing. A block within a block diagram defines a dynamic system in itself. The relationships between each elementary dynamic system in a block diagram are illustrated by the use of signals connecting the blocks. Collectively the blocks and lines in a block diagram describe an overall dynamic system.

Simulink extends these classic block diagram models by introducing the notion of two classes of blocks, nonvirtual block and virtual blocks. Nonvirtual blocks represent elementary systems. A virtual block is provided for graphical organizational convenience and plays no role in the definition of the system of equations described by the block diagram model. Examples of virtual blocks are the Bus Creator and Bus Selector which are used to reduce block diagram clutter by managing groups of signals as a "bundle." You can use virtual blocks to improve the readability of your models.

In general, block and lines can be used to describe many "models of computations." One example would be a flow chart. A flow chart consists of blocks and lines, but one cannot describe general dynamic systems using flow chart semantics.

The term "time-based block diagram" is used to distinguish block diagrams that describe dynamic systems from that of other forms of block diagrams. In Simulink, we use the term block diagram (or model) to refer to a time-based block diagram unless the context requires explicit distinction.

To summarize the meaning of time-based block diagrams:

• Simulink block diagrams define time-based relationships between signals and state variables. The solution of a block diagram is obtained by evaluating these relationships over time, where time starts at a user specified "start time" and ends at a user specified "stop time." Each evaluation of these relationships is referred to as a time step.

- Signals represent quantities that change over time and are defined for all points in time between the block diagram's start and stop time.

- The relationships between signals and state variables are defined by a set of equations represented by blocks. Each block consists of a set of equations (block methods). These equations define a relationship between the input signals, output signals and the state variables. Inherent in the definition of a equation is the notion of parameters, which are the coefficients found within the equation.

Creating Models

Simulink provides a graphical editor that allows you to create and connect instances of block types (see Chapter 5, "Creating a Model") selected from libraries of block types (see the "Block Reference" in the online Simulink Help) via a library browser. Simulink provides libraries of blocks representing elementary systems that can be used a building blocks. The blocks supplied with Simulink are called built-in blocks. Simulink users can also create their own block types and use the Simulink editor to create instances of them in a diagram. Customer-defined blocks are called custom blocks.

Time

Time is an inherit component of block diagrams in that the results of a block diagram simulation change with time. Put another way, a block diagram represents the instantaneous behavior of a dynamic system. Determining a system's behavior over time thus entails repeatedly executing the model at intervals, called time steps, from the start of the time span to the end of the time span. Simulink refers to the repeated execution of a model at successive time steps as simulating the system that the model represents. It is possible to simulate a system manually, i.e., to execute its model manually. However, this is unnecessary as the Simulink engine performs this task automatically on command from the user.

States

Typically the current values of some system, and hence model, outputs are functions of the previous values of temporal variables. Such variables are called states. Computing a model's outputs from a block diagram hence entails saving the value of states at the current time step for use in computing the outputs at a subsequent time step. Simulink performs this task during simulation for models that define states.

Two types of states can occur in a Simulink model: discrete and continuous states. A continuous state changes continuously. Examples of continuous states are the position and speed of a car. A discrete state is an approximation of a continuous state where the state is updated (recomputed) using finite (periodic or aperiodic) intervals. An example of a discrete state would be the position of a car shown on a digital odometer where it is updated every second as opposed to continuously. In the limit, as the discrete state time interval approaches zero, a discrete state becomes equivalent to a continuous state.

Blocks implicitly define a model's states. In particular, a block that needs some or all of its previous outputs to compute its current outputs implicitly defines a set of states that need to be saved between time steps. Such a block is said to have states.

The following is a graphical representation of a block that has states.

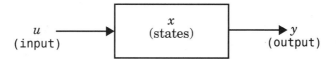

Blocks that define continuous states include the following standard Simulink blocks:

- Integrator
- State-Space
- Transfer Fcn
- Zero-Pole

The total number of a model's states is the sum of all the states defined by all its blocks. Determining the number of states in a diagram requires parsing the diagram to determine the types of blocks that it contains and then aggregating the number of states defined by each instance of a block type that defines states. Simulink performs this task during the Compilation phase of a simulation.

Continuous States

Computing a continuous state entails knowing its rate of change, or derivative. Since the rate of change of a continuous state typically itself changes continuously (i.e., is itself a state), computing the value of a continuous state at the current time step entails integration of its derivative from the start of a simulation. Thus modeling a continuous state entails representing the operation of integration and the process of computing the state's derivative at each point in time. Simulink block diagrams use Integrator blocks to indicate integration and a chain of operator blocks connected to the integrator block to represent the method for computing the state's derivative. The chain of block's connected to the Integrator's is the graphical counterpart to an ordinary differential equation (ODE).

In general, excluding simple dynamic systems, analytical methods do not exist for integrating the states of real-world dynamic systems represented by ordinary differential equations. Integrating the states requires the use of numerical methods called ODE solvers. These various methods trade computational accuracy for computational workload. Simulink comes with computerized implementations of the most common ODE integration methods and allows a user to determine which it uses to integrate states represented by Integrator blocks when simulating a system.

Computing the value of a continuous state at the current time step entails integrating its values from the start of the simulation. The accuracy of numerical integration in turn depends on the size of the intervals between time steps. In general, the smaller the time step, the more accurate the simulation. Some ODE solvers, called variable time step solvers, can automatically vary the size of the time step, based on the rate of change of the state, to achieve a specified level of accuracy over the course of a simulation. Simulink allows the user to specify the size of the time step in the case of fixed-step solvers or allow the solver to determine the step size in the case of variable-step solvers. To minimize the computation workload, the variable-step solver chooses the largest step size consistent with achieving an overall level of precision specified by the user for the most rapidly changing model state. This ensures that all model states are computed to the accuracy specified by the user.

Discrete States

Computing a discrete state requires knowing the relationship between the current time and its value at the time at which it previously changed value. Simulink refers to this relationship as the state's update function. A discrete state depends not only on its value at the previous time step but also on the values of a model's inputs. Modeling a discrete state thus entails modeling the state's dependency on the systems' inputs at the previous time step. Simulink block diagrams use specific types of blocks, called discrete blocks, to specify update functions and chains of blocks connected to the inputs of the block's to model the state's dependency on system inputs.

As with continuous states, discrete states set a constraint on the simulation time step size. Specifically a step size must be chosen that ensure that all the sample times of the model's states are hit. Simulink assigns this task to a component of the Simulink system called a discrete solver. Simulink provides two discrete solvers: a fixed-step discrete solver and a variable-step discrete solver. The fixed-step discrete solver determines a fixed step size that hits all the sample times of all the model's discrete states, regardless of whether the states actually change value at the sample time hits. By contrast, the variable-step discrete solver varies the step size to ensure that sample time hits occur only at times when the states change value.

Modeling Hybrid Systems

A hybrid system is a a system that has both discrete and continuous states Strictly speaking a hybrid model is identified as having continuous and discrete sample times from which it follows that the model will have continuous and discrete states. Solving a model of such a system entails choosing a step size that satisfies both the precision constraint on the continuous state integration and the sample time hit constraint on the discrete states. Simulink meets this requirement by passing the next sample time hit as determined by the discrete solver as an additional constraint on the continuous solver. The continuous solver must choose a step size that advances the simulation up to but not beyond the time of the next sample time hit. The continuous solver can take a time step short of the next sample time hit to meet its accuracy constraint but it cannot take a step beyond the next sample time hit even if its accuracy constraint allows it to.

Block Parameters

Key properties of many standard blocks are parameterized. For example, the Constant value of the Simulink Constant block is a parameter. Each parameterized block has a block dialog that lets you set the values of the parameters. You can use MATLAB expressions to specify parameter values. Simulink evaluates the expressions before running a simulation. You can change the values of parameters during a simulation. This allows you to determine interactively the most suitable value for a parameter.

A parameterized block effectively represents a family of similar blocks. For example, when creating a model, you can set the Constant value parameter of each instance of the Constant block separately so that each instance behaves differently. Because it allows each standard block to represent a family of blocks, block parameterization greatly increases the modeling power of the standard Simulink libraries.

Each time you change parameters, you change the meaning of the model. Simulink lets you modify the parameter values during execution of your model. For example, you can pause simulation, change parameter values, and continue simulation. It should be pointed out that parameter changes do not immediately occur, but are queued up and then applied at the start of the next time step during model execution. Returning to our example of the constant block, the function it defines is $signal(t) = Cons \tan t Value$ for all time. If we were to allow the constant value to be changed immediately, then the solution at the point in time at which the change occurred would be invalid, thus we must queue the change for processing on the next time step.

Tunable Parameters

Many block parameters are tunable. A *tunable parameter* is a parameter whose value can change while Simulink is executing a model. For example, the gain parameter of the Gain block is tunable. You can alter the block's gain while a simulation is running. If a parameter is not tunable and the simulation is running, Simulink disables the dialog box control that sets the parameter. Simulink allows you to specify that all parameters in your model are nontunable except for those that you specify. This can speed up execution of large models and enable generation of faster code from your model. See "Model Parameter Configuration Dialog Box" on page 8-46 for more information.

Block Sample Times

Every Simulink block is considered to have a sample time, even continuous blocks (e.g., blocks that define continuous states, such as the Integrator block) and blocks that do not define states, such as the Gain block. Discrete blocks allows you to specify their sample times via a Sample Time parameter. Continuous blocks are considered to have an infinitesimal sample time called a continuous sample time. A block that is neither discrete or continuous is said to have an implicit sample time that it inherits from its inputs. The implicit sample time is continuous if any of the block's inputs are continuous. Otherwise, the implicit sample time is discrete. An implicit discrete sample time is equal to the shortest input sample time if all the input sample times are integer multiples of the shortest time. Otherwise, the implicit sample time is equal to the *fundamental sample time* of the inputs, where the fundamental sample time of a set of sample times is defined as the greatest integer divisor of the set of sample times.

Simulink can optionally color code a block diagram to indicate the sample times of the blocks it contains, e.g., black (continuous), magenta (constant), yellow (hybrid), red (fastest discrete), and so on. See "Mixed Continuous and Discrete Systems" on page 3-40 for more information.

Custom Blocks

Simulink allows you to create libraries of custom blocks that you can then use in your models. You can create a custom block either graphically or programmatically. To create a custom block graphically, you draw a block diagram representing the block's behavior, wrap this diagram in an instance of the Simulink Subsystem block, and provide the block with a parameter dialog, using the Simulink block mask facility. To create a block programmatically, you create an M-file or a MEX-file that contains the block's system functions (see *Writing S-Functions* in the online Help for Simulink). The resulting file is called an S-function. You then associate the S-function with instances of the Simulink S-Function block in your model. You can add a parameter dialog to your S-Function block by wrapping it in a Subsystem block and adding the parameter dialog to the Subsystem block.

Systems and Subsystems

A Simulink block diagram can consist of layers. Each layer is defined by a subsystem. A subsystem is part of the overall block diagram and ideally has no impact on the meaning of the block diagram. Subsystems are provided primarily to help in the organization aspects a block diagram. Subsystem do not define a separate block diagram.

Simulink differentiates between two different types of subsystems virtual and nonvirtual subsystems. The main difference is that nonvirtual subsystems provide the ability to control when the contents of the subsystem are evaluated.

Flattening the Model Hierarchy

While preparing a model for execution, Simulink generates internal "systems" that are collections of block methods (equations) that are evaluated together. The semantics of time-based block diagrams doesn't require creation of these systems. Simulink creates these internal systems as a means to manage the execution of the model. Roughly speaking, there will be one system for the top-level block diagram window which is referred to as the root system, and several lower-level system derived from the nonvirtual subsystem and other elements within the block diagram. You will see these systems within the Simulink Debugger. The act of creating these "internal" systems is often referred to as flattening the model hierarchy.

Conditionally Executed Subsystems

You can create conditionally executed subsystems that are executed only when a transition occurs on a triggering, function-call, action, or enabling input (see "Creating Conditionally Executed Subsystems" on page 5-26).

Conditionally executed subsystems are atomic. Unconditionally executed subsystems are virtual by default. You can, however, designate an unconditionally executed subsystem as atomic. This is useful if you need to ensure that the equations defined by a subsystem are evaluated "together" as a unit.

Signals

Simulink uses the term *signal* to refer to a time varying quantity that has values at all points in time. Simulink allows you to specify a wide range of signal attributes, including signal name, data type (e.g., 8-bit, 16-bit, or 32-bit integer), numeric type (real or complex), and dimensionality (one-dimensional or two-dimensional array). Many blocks can accept or output signals of any data or numeric type and dimensionality. Others impose restrictions on the attributes of the signals they can handle.

On the block diagram, you will find that the signals are represented with lines that have an arrow head. The source of the signal corresponds to the block that writes to the signal during evaluation of its block methods (equations). The destinations of the signal are blocks that read the signal during the evaluation of its block methods (equations). A good analogy of the meaning of a signal is to consider a classroom. The teacher is the one responsible for writing on the white board and the students read what is written on the white board when they choose to. This is also true of Simulink signals, a reader of the signal (a block method) can choose to read the signal as frequently or infrequently as so desired.

Block Methods

Blocks represent multiple equations. These equations are represented as block methods within Simulink. These block methods are evaluated (executed) during the execution of a block diagram. The evaluation of these block methods is performed within a simulation loop, where each cycle through the simulation loop represent evaluation of the block diagram at a given point in time.

Method Types

Simulink assigns names to the types of functions performed by block methods. Common method types include:

- Outputs

  Computes the outputs of a block given its inputs at the current time step and its states at the previous time step.

- Update

  Computes the value of the block's discrete states at the current time step, given its inputs at the current time step and its discrete states at the previous time step.

- Derivatives

  Computes the derivatives of the block's continuous states at the current time step, given the block's inputs and the values of the states at the previous time step.

Method Naming Convention

Block methods perform the same types of operations in different ways for different types of blocks. The Simulink user interface and documentation uses dot notation to indicate the specific function performed by a block method:

```
BlockType.MethodType
```

For example, Simulink refers to the method that computes the outputs of a Gain block as

```
Gain.Outputs
```

The Simulink debugger takes the naming convention one step further and uses the instance name of a block to specify both the method type and the block instance on which the method is being invoked during simulation, e.g.,

```
g1.Outputs
```

Model Methods

In addition to block methods, Simulink also provides a set of methods that compute the model's properties and its outputs. Simulink similarly invokes these methods during simulation to determine a model's properties and its outputs. The model methods generally perform their tasks by invoking block methods of the same type. For example, the model Outputs method invokes the Outputs methods of the blocks that it contains in the order specified by the model to compute its outputs. The model Derivatives method similarly invokes the Derivatives methods of the blocks that it contains to determine the derivatives of its states.

Simulating Dynamic Systems

Simulating a dynamic system refers to the process of computing a system's states and outputs over a span of time, using information provided by the system's model. Simulink simulates a system when you choose **Start** from the model editor's **Simulation** menu, with the system's model open.

A Simulink component called the Simulink Engine responds to a Start command, performing the following steps.

Model Compilation

First, the Simulink engine invokes the model compiler. The model compiler converts the model to an executable form, a process called compilation. In particular, the compiler

- Evaluates the model's block parameter expressions to determine their values.
- Determines signal attributes, e.g., name, data type, numeric type, and dimensionality, not explicitly specified by the model and checks that each block can accept the signals connected to its inputs.
- Simulink uses a process called attribute propagation to determine unspecified attributes. This process entails propagating the attributes of a source signal to the inputs of the blocks that it drives.
- Performs block reduction optimizations.
- Flattens the model hierarchy by replacing virtual subsystems with the blocks that they contain (see "Solvers" on page 3-17).
- Sorts the blocks into the order in which they need to be executed during the execution phase (see "Solvers" on page 3-17).
- Determines the sample times of all blocks in the model whose sample times you did not explicitly specify.

Determining Block Update Order

During a simulation, Simulink updates the states and outputs of a model's blocks once per time step. The order in which the blocks are updated is therefore critical to the validity of the results. In particular, if a block's outputs are a function of its inputs at the current time step, the block must be updated after the blocks that drive its inputs. Otherwise, the block's outputs will be

invalid. Simulink sorts the blocks into the correct order during the model
initialization phase.

Direct-Feedthrough Ports. In order to create a valid update ordering, Simulink
categorizes a block's input ports according to the relationship of outputs to
inputs. An input port whose current value determines the current value of one
of the block's outputs is called a *direct-feedthrough* port. Examples of blocks
that have direct-feedthrough ports include the Gain, Product, and Sum blocks.
Examples of blocks that have non-direct-feedthrough inputs include the
Integrator block (its output is a function purely of its state), the Constant block
(it does not have an input), and the Memory block (its output is dependent on
its input in the previous time step).

Block Sorting Rules. Simulink uses the following basic update rules to sort the
blocks:

- Each block must be updated before any of the blocks whose
  direct-feedthrough ports it drives.

  This rule ensures that the direct-feedthrough inputs to blocks will be valid
  when the blocks are updated.

- Blocks that do not have direct feedthrough inputs can be updated in any
  order as long as they are updated before any blocks whose direct-feedthrough
  inputs they drive.

  Putting all blocks that do not have direct-feedthrough ports at the head of
  the update list in any order satisfies this rule. It thus allows Simulink to
  ignore these blocks during the sorting process.

The result of applying these rules is an update list in which blocks without
direct feedthrough ports appear at the head of the list in no particular order
followed by blocks with direct-feedthrough ports in the order required to supply
valid inputs to the blocks they drive.

During the sorting process, Simulink checks for and flags the occurrence of
algebraic loops, that is, signal loops in which a direct-feedthrough output of a
block is connected directly or indirectly to the corresponding
direct-feedthrough input of the block. Such loops seemingly create a deadlock
condition, because Simulink needs the value of the direct-feedthrough input to
compute the output. However, an algebraic loop can represent a set of
simultaneous algebraic equations (hence the name) where the block's input
and output are the unknowns. Further, these equations can have valid

solutions at each time step. Accordingly, Simulink assumes that loops involving direct-feedthrough ports do, in fact, represent a solvable set of algebraic equations and attempts to solve them each time the block is updated during a simulation. For more information, see "Algebraic Loops" on page 3-24.

Link Phase

In this phase, the Simulink Engine allocates memory needed for working areas (signals, states, and run-time parameters) for execution of the block diagram. It also allocates and initializes memory for data structures that store run-time information for each block. For built-in blocks, the principal run-time data structure for a block is called the SimBlock. It stores pointers to a block's input and output buffers and state and work vectors.

Method Execution Lists

In the Link phase, the Simulink engine also creates method execution lists. These lists list the most efficient order in which to execute a model's block methods to compute its outputs. Simulink uses the sorted lists generated during the Compile phase to construct the method execution lists.

Block Priorities

Simulink allows you to assign update priorities to blocks (see "Assigning Block Priorities" in the online Simulink documentation). Simulink executes the output methods of higher priority blocks before those of lower priority blocks. Simulink honors the priorities only if they are consistent with its block sorting rules.

Simulation Loop Phase

The simulation now enters the simulation loop phase. In this phase, the Simulink engine successively computes the states and outputs of the system at intervals from the simulation start time to the finish time, using information provided by the model. The successive time points at which the states and outputs are computed are called time steps. The length of time between steps is called the step size. The step size depends on the type of solver (see "Solvers" on page 3-17) used to compute the system's continuous states, the system's fundamental sample time (see "Modeling and Simulating Discrete Systems" on page 3-31), and whether the system's continuous states have discontinuities (see "Zero-Crossing Detection" on page 3-19).

The Simulation Loop phase has two subphases: the Loop Initialization phase and the Loop Iteration phase. The initialization phase occurs once, at the start of the loop. The iteration phase is repeated once per time step from the simulation start time to the simulation stop time.

At the start of the simulation, the model specifies the initial states and outputs of the system to be simulated. At each step, Simulink computes new values for the system's inputs, states, and outputs and updates the model to reflect the computed values. At the end of the simulation, the model reflects the final values of the system's inputs, states, and outputs. Simulink provides data display and logging blocks. You can display and/or log intermediate results by including these blocks in your model.

Loop Iteration

At each time step, the Simulink Engine

1 Computes the model's outputs.

   The Simulink Engine initiates this step by invoking the Simulink model Outputs method. The model Outputs method in turn invokes the model system Outputs method, which invokes the Outputs methods of the blocks that the model contains in the order specified by the Outputs method execution lists generated in the Link phase of the simulation (see "Solvers" on page 3-17).

   The system Outputs method passes the following arguments to each block Outputs method: a pointer to the block's data structure and to its SimBlock structure. The SimBlock data structures point to information that the Outputs method needs to compute the block's outputs, including the location of its input buffers and its output buffers.

2 Computes the model's states.

   The Simulink Engine computes a model's states by invoking a solver. Which solver it invokes depends on whether the model has no states, only discrete states, only continuous states, or both continuous and discrete states.

   If the model has only discrete states, the Simulink Engine invokes the discrete solver selected by the user. The solver computes the size of the time step needed to hit the model's sample times. It then invokes the Update method of the model. The model Update method invokes the Update method of its system, which invokes the Update methods of each of the blocks that the system contains in the order specified by the Update method lists generated in the Link phase.

If the model has only continuous states, the Simulink Engine invokes the continuous solver specified by the model. Depending on the solver, the solver either in turn calls the Derivatives method of the model once or enters a subcycle of minor time steps where the solver repeatedly calls the model's Outputs methods and Derivatives methods to compute the model's outputs and derivatives at successive intervals within the major time step. This is done to increase the accuracy of the state computation. The model Outputs method and Derivatives methods in turn invoke their corresponding system methods, which invoke the block Outputs and Derivatives in the order specified by the Outputs and Derivatives methods execution lists generated in the Link phase.

3 Optionally checks for discontinuities in the continuous states of blocks.

Simulink uses a technique called zero-crossing detection to detect discontinuities in continuous states. See "Zero-Crossing Detection" on page 3-19 for more information.

4 Computes the time for the next time step.

Simulink repeats steps 1 through 4 until the simulation stop time is reached.

Solvers

Simulink simulates a dynamic system by computing its states at successive time steps over a specified time span, using information provided by the model. The process of computing the successive states of a system from its model is known as solving the model. No single method of solving a model suffices for all systems. Accordingly, Simulink provides a set of programs, known as *solvers*, that each embody a particular approach to solving a model. The **Configuration Parameters** dialog box allows you to choose the solver most suitable for your model (see "Choosing a Solver Type" on page 8-7).

Fixed-Step Solvers Versus Variable-Step Solvers

Simulink solvers fall into two basic categories: fixed-step and variable-step.

Fixed-step solvers solve the model at regular time intervals from the beginning to the end of the simulation. The size of the interval is known as the step size. You can specify the step size or let the solver choose the step size. Generally, decreasing the step size increases the accuracy of the results while increasing the time required to simulate the system.

Variable-step solvers vary the step size during the simulation, reducing the step size to increase accuracy when a model's states are changing rapidly and increasing the step size to avoid taking unnecessary steps when the model's states are changing slowly. Computing the step size adds to the computational overhead at each step but can reduce the total number of steps, and hence simulation time, required to maintain a specified level of accuracy for models with rapidly changing or piecewise continuous states.

Continuous Versus Discrete Solvers

Simulink provides both continuous and discrete solvers.

Continuous solvers use numerical integration to compute a model's continuous states at the current time step from the states at previous time steps and the state derivatives. Continuous solvers rely on the model's blocks to compute the values of the model's discrete states at each time step.

Mathematicians have developed a wide variety of numerical integration techniques for solving the ordinary differential equations (ODEs) that represent the continuous states of dynamic systems. Simulink provides an extensive set of fixed-step and variable-step continuous solvers, each implementing a specific ODE solution method (see "Choosing a Solver Type" on page 8-7).

Discrete solvers exist primarily to solve purely discrete models. They compute the next simulation time step for a model and nothing else. They do not compute continuous states and they rely on the model's blocks to update the model's discrete states.

Note You can use a continuous solver, but not a discrete solver, to solve a model that contains both continuous and discrete states. This is because a discrete solver does not handle continuous states. If you select a discrete solver for a continuous model, Simulink disregards your selection and uses a continuous solver instead when solving the model.

Simulink provides two discrete solvers, a fixed-step discrete solver and a variable-step discrete solver. The fixed-step solver by default chooses a step size and hence simulation rate fast enough to track state changes in the fastest block in your model. The variable-step solver adjusts the simulation step size to keep pace with the actual rate of discrete state changes in your model. This can avoid unnecessary steps and hence shorten simulation time for multirate models (see "Determining Step Size for Discrete Systems" on page 3-36 for more information).

Minor Time Steps

Some continuous solvers subdivide the simulation time span into major and minor time steps, where a minor time step represents a subdivision of the major time step. The solver produces a result at each major time step. It uses results at the minor time steps to improve the accuracy of the result at the major time step.

Zero-Crossing Detection

When simulating a dynamic system, Simulink checks for discontinuities in the system's state variables at each time step, using a technique known as zero-crossing detection. If Simulink detects a discontinuity within the current time step, it determines the precise time at which the discontinuity occurs and takes additional time steps before and after the discontinuity. This section explains why zero-crossing detection is important and how it works.

Discontinuities in state variables often coincide with significant events in the evolution of a dynamic system. For example, the instant when a bouncing ball hits the floor coincides with a discontinuity in its position. Because discontinuities often indicate a significant change in a dynamic system, it is important to simulate points of discontinuity precisely. Otherwise, a simulation could lead to false conclusions about the behavior of the system under investigation. Consider, for example, a simulation of a bouncing ball. If the point at which the ball hits the floor occurs between simulation steps, the simulated ball appears to reverse position in midair. This might lead an investigator to false conclusions about the physics of the bouncing ball.

To avoid such misleading conclusions, it is important that simulation steps occur at points of discontinuity. A simulator that relies purely on solvers to determine simulation times cannot efficiently meet this requirement. Consider, for example, a fixed-step solver. A fixed-step solver computes the values of state variables at integral multiples of a fixed step size. However, there is no guarantee that a point of discontinuity will occur at an integral multiple of the step size. You could reduce the step size to increase the probability of hitting a discontinuity, but this would greatly increase the execution time.

A variable-step solver appears to offer a solution. A variable-step solver adjusts the step size dynamically, increasing the step size when a variable is changing slowly and decreasing the step size when the variable changes rapidly. Around a discontinuity, a variable changes extremely rapidly. Thus, in theory, a variable-step solver should be able to hit a discontinuity precisely. The problem is that to locate a discontinuity accurately, a variable-step solver must again take many small steps, greatly slowing down the simulation.

How Zero-Crossing Detection Works

Simulink uses a technique known as zero-crossing detection to address this problem. With this technique, a block can register a set of zero-crossing variables with Simulink, each of which is a function of a state variable that can have a discontinuity. The zero-crossing function passes through zero from a positive or negative value when the corresponding discontinuity occurs. At the end of each simulation step, Simulink asks each block that has registered zero-crossing variables to update the variables. Simulink then checks whether any variable has changed sign since the last step. Such a change indicates that a discontinuity occurred in the current time step.

If any zero crossings are detected, Simulink interpolates between the previous and current values of each variable that changed sign to estimate the times of the zero crossings (e.g., discontinuities). Simulink then steps up to and over each zero crossing in turn. In this way, Simulink avoids simulating exactly at the discontinuity, where the value of the state variable might be undefined.

Zero-crossing detection enables Simulink to simulate discontinuities accurately without resorting to excessively small step sizes. Many Simulink blocks support zero-crossing detection. The result is fast and accurate simulation of all systems, including systems with discontinuities.

Implementation Details

An example of a Simulink block that uses zero crossings is the Saturation block. Zero crossings detect these state events in the Saturation block:

- The input signal reaches the upper limit.
- The input signal leaves the upper limit.
- The input signal reaches the lower limit.
- The input signal leaves the lower limit.

Simulink blocks that define their own state events are considered to have *intrinsic zero crossings*. If you need explicit notification of a zero-crossing event, use the Hit Crossing block. See "Blocks with Zero Crossings" on page 3-23 for a list of blocks that incorporate zero crossings.

The detection of a state event depends on the construction of an internal zero-crossing signal. This signal is not accessible by the block diagram. For the Saturation block, the signal that is used to detect zero crossings for the upper limit is zcSignal = UpperLimit - u, where u is the input signal.

Zero-crossing signals have a direction attribute, which can have these values:

- *rising* – A zero crossing occurs when a signal rises to or through zero, or when a signal leaves zero and becomes positive.
- *falling* – A zero crossing occurs when a signal falls to or through zero, or when a signal leaves zero and becomes negative.
- *either* – A zero crossing occurs if either a rising or falling condition occurs.

For the Saturation block's upper limit, the direction of the zero crossing is *either*. This enables the entering and leaving saturation events to be detected using the same zero-crossing signal.

If the error tolerances are too large, it is possible for Simulink to fail to detect a zero crossing. For example, if a zero crossing occurs within a time step, but the values at the beginning and end of the step do not indicate a sign change, the solver steps over the crossing without detecting it.

The following figure shows a signal that crosses zero. In the first instance, the integrator steps over the event. In the second, the solver detects the event.

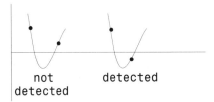

If you suspect this is happening, tighten the error tolerances to ensure that the solver takes small enough steps. For more information, see "Maximum order" on page 8-34.

Note Using the Refine output option (see "Output options" on page 8-41) does not help locate the missed zero crossings. You should alter the maximum step size or output times.

Caveat

It is possible to create models that exhibit high-frequency fluctuations about a discontinuity (chattering). Such systems typically are not physically realizable; a massless spring, for example. Because chattering causes repeated detection of zero crossings, the step sizes of the simulation become very small, essentially halting the simulation.

If you suspect that this behavior applies to your model, you can use the **Zero crossing control** option on the **Solver** pane of the **Configuration Parameters** dialog box (see "Zero crossing control" on page 8-32) to disable zero-crossing detection. Although disabling zero-crossing detection can alleviate the symptoms of this problem, you no longer benefit from the increased accuracy that zero-crossing detection provides. A better solution is to try to identify the source of the underlying problem in the model.

Blocks with Zero Crossings

The following table lists blocks that use zero crossings and explains how the blocks use the zero crossings:

Block	Description of Zero Crossing
Abs	One: to detect when the input signal crosses zero in either the rising or falling direction.
Backlash	Two: one to detect when the upper threshold is engaged, and one to detect when the lower threshold is engaged.
Dead Zone	Two: one to detect when the dead zone is entered (the input signal minus the lower limit), and one to detect when the dead zone is exited (the input signal minus the upper limit).
Hit Crossing	One: to detect when the input crosses the threshold.
Integrator	If the reset port is present, to detect when a reset occurs. If the output is limited, there are three zero crossings: one to detect when the upper saturation limit is reached, one to detect when the lower saturation limit is reached, and one to detect when saturation is left.
MinMax	One: for each element of the output vector, to detect when an input signal is the new minimum or maximum.
Relay	One: if the relay is off, to detect the switch on point. If the relay is on, to detect the switch off point.
Relational Operator	One: to detect when the output changes.
Saturation	Two: one to detect when the upper limit is reached or left, and one to detect when the lower limit is reached or left.
Sign	One: to detect when the input crosses through zero.
Step	One: to detect the step time.

Block	Description of Zero Crossing (Continued)
Subsystem	For conditionally executed subsystems: one for the enable port if present, and one for the trigger port, if present.
Switch	One: to detect when the switch condition occurs.

Algebraic Loops

Some Simulink blocks have input ports with *direct feedthrough*. This means that the output of these blocks cannot be computed without knowing the values of the signals entering the blocks at these input ports. Some examples of blocks with direct feedthrough inputs are as follows:

- The Math Function block
- The Gain block
- The Integrator block's initial condition ports
- The Product block
- The State-Space block when there is a nonzero D matrix
- The Sum block
- The Transfer Fcn block when the numerator and denominator are of the same order
- The Zero-Pole block when there are as many zeros as poles

An *algebraic loop* generally occurs when an input port with direct feedthrough is driven by the output of the same block, either directly, or by a feedback path through other blocks with direct feedthrough. An example of an algebraic loop is this simple scalar loop.

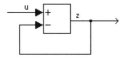

Mathematically, this loop implies that the output of the Sum block is an algebraic state z constrained to equal the first input u minus z (i.e. $z = u - z$). The solution of this simple loop is $z = u/2$, but most algebraic loops cannot be solved by inspection.

It is easy to create vector algebraic loops with multiple algebraic state variables $z1$, $z2$, etc., as shown in this model.

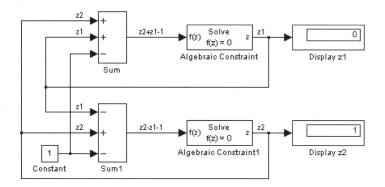

The Algebraic Constraint block is a convenient way to model algebraic equations and specify initial guesses. The Algebraic Constraint block constrains its input signal $F(z)$ to zero and outputs an algebraic state z. This block outputs the value necessary to produce a zero at the input. The output must affect the input through some feedback path. You can provide an initial guess of the algebraic state value in the block's dialog box to improve algebraic loop solver efficiency.

A scalar algebraic loop represents a scalar algebraic equation or constraint of the form $F(z) = 0$, where z is the output of one of the blocks in the loop and the function F consists of the feedback path through the other blocks in the loop to the input of the block. In the simple one-block example shown on the previous page, $F(z) = z - (u - z)$. In the vector loop example shown above, the equations are

$$z2 + z1 - 1 = 0$$
$$z2 - z1 - 1 = 0$$

Algebraic loops arise when a model includes an algebraic constraint $F(z) = 0$. This constraint might arise as a consequence of the physical interconnectivity of the system you are modeling, or it might arise because you are specifically trying to model a differential/algebraic system (DAE).

When a model contains an algebraic loop, Simulink calls a loop solving routine at each time step. The loop solver performs iterations to determine the solution to the problem (if it can). As a result, models with algebraic loops run slower than models without them.

To solve $F(z) = 0$, the Simulink loop solver uses Newton's method with weak line search and rank-one updates to a Jacobian matrix of partial derivatives. Although the method is robust, it is possible to create loops for which the loop solver will not converge without a good initial guess for the algebraic states z. You can specify an initial guess for a line in an algebraic loop by placing an IC block (which is normally used to specify an initial condition for a signal) on that line. As shown above, another way to specify an initial guess for a line in an algebraic loop is to use an Algebraic Constraint block.

Whenever possible, use an IC block or an Algebraic Constraint block to specify

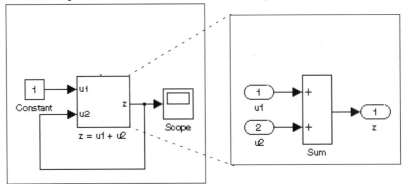

In this case, the input at the u2 port of the adder subsystem is equal to the subsystem's output at the current time step for every time step. The mathematical representation of this system

    z = z + 1

reveals that it has no mathematically valid solution.

Highlighting Algebraic Loops

You can cause Simulink to highlight algebraic loops when you update, simulate, or debug a model. Use the ashow command to highlight algebraic loops when debugging a model.

To cause Simulink to highlight algebraic loops that it detects when updating or simulating a model, set the Algebraic loop diagnostic on the **Diagnostics** pane of the **Configuration Parameters** dialog box to Error (see "The

Configuration Parameters Dialog Box" on page 8-29 for more information). This causes Simulink to display an error dialog (the Diagnostics Viewer) and recolor portions of the diagram that represent the algebraic loops that it detects. Simulink uses red to color the blocks and lines that constitute the loops. Closing the error dialog restores the diagram to its original colors.

For example, the following figure shows the block diagram of the hydcyl demo model in its original colors.

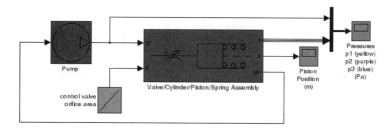

The following figure shows the diagram after updating when the Algebraic loop diagnostic is set to Error.

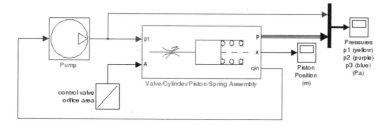

In this example, Simulink has colored the algebraic loop red, making it stand out from the rest of the diagram.

Eliminating Algebraic Loops

Simulink can eliminate some algebraic loops that include any of the following types of blocks:

- Atomic Subsystem
- Enabled Subsystem
- Model

To enable automatic algebraic loop elimination for a loop involving a particular instance of an Atomic Subsystem or Enabled Subsystem block, select the **Minimize algebraic loop occurrences** parameter on the block's parameters dialog box. To enable algebraic loop elimination for a loop involving a Model block, check the **Minimize algebraic loop occurrences** parameter on the **Model Referencing** configuration parameters dialog (see "Model Referencing Pane" on page 8-63) of the model referenced by the Model block. If a loop includes more than one instance of these blocks, you should enable algebraic loop elimination for all of them, including nested blocks.

The Simulink **Minimize algebraic loop** solver diagnostic allows you to specify the action Simulink should take, for example, display a warning message, if it is unable to eliminate an algebraic loop involving a block for which algebraic loop elimination is enabled. See "The Diagnostics Pane" on page 8-47 for more information.

Algebraic loop minimization is off by default because it is incompatible with conditional input branch optimization in Simulink (see "The Optimization Pane" on page 8-42) and with single output/update function optimization in Real-Time Workshop®. If you need these optimizations for an atomic or enabled subsystem or referenced model involved in an algebraic loop, you must eliminate the algebraic loop yourself.

As an example of the ability of Simulink to eliminate algebraic loops, consider the following model.

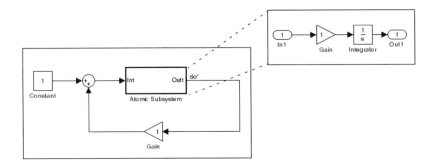

Simulating this model with the solver's Algebraic Loop diagnostic set to error (see "The Diagnostics Pane" on page 8-47) reveals that this model contains an algebraic loop involving its atomic subsystem.

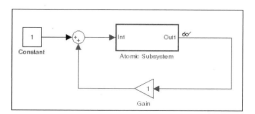

Checking the atomic subsystem's **Minimize algebraic loop occurrences** parameter causes Simulink to eliminate the algebraic loop from the compiled version of the model.

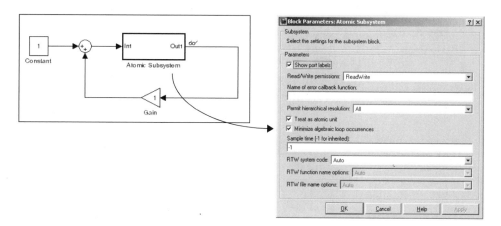

As a result, the model now simulates without error.

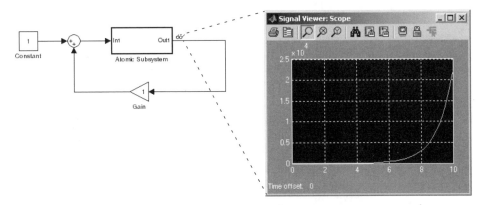

Note that Simulink is able to eliminate the algebraic loop involving this model's atomic subsystem because the atomic subsystem contains a block with a port that does not have direct feed through, i.e., the Integrator block.

If you remove the Integrator block from the atomic subsystem, Simulink is unable to eliminate the algebraic loop. Hence, attempting to simulate the model results in an error.

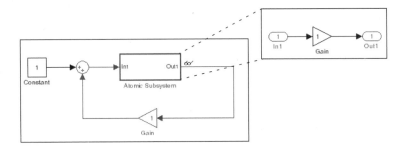

Modeling and Simulating Discrete Systems

Simulink has the ability to simulate discrete (sampled data) systems, including systems whose components operate at different rates (*multirate systems*) and systems that mix discrete and continuous components (*hybrid systems*). This capability stems from two key Simulink features:

- SampleTime block parameter

  Some Simulink blocks have a SampleTime parameter that you can use to specify the block's sample time, i.e., the rate at which it executes during simulation. All blocks have either an explicit or implicit sample time parameter. Continuous blocks are examples of blocks that have an implicit (continuous) sample time. It is possible for a block to have multiple sample times as provided with blocksets such as the Signal Processing Blockset or created by a user using the S-Function block.

- Sample-time inheritance

  Most standard Simulink blocks can inherit their sample time from the blocks connected to their inputs. Exceptions include blocks in the Continuous library and blocks that do not have inputs (e.g., blocks from the Sources library). In some cases, source blocks can inherit the sample time of the block connected to its input.

The ability to specify sample times on a block-by-block basis, either directly through the SampleTime parameter or indirectly through inheritance, enables you to model systems containing discrete components operating at different rates and hybrid systems containing discrete and continuous components.

Specifying Sample Time

Simulink allows you to specify the sample time of any block that has a `SampleTime` parameter. You can use the block's parameter dialog box to set this parameter. You do this by entering the sample time in the **Sample time** field on the dialog box. You can enter either the sample time alone or a vector whose first element is the sample time and whose second element is an offset: $[T_s, T_o]$. Various values of the sample time and offset have special meanings.

The following table summarizes valid values for this parameter and how Simulink interprets them to determine a block's sample time.

Sample Time	Usage
$[T_s, T_o]$ $0 > T_s < T_{sim}$ $\|T_o\| < T_p$	Specifies that updates occur at simulation times $$t_n = n * T_s + \|T_o\|$$ where n is an integer in the range $1 .. T_{sim}/T_s$ and T_{sim} is the length of the simulation. Blocks that have a sample time greater than 0 are said to have a *discrete sample time*. The offset allows you to specify that Simulink update the block later in the sample interval than other blocks operating at the same rate.
$[0, 0], 0$	Specifies that updates occur at every major and minor time step. A block that has a sample time of 0 is said to have a *continuous sample time*.
$[0, 1]$	Specifies that updates occur only at major time steps, skipping minor time steps (see "Minor Time Steps" on page 3-19). This setting avoids unnecessary computations for blocks whose sample time cannot change between major time steps. The sample time of a block that executes only at major time steps is said to be *fixed in minor time step*.

Sample Time	Usage
[-1, 0], -1	If the block is not in a triggered subsystem, this setting specifies that the block inherits its sample time from the block connected to its input (inheritance) or, in some cases, from the block connected to its output (back inheritance). If the block is in a triggered subsystem, you must set the SampleTime parameter to this setting. Note that specifying sample-time inheritance for a source block can cause Simulink to assign an inappropriate sample time to the block if the source drives more than one block. For this reason, you should avoid specifying sample-time inheritance for source blocks. If you do, Simulink displays a warning message when you update or simulate the model.
inf	The meaning of this sample time depends on whether the active model configuration's inline parameters optimization (see "Inline parameters" on page 8-43) is enabled. If the inline parameters optimization is enabled, inf signifies that the block's output can never change (see "Invariant Constants" on page 3-39). This speeds up simulation and the generated code by eliminating the need to recompute the block's output at each time step. If the inline parameters optimization is disabled or the block with inf sample time drives an output port of a conditionally executed subsystem, Simulink treats inf as -1, i.e., as inherited sample time. This allows you to tune the block's parameters during simulation.

Changing a Block's Sample Time

You cannot change the SampleTime parameter of a block while a simulation is running. If you want to change a block's sample time, you must stop and restart the simulation for the change to take effect.

Compiled Sample Time

During the compilation phase of a simulation, Simulink determines the sample time of the block from its SampleTime parameter (if it has a SampleTime parameter), sample-time inheritance, or block type (Continuous blocks always have a continuous sample time). It is this compiled sample time that determines the sample rate of a block during simulation. You can determine the compiled sample time of any block in a model by first updating the model and then getting the block's CompiledSampleTime parameter, using the get_param command.

Purely Discrete Systems

Purely discrete systems can be simulated using any of the solvers; there is no difference in the solutions. To generate output points only at the sample hits, choose one of the discrete solvers.

Multirate Systems

Multirate systems contain blocks that are sampled at different rates. These systems can be modeled with discrete blocks or with both discrete and continuous blocks. For example, consider this simple multirate discrete model.

For this example the DTF1 Discrete Transfer Fcn block's **Sample time** is set to [1 0.1], which gives it an offset of 0.1. The DTF2 Discrete Transfer Fcn block's **Sample time** is set to 0.7, with no offset.

Starting the simulation and plotting the outputs using the stairs function

```
[t,x,y] = sim('multirate', 3);
stairs(t,y)
```

produces this plot

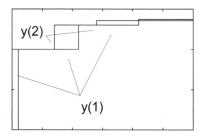

For the DTF1 block, which has an offset of 0.1, there is no output until t = 0.1. Because the initial conditions of the transfer functions are zero, the output of DTF1, y(1), is zero before this time.

Determining Step Size for Discrete Systems

Simulating a discrete system requires that the simulator take a simulation step at every *sample time hit*, that is, at integer multiples of the system's shortest sample time. Otherwise, the simulator might miss key transitions in the system's states. Simulink avoids this by choosing a simulation step size to ensure that steps coincide with sample time hits. The step size that Simulink chooses depends on the system's fundamental sample time and the type of solver used to simulate the system.

The *fundamental sample time* of a discrete system is the greatest integer divisor of the system's actual sample times. For example, suppose that a system has sample times of 0.25 and 0.5 second. The fundamental sample time in this case is 0.25 second. Suppose, instead, the sample times are 0.5 and 0.75 second. In this case, the fundamental sample time is again 0.25 second.

You can direct Simulink to use either a fixed-step or a variable-step discrete solver to solve a discrete system. A fixed-step solver sets the simulation step size equal to the discrete system's fundamental sample time. A variable-step solver varies the step size to equal the distance between actual sample time hits. The following diagram illustrates the difference between a fixed-step and a variable-size solver.

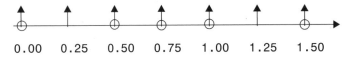

| 0.00 | 0.25 | 0.50 | 0.75 | 1.00 | 1.25 | 1.50 |

Fixed-Step Solver

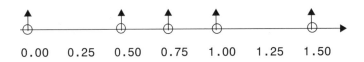

| 0.00 | 0.25 | 0.50 | 0.75 | 1.00 | 1.25 | 1.50 |

Variable-Step Solver

In the diagram, arrows indicate simulation steps and circles represent sample time hits. As the diagram illustrates, a variable-step solver requires fewer simulation steps to simulate a system, if the fundamental sample time is less than any of the actual sample times of the system being simulated. On the other hand, a fixed-step solver requires less memory to implement and is faster if one of the system's sample times is fundamental. This can be an advantage in applications that entail generating code from a Simulink model (using Real-Time Workshop®).

Sample Time Propagation

When updating a model's diagram, for example, at the beginning of a simulation, Simulink uses a process called sample time propagation to determine the sample times of blocks that inherit their sample times. The figure below illustrates a Discrete Filter block with a sample time of Ts driving a Gain block.

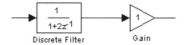

Because the Gain block's output is simply the input multiplied by a constant, its output changes at the same rate as the filter. In other words, the Gain block has an effective sample rate equal to that of the filter's sample rate. This is the fundamental mechanism behind sample time propagation in Simulink.

Simulink assigns an inherited sample time to a block based on the sample times of the blocks connected to its inputs. If all the inputs have the same sample time, Simulink assigns that sample time to the block. If the inputs have different sample times, if all sample times are integer multiples of the fastest sample time, the block is assigned the sample time of the fastest input. If a variable-step solver is being used, the block is assigned the continuous sample time. If a fixed-step solver is being used and the greatest common divisor of the sample times (the fundamental sample time) can be computed, it is used. Otherwise continuous is used.

Under some circumstances, Simulink also back propagates sample times to source blocks if it can do so without affecting the output of a simulation. For instance, in the model below, Simulink recognizes that the Signal Generator block is driving a Discrete-Time Integrator block, so it assigns the Signal

Generator block and the Gain block the same sample time as the Discrete-Time Integrator block.

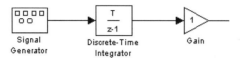

You can verify this by selecting **Sample Time Colors** from the Simulink **Format** menu and noting that all blocks are colored red. Because the Discrete-Time Integrator block only looks at its input at its sample times, this change does not affect the outcome of the simulation but does result in a performance improvement.

Replacing the Discrete-Time Integrator block with a continuous Integrator block, as shown below, and recoloring the model by choosing **Update diagram** from the **Edit** menu cause the Signal Generator and Gain blocks to change to continuous blocks, as indicated by their being colored black.

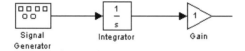

Invariant Constants

Simulink by default assigns Constant blocks a sample time of infinity, also referred to as a *constant sample time*. This means that the outputs of any blocks that inherit a constant sample time from a Constant block do not change during the simulation unless the parameters are explicitly modified by the model user.

For example, in this model, both the Constant and Gain blocks have constant sample time.

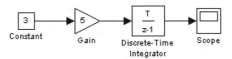

Because Simulink supports the ability to change block parameters during a simulation, all blocks, even blocks having constant sample time, must generate their output at the model's effective sample time.

Note You can determine which blocks have constant sample time by selecting **Sample Time Colors** from the **Format** menu. Blocks having constant sample time are colored magenta.

Because of this feature, *all* blocks compute their output at each sample time hit, or, in the case of purely continuous systems, at every simulation step. For blocks having constant sample time whose parameters do not change during a simulation, evaluating these blocks during the simulation is inefficient and slows down the simulation.

You can set the inline parameters option (see "Inline parameters" on page 8-43) to remove all blocks having constant sample times from the simulation "loop." The effect of this feature is twofold. First, parameters for these blocks cannot be changed during a simulation. Second, simulation speed is improved. The speed improvement depends on model complexity, the number of blocks with constant sample time, and the effective sampling rate of the simulation.

Note Simulink displays an error if you connect a Constant, Model, or S-Function block with constant sample time to the output port of a conditionally executed subsystem. To avoid the error, either change the sample time of the block to a nonconstant sample time or insert a Signal Conversion block between the block with constant sample time and the output port.

Mixed Continuous and Discrete Systems

Mixed continuous and discrete systems are composed of both sampled and continuous blocks. Such systems can be simulated using any of the integration methods, although certain methods are more efficient and accurate than others. For most mixed continuous and discrete systems, the Runge-Kutta variable-step methods, ode23 and ode45, are superior to the other methods in terms of efficiency and accuracy. Because of discontinuities associated with the sample and hold of the discrete blocks, the ode15s and ode113 methods are not recommended for mixed continuous and discrete systems.

4

Simulink Basics

The following sections explain how to perform basic Simulink tasks.

Starting Simulink

To start Simulink, you must first start MATLAB. Consult your MATLAB documentation for more information. You can then start Simulink in two ways:

- Click the Simulink icon  on the MATLAB toolbar.
- Enter the `simulink` command at the MATLAB prompt.

On Microsoft Windows platforms, starting Simulink displays the Simulink Library Browser.

The Library Browser displays a tree-structured view of the Simulink block libraries installed on your system. You can build models by copying blocks from the Library Browser into a model window (see "Editing Blocks" on page 6-4).

On Macintosh or Linux platforms, starting Simulink displays the Simulink block library window.

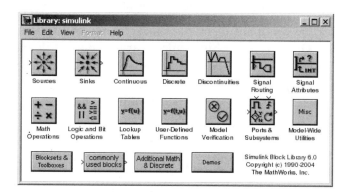

The Simulink library window displays icons representing the block libraries that come with Simulink. You can create models by copying blocks from the library into a model window.

Note On Windows, you can display the Simulink library window by right-clicking the Simulink node in the Library Browser window.

Opening Models

To edit an existing model diagram, either

- Click the **Open** button on the Library Browser's toolbar (Windows only) or select **Open** from the Simulink library window's **File** menu and then choose or enter the file name for the model to edit.
- Enter the name of the model (without the .mdl extension) in the MATLAB Command Window. The model must be in the current directory or on the path.

Note If the character encoding of the model to be opened differs from the character encoding of the current MATLAB session, you should change the MATLAB encoding to the model encoding before opening the model, using the slCharacterEncoding command.

Avoiding Initial Model Open Delay

You may notice that the first model that you open in a MATLAB session takes longer to open than do subsequent models. This is because to reduce its own startup time and to avoid unnecessary consumption of your system's memory, MATLAB does not load Simulink into memory until the first time you open a Simulink model. You can cause MATLAB to load Simulink at MATLAB startup, and thus avoid the initial model opening delay, using either the -r MATLAB command line option or your MATLAB startup.m file to run either load_simulink (loads Simulink) or simulink (loads Simulink and opens the Simulink Library browser) at MATLAB startup. For example, to load Simulink at MATLAB startup on Microsoft Windows systems, create a desktop shortcut with the following target:

```
<matlabroot>\bin\win32\matlab.exe -r load_simulink
```

Similarly, the following command loads Simulink at MATLAB startup on UNIX systems:

```
matlab -r load_simulink
```

Entering Simulink Commands

You run Simulink and work with your model by entering commands. You can enter commands by

- Selecting items from the Simulink menu bar
- Selecting items from a context-sensitive Simulink menu (Windows only)
- Clicking buttons on the Simulink toolbar (Windows only)
- Entering commands in the MATLAB Command Window

Using the Simulink Menu Bar to Enter Commands

The Simulink menu bar appears near the top of each model window. The menu commands apply to the contents of that window.

Using Context-Sensitive Menus to Enter Commands

Simulink displays a context-sensitive menu when you click the right mouse button over a model or block library window. The contents of the menu depend on whether a block is selected. If a block is selected, the menu displays commands that apply only to the selected block. If no block is selected, the menu displays commands that apply to a model or library as a whole.

Using the Simulink Toolbar to Enter Commands

Model windows in the Windows version of Simulink optionally display a toolbar beneath the Simulink menu bar. To display the toolbar, select the **Toolbar** option on the Simulink **View** menu.

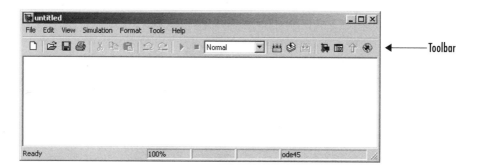

The toolbar contains buttons corresponding to frequently used Simulink commands, such as those for opening, running, and closing models. You can run such commands by clicking the corresponding button. For example, to open a Simulink model, click the button containing the open folder icon. You can determine which command a button executes by moving the mouse pointer over the button. A small window appears containing text that describes the button. The window is called a tooltip. Each button on the toolbar displays a tooltip when the mouse pointer hovers over it. You can hide the toolbar by clearing the **Toolbar** option on the Simulink **View** menu.

Using the MATLAB Window to Enter Commands

When you run a simulation and analyze its results, you can enter MATLAB commands in the MATLAB Command Window. See Chapter 8, "Running Simulations," and Chapter 9, "Analyzing Simulation Results," for more information.

Undoing a Command

You can cancel the effects of up to 101 consecutive operations by choosing **Undo** from the **Edit** menu. You can undo these operations:

- Adding, deleting, or moving a block
- Adding, deleting, or moving a line
- Adding, deleting, or moving a model annotation
- Editing a block name
- Creating a subsystem (see "Undoing Subsystem Creation" on page 5-22 for more information)

You can reverse the effects of an **Undo** command by choosing **Redo** from the **Edit** menu.

Simulink Windows

Simulink uses separate windows to display a block library browser, a block library, a model, and graphical (scope) simulation output. These windows are not MATLAB figure windows and cannot be manipulated using Handle Graphics® commands.

Simulink windows are sized to accommodate the most common screen resolutions available. If you have a monitor with exceptionally high or low resolution, you might find the window sizes too small or too large. If this is the case, resize the window and save the model to preserve the new window dimensions.

Status Bar

The Windows version of Simulink displays a status bar at the bottom of each model and library window.

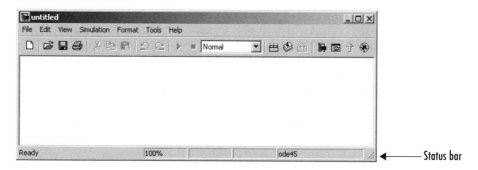

Status bar

When a simulation is running, the status bar displays the status of the simulation, including the current simulation time and the name of the current solver. You can display or hide the status bar by selecting or clearing the **Status Bar** option on the Simulink **View** menu.

Zooming Block Diagrams

Simulink allows you to enlarge or shrink the view of the block diagram in the current Simulink window. To zoom a view:

- Select **Zoom In** from the **View** menu (or type r) to enlarge the view.
- Select **Zoom Out** from the **View** menu (or type v) to shrink the view.

- Select **Fit System to View** from the **View** menu (or press the space bar) to fit the diagram to the view.
- Select **Normal** from the **View** menu to view the diagram at actual size.

By default, Simulink fits a block diagram to view when you open the diagram either in the model browser's content pane or in a separate window. If you change a diagram's zoom setting, Simulink saves the setting when you close the diagram and restores the setting the next time you open the diagram. If you want to restore the default behavior, choose **Fit System to View** from the **View** menu the next time you open the diagram.

Panning Block Diagrams

You can use the mouse to pan model diagrams that are too large to fit in the model editor's window. To do this, position the mouse over the diagram and hold down the left mouse button and the P or Q key on the keyboard. Moving the mouse now pans the model diagram in the editor window.

Saving a Model

You can save a model by choosing either the **Save** or **Save As** command from the **File** menu. Simulink saves the model by generating a specially formatted file called the *model file* (with the `.mdl` extension) that contains the block diagram and block properties.

If you are saving a model for the first time, use the **Save** command to provide a name and location for the model file. Model file names must start with a letter and can contain no more than 63 letters, numbers, and underscores. The file name must not be the same as that of a MATLAB command.

If you are saving a model whose model file was previously saved, use the **Save** command to replace the file's contents or the **Save As** command to save the model with a new name or location. You can also use the **Save As** command to save the model in a format compatible with previous releases of Simulink (see "Saving a Model in Earlier Formats" on page 4-9).

Simulink follows this procedure while saving a model:

1 If the `mdl` file for the model already exists, it is renamed as a temporary file.

2 Simulink executes all block `PreSaveFcn` callback routines, then executes the block diagram's `PreSaveFcn` callback routine.

3 Simulink writes the model file to a new file using the same name and an extension of `mdl`.

4 Simulink executes all block `PostSaveFcn` callback routines, then executes the block diagram's `PostSaveFcn` callback routine.

5 Simulink deletes the temporary file.

If an error occurs during this process, Simulink renames the temporary file to the name of the original model file, writes the current version of the model to a file with an `.err` extension, and issues an error message. Simulink performs steps 2 through 4 even if an error occurs in an earlier step.

Saving a Model in Earlier Formats

The **Save As** command allows you to save a model created with the latest version of Simulink in formats used by earlier versions of Simulink, including

Simulink 3 (Release 11), Simulink 4 (Release 12), and Simulink 4.1 (Release 12.1). You might want to do this, for example, if you need to make a model available to colleagues who have access only to one of these earlier versions of Simulink.

To save a model in earlier format:

1 Select **Save As** from the Simulink **File** menu.

Simulink displays the **Save As** dialog box.

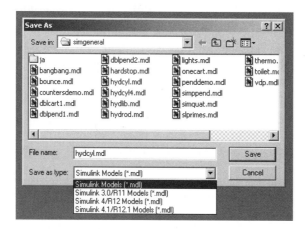

2 Select a format from the **Save as type** list on the dialog box.

3 Click the **Save** button.

When saving a model in an earlier version's format, Simulink saves the model in that format regardless of whether the model contains blocks and features that were introduced after that version. If the model does contain blocks or use features that postdate the earlier version, the model might not give correct results when run by the earlier version. For example, matrix and frame signals do not work in Release 11, because Release 11 does not have matrix and frame support. Similarly, models that contain unconditionally executed subsystems marked "Treat as atomic unit" might produce different results in Release 11, because Release 11 does not support unconditionally executed atomic subsystems.

The command converts blocks that postdate the earlier version into empty masked subsystem blocks colored yellow. For example, post-Release 11 blocks include

- Lookup Table (n-D)
- Assertion
- Rate Transition
- PreLookup Index Search
- Interpolation (n-D)
- Direct Lookup Table (n-D)
- Polynomial
- Matrix Concatenation
- Signal Specification
- Bus Creator
- If, WhileIterator, ForIterator, Assignment
- SwitchCase
- Bitwise Logical Operator

Post-Release 11 blocks from Simulink blocksets appear as unlinked blocks.

Printing a Block Diagram

You can print a block diagram by selecting **Print** from the **File** menu (on a Microsoft Windows system) or by using the print command in the MATLAB Command Window (on all platforms).

On a Microsoft Windows system, the **Print** menu item prints the block diagram in the current window.

Print Dialog Box

When you select the **Print** menu item, the **Print** dialog box appears. The **Print** dialog box enables you to selectively print systems within your model. Using the dialog box, you can print

- The current system only
- The current system and all systems above it in the model hierarchy
- The current system and all systems below it in the model hierarchy, with the option of looking into the contents of masked and library blocks
- All systems in the model, with the option of looking into the contents of masked and library blocks
- An overlay frame on each diagram

The portion of the **Print** dialog box that supports selective printing is similar on supported platforms. This figure shows how it looks on a Microsoft Windows system. In this figure, only the current system is to be printed.

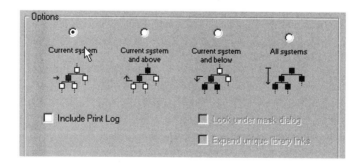

When you select either the **Current system and below** or **All systems** option, two check boxes become enabled. In this figure, **All systems** is selected.

Selecting the **Look Under Mask Dialog** check box prints the contents of masked subsystems when encountered at or below the level of the current block. When you are printing all systems, the top-level system is considered the current block, so Simulink looks under any masked blocks encountered.

Selecting the **Expand Unique Library Links** check box prints the contents of library blocks when those blocks are systems. Only one copy is printed regardless of how many copies of the block are contained in the model. For more information about libraries, see "Working with Block Libraries" on page 6-18.

The print log lists the blocks and systems printed. To print the print log, select the **Include Print Log** check box.

Selecting the **Frame** check box prints a title block frame on each diagram. Enter the path to the title block frame in the adjacent edit box. You can create a customized title block frame, using the MATLAB frame editor. See frameedit in the online MATLAB reference for information on using the frame editor to create title block frames.

Print Command

The format of the print command is

```
print -ssys -device filename
```

sys is the name of the system to be printed. The system name must be preceded by the s switch identifier and is the only required argument. sys must be open or must have been open during the current session. If the system name contains spaces or takes more than one line, you need to specify the name as a string. See the examples below.

device specifies a device type. For a list and description of device types, see the documentation for the MATLAB print function.

filename is the PostScript file to which the output is saved. If filename exists, it is replaced. If filename does not include an extension, an appropriate one is appended.

For example, this command prints a system named untitled.

```
print -suntitled
```

This command prints the contents of a subsystem named Sub1 in the current system.

```
print -sSub1
```

This command prints the contents of a subsystem named Requisite Friction.

```
print (['-sRequisite Friction'])
```

The next example prints a system named Friction Model, a subsystem whose name appears on two lines. The first command assigns the newline character to a variable; the second prints the system.

```
cr = sprintf('\n');
print (['-sFriction' cr 'Model'])
```

To print the currently selected subsystem, enter

```
print(['-s', gcb])
```

Specifying Paper Size and Orientation

Simulink lets you specify the type and orientation of the paper used to print a model diagram. You can do this on all platforms by setting the model's PaperType and PaperOrientation properties, respectively (see "Model and Block Parameters" in the online documentation), using the set_param command. You can set the paper orientation alone, using the MATLAB orient command. On Windows, the **Print** and **Printer Setup** dialog boxes let you set the page type and orientation properties as well.

Positioning and Sizing a Diagram

You can use a model's PaperPositionMode and PaperPosition parameters to position and size the model's diagram on the printed page. The value of the PaperPosition parameter is a vector of form [left bottom width height]. The first two elements specify the bottom left corner of a rectangular area on the page, measured from the page's bottom left corner. The last two elements specify the width and height of the rectangle. When the model's PaperPositionMode is manual, Simulink positions (and scales, if necessary) the model's diagram to fit inside the specified print rectangle. For example, the following commands

```
vdp
set_param('vdp', 'PaperType', 'usletter')
set_param('vdp', 'PaperOrientation', 'landscape')
set_param('vdp', 'PaperPositionMode', 'manual')
set_param('vdp', 'PaperPosition', [0.5 0.5 4 4])
print -svdp
```

print the block diagram of the vdp sample model in the lower left corner of a U.S. letter-size page in landscape orientation.

If PaperPositionMode is auto, Simulink centers the model diagram on the printed page, scaling the diagram, if necessary, to fit the page.

Generating a Model Report

A Simulink model report is an HTML document that describes a model's structure and content. The report includes block diagrams of the model and its subsystems and the settings of its block parameters.

To generate a report for the current model:

1 Select **Print details** from the model's **File** menu.

The **Print Details** dialog box appears.

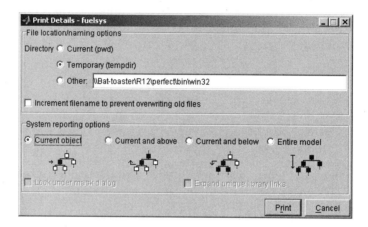

The dialog box allows you to select various report options (see "Model Report Options" on page 4-17).

2 Select the desired report options on the dialog box.

3 Select **Print**.

Simulink generates the HTML report and displays the in your system's default HTML browser.

While generating the report, Simulink displays status messages on a messages pane that replaces the options pane on the **Print Details** dialog box.

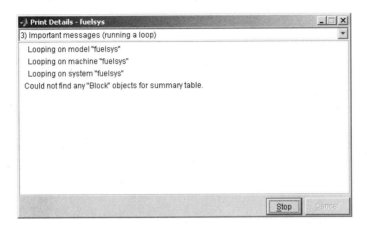

You can select the detail level of the messages from the list at the top of the messages pane. When the report generation process begins, the **Print** button on the **Print Details** dialog box changes to a **Stop** button. Clicking this button terminates the report generation. When the report generation process finishes, the **Stop** button changes to an **Options** button. Clicking this button redisplays the report generation options, allowing you to generate another report without having to reopen the **Print Details** dialog box.

Model Report Options

The **Print Details** dialog box allows you to select the following report options.

Directory

The directory where Simulink stores the HTML report that it generates. The options include your system's temporary directory (the default), your system's current directory, or another directory whose path you specify in the adjacent edit field.

Increment filename to prevent overwriting old files

Creates a unique report file name each time you generate a report for the same model in the current session. This preserves each report.

Current object

Include only the currently selected object in the report.

Current and above

Include the current object and all levels of the model above the current object in the report.

Current and below

Include the current object and all levels below the current object in the report.

Entire model

Include the entire model in the report.

Look under mask dialog

Include the contents of masked subsystems in the report.

Expand unique library links

Include the contents of library blocks that are subsystems. The report includes a library subsystem only once even if it occurs in more than one place in the model.

Summary of Mouse and Keyboard Actions

These tables summarize the use of the mouse and keyboard to manipulate blocks, lines, and signal labels. LMB means press the left mouse button; CMB, the center mouse button; and RMB, the right mouse button.

Manipulating Blocks

The following table lists mouse and keyboard actions that apply to blocks.

Task	Microsoft Windows	Macintosh or Linux
Select one block	LMB	LMB
Select multiple blocks	**Shift** + LMB	**Shift** + LMB; or CMB alone
Copy block from another window	Drag block	Drag block
Move block	Drag block	Drag block
Duplicate block	**Ctrl** + LMB and drag; or RMB and drag	**Ctrl** + LMB and drag; or RMB and drag
Connect blocks	LMB	LMB
Disconnect block	**Shift** + drag block	**Shift** + drag block; or CMB and drag
Open selected subsystem	**Enter**	**Return**
Go to parent of selected subsystem	**Esc**	**Esc**

Manipulating Lines

The following table lists mouse and keyboard actions that apply to lines.

Task	Microsoft Windows	Macintosh or Linux
Select one line	LMB	LMB
Select multiple lines	**Shift** + LMB	**Shift** + LMB; or CMB alone
Draw branch line	**Ctrl** + drag line; or RMB and drag line	**Ctrl** + drag line; or RMB + drag line
Route lines around blocks	**Shift** + draw line segments	**Shift** + draw line segments; or CMB and draw segments
Move line segment	Drag segment	Drag segment
Move vertex	Drag vertex	Drag vertex
Create line segments	**Shift** + drag line	**Shift** + drag line; or CMB + drag line

Manipulating Signal Labels

The next table lists mouse and keyboard actions that apply to signal labels.

Action	Microsoft Windows	Macintosh or Linux
Create signal label	Double-click line, then enter label	Double-click line, then enter label
Copy signal label	**Ctrl** + drag label	**Ctrl** + drag label
Move signal label	Drag label	Drag label
Edit signal label	Click in label, then edit	Click in label, then edit
Delete signal label	**Shift** + click label, then press **Delete**	**Shift** + click label, then press **Delete**

Manipulating Annotations

The next table lists mouse and keyboard actions that apply to annotations.

Action	Microsoft Windows	Macintosh or Linux
Create annotation	Double-click in diagram, then enter text	Double-click in diagram, then enter text
Copy annotation	**Ctrl** + drag label	**Ctrl** + drag label
Move annotation	Drag label	Drag label
Edit annotation	Click in text, then edit	Click in text, then edit
Delete annotation	**Shift** + select annotation, then press **Delete**	**Shift** + select annotation, then press **Delete**

Ending a Simulink Session

Terminate a Simulink session by closing all Simulink windows.

Terminate a MATLAB session by choosing one of these commands from the **File** menu:

- On a Microsoft Windows system: **Exit MATLAB**
- On a Macintosh or Linux system: **Quit MATLAB**

Creating a Model

The following sections explain how to create Simulink models.

Creating a New Model

To create a new model, click the **New** button on the Library Browser's toolbar (Windows only) or choose **New** from the library window's **File** menu and select **Model**. You can move the window as you do other windows. Chapter 2, "Getting Started" describes how to build a simple model. "Modeling Equations" on page 8-2 describes how to build systems that model equations.

Selecting Objects

Many model building actions, such as copying a block or deleting a line, require that you first select one or more blocks and lines (objects).

Selecting One Object

To select an object, click it. Small black square "handles" appear at the corners of a selected block and near the end points of a selected line. For example, the figure below shows a selected Sine Wave block and a selected line.

When you select an object by clicking it, any other selected objects are deselected.

Selecting More Than One Object

You can select more than one object either by selecting objects one at a time, by selecting objects located near each other using a bounding box, or by selecting the entire model.

Selecting Multiple Objects One at a Time

To select more than one object by selecting each object individually, hold down the **Shift** key and click each object to be selected. To deselect a selected object, click the object again while holding down the **Shift** key.

Selecting Multiple Objects Using a Bounding Box

An easy way to select more than one object in the same area of the window is to draw a bounding box around the objects:

1 Define the starting corner of a bounding box by positioning the pointer at one corner of the box, then pressing and holding down the mouse button. Notice the shape of the cursor.

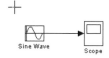

2 Drag the pointer to the opposite corner of the box. A dotted rectangle encloses the selected blocks and lines.

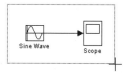

3 Release the mouse button. All blocks and lines at least partially enclosed by the bounding box are selected.

Selecting the Entire Model

To select all objects in the active window, choose **Select All** from the **Edit** menu. You cannot create a subsystem by selecting blocks and lines in this way. For more information, see "Creating Subsystems" on page 5-20.

Specifying Block Diagram Colors

Simulink allows you to specify the foreground and background colors of any block or annotation in a diagram, as well as the diagram's background color. To set the background color of a block diagram, select **Screen color** from the Simulink **Format** menu. To set the background color of a block or annotation or group of such items, first select the item or items. Then select **Background color** from the Simulink **Format** menu. To set the foreground color of a block or annotation, first select the item. Then select **Foreground color** from the Simulink **Format** menu.

In all cases, Simulink displays a menu of color choices. Choose the desired color from the menu. If you select a color other than **Custom**, Simulink changes the background or foreground color of the diagram or diagram element to the selected color.

Choosing a Custom Color

If you choose **Custom**, Simulink displays the Simulink **Choose Custom Color** dialog box.

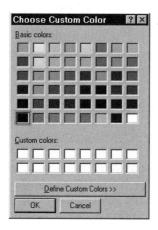

The dialog box displays a palette of basic colors and a palette of custom colors that you previously defined. If you have not previously created any custom colors, the custom color palette is all white. To choose a color from either palette, click the color, and then click the **OK** button.

Defining a Custom Color

To define a custom color, click the **Define Custom Colors** button on the **Choose Custom Color** dialog box. The dialog box expands to display a custom color definer.

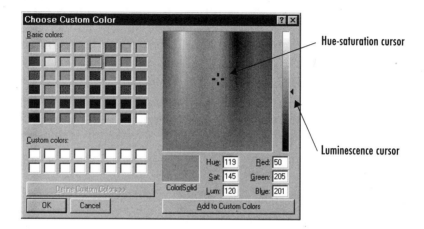

The color definer allows you to specify a custom color by

- Entering the red, green, and blue components of the color as values between 0 (darkest) and 255 (brightest)
- Entering hue, saturation, and luminescence components of the color as values in the range 0 to 255
- Moving the hue-saturation cursor to select the hue and saturation of the desired color and the luminescence cursor to select the luminescence of the desired color

The color that you have defined in any of these ways appears in the **Color|Solid** box. To redefine a color in the **Custom colors** palette, select the color and define a new color, using the color definer. Then click the **Add to Custom Colors** button on the color definer.

Specifying Colors Programmatically

You can use the set_param command at the MATLAB command line or in an M-file program to set parameters that determine the background color of a diagram and the background color and foreground color of diagram elements.

The following table summarizes the parameters that control block diagram colors.

Parameter	Determines
ScreenColor	Background color of block diagram
BackgroundColor	Background color of blocks and annotations
ForegroundColor	Foreground color of blocks and annotations

You can set these parameters to any of the following values:

- 'black', 'white', 'red', 'green', 'blue', 'cyan', 'magenta', 'yellow', 'gray', 'lightBlue', 'orange', 'darkGreen'
- '[r,g,b]'

  where r, g, and b are the red, green, and blue components of the color normalized to the range 0.0 to 1.0.

For example, the following command sets the background color of the currently selected system or subsystem to a light green color:

```
set_param(gcs, 'ScreenColor', '[0.3, 0.9, 0.5]')
```

Displaying Sample Time Colors

Simulink can color code the blocks and lines in your model to indicate the sample rates at which the blocks operate.

Color	Use
Black	Continuous blocks
Magenta	Constant blocks
Yellow	Hybrid (subsystems grouping blocks, or Mux or Demux blocks grouping signals with varying sample times)
Red	Fastest discrete sample time
Green	Second fastest discrete sample time

Color	Use
Blue	Third fastest discrete sample time
Light Blue	Fourth fastest discrete sample time
Dark Green	Fifth fastest discrete sample time
Orange	Sixth fastest discrete sample time
Cyan	Blocks in triggered subsystems
Gray	Fixed in minor step

To enable the sample time colors feature, select **Sample Time Colors** from the **Format** menu.

Simulink does not automatically recolor the model with each change you make to it, so you must select **Update Diagram** from the **Edit** menu to explicitly update the model coloration. To return to your original coloring, disable sample time coloration by again choosing **Sample Time Colors**.

It is important to note that Mux and Demux blocks are simply grouping operators; signals passing through them retain their timing information. For this reason, the lines emanating from a Demux block can have different colors if they are driven by sources having different sample times. In this case, the Mux and Demux blocks are color coded as hybrids (yellow) to indicate that they handle signals with multiple rates.

Similarly, Subsystem blocks that contain blocks with differing sample times are also colored as hybrids, because there is no single rate associated with them. If all the blocks within a subsystem run at a single rate, the Subsystem block is colored according to that rate.

Connecting Blocks

Simulink block diagrams use lines to represent pathways for signals among blocks in a model (see "Annotating Diagrams" on page 5-16 for information on signals). Simulink can connect blocks for you or you can connect the blocks yourself by drawing lines from their output ports to their input ports.

Automatically Connecting Blocks

You can command Simulink to connect blocks automatically. This eliminates the need for you to draw the connecting lines yourself. When connecting blocks, Simulink routes lines around intervening blocks to avoid cluttering the diagram.

Connecting Two Blocks

To autoconnect two blocks:

1 Select the source block.

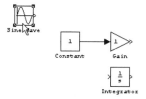

2 Hold down **Ctrl** and left-click the destination block.

Simulink connects the source block to the destination block, routing the line around intervening blocks if necessary.

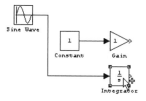

When connecting two blocks, Simulink draws as many connections as possible between the two blocks as illustrated in the following example.

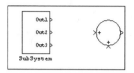 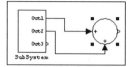

Before autoconnect   After autoconnect

Connecting Groups of Blocks

Simulink can connect a group of source blocks to a destination block or a source block to a group of destination blocks.

To connect a group of source blocks to a destination block:

1 Select the source blocks.

2 Hold down **Ctrl** and left-click the destination block.

To connect a source block to a group of destination blocks:

1 Select the *destination* blocks.

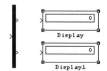

2 Hold down **Ctrl** and left-click the *source* block.

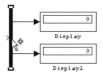

Manually Connecting Blocks

Simulink allows you to draw lines manually between blocks or between lines and blocks. You might want to do this if you need to control the path of the line or to create a branch line.

Drawing a Line Between Blocks

To connect the output port of one block to the input port of another block:

1 Position the cursor over the first block's output port. It is not necessary to position the cursor precisely on the port. The cursor shape changes to crosshairs.

2 Press and hold down the mouse button.

3 Drag the pointer to the second block's input port. You can position the cursor on or near the port or in the block. If you position the cursor in the block, the line is connected to the closest input port. The cursor shape changes to double crosshairs.

4 Release the mouse button. Simulink replaces the port symbols by a connecting line with an arrow showing the direction of the signal flow. You can create lines either from output to input, or from input to output. The arrow is drawn at the appropriate input port, and the signal is the same.

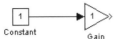

Simulink draws connecting lines using horizontal and vertical line segments. To draw a diagonal line, hold down the **Shift** key while drawing the line.

Drawing a Branch Line

A *branch line* is a line that starts from an existing line and carries its signal to the input port of a block. Both the existing line and the branch line carry the same signal. Using branch lines enables you to cause one signal to be carried to more than one block.

In this example, the output of the Product block goes to both the Scope block and the To Workspace block.

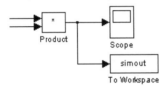

To add a branch line, follow these steps:

1 Position the pointer on the line where you want the branch line to start.

2 While holding down the **Ctrl** key, press and hold down the left mouse button.

3 Drag the pointer to the input port of the target block, then release the mouse button and the **Ctrl** key.

You can also use the right mouse button instead of holding down the left mouse button and the **Ctrl** key.

Drawing a Line Segment

You might want to draw a line with segments exactly where you want them instead of where Simulink draws them. Or you might want to draw a line before you copy the block to which the line is connected. You can do either by drawing line segments.

To draw a line segment, you draw a line that ends in an unoccupied area of the diagram. An arrow appears on the unconnected end of the line. To add another line segment, position the cursor over the end of the segment and draw another segment. Simulink draws the segments as horizontal and vertical lines. To draw diagonal line segments, hold down the **Shift** key while you draw the lines.

Moving a Line Segment

To move a line segment, follow these steps:

1 Position the pointer on the segment you want to move.

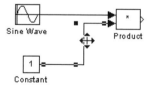

2 Press and hold down the left mouse button.

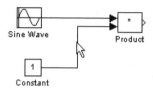

3 Drag the pointer to the desired location.

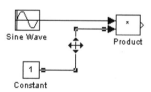

4 Release the mouse button.

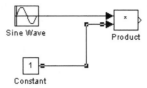

To move the segment connected to an input port, position the pointer over the port and drag the end of the segment to the new location. You cannot move the segment connected to an output port.

Moving a Line Vertex

To move a vertex of a line, follow these steps:

1 Position the pointer on the vertex, then press and hold down the mouse button. The cursor changes to a circle that encloses the vertex.

2 Drag the pointer to the desired location.

3 Release the mouse button.

Inserting Blocks in a Line

You can insert a block in a line by dropping the block on the line. Simulink inserts the block for you at the point where you drop the block. The block that you insert can have only one input and one output.

To insert a block in a line:

1 Position the pointer over the block and press the left mouse button.

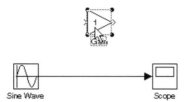

2 Drag the block over the line in which you want to insert the block.

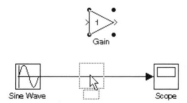

3 Release the mouse button to drop the block on the line. Simulink inserts the block where you dropped it.

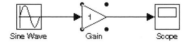

Disconnecting Blocks

To disconnect a block from its connecting lines, hold down the **Shift** key, then drag the block to a new location.

Annotating Diagrams

Annotations provide textual information about a model. You can add an annotation to any unoccupied area of your block diagram.

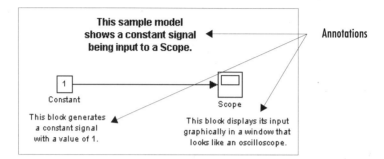

To create a model annotation, double-click an unoccupied area of the block diagram. A small rectangle appears and the cursor changes to an insertion point. Start typing the annotation contents. Each line is centered within the rectangle that surrounds the annotation.

To move an annotation, drag it to a new location.

To edit an annotation, select it:

- To replace the annotation, click the annotation, then double-click or drag the cursor to select it. Then, enter the new annotation.
- To insert characters, click between two characters to position the insertion point, then insert text.
- To replace characters, drag the mouse to select a range of text to replace, then enter the new text.

To delete an annotation, hold down the **Shift** key while you select the annotation, then press the **Delete** or **Backspace** key.

To change the font of all or part of an annotation, select the text in the annotation you want to change, then choose **Font** from the **Format** menu. Select a font and size from the dialog box.

To change the text alignment (e.g., left, center, or right) of the annotation, select the annotation and choose **Text Alignment** from the model window's

Format or context menu. Then choose one of the alignment options (e.g., **Center**) from the **Text Alignment** submenu.

Using TeX Formatting Commands in Annotations

You can use TeX formatting commands to include mathematical and other symbols and Greek letters in block diagram annotations.

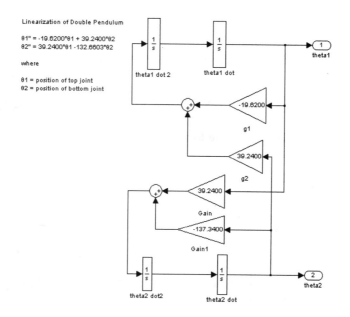

To use TeX commands in an annotation:

1 Select the annotation.

2 Select **Enable TeX Commands** from the **Edit** menu on the model window.

3 Enter or edit the text of the annotation, using TeX commands where needed to achieve the desired appearance.

```
Linearization of Double Pendulum

\theta1" = -19.6200*\theta1 + 39.2400*\theta2
\theta2" = 39.2400*\theta1 -132.6603*\theta2

where

\theta1 = position of top joint
\theta2 = position of bottom joint
```

See "Mathematical Symbols, Greek Letters, and TeX Characters" in the MATLAB documentation for information on the TeX formatting commands supported by Simulink.

4 Deselect the annotation by clicking outside it or typing **Esc**.

Simulink displays the formatted text.

```
Linearization of Double Pendulum

θ1" = -19.6200*θ1 + 39.2400*θ2
θ2" = 39.2400*θ1 -132.6603*θ2

where

θ1 = position of top joint
θ2 = position of bottom joint
```

Creating Annotations Programmatically

You can use the Simulink add_block command to create annotations at the command line or in an M-file program. Use the following syntax to create the annotation:

```
add_block('built-in/Note','path/text','Position', [center_x, 0,
0, center_y]);
```

where path is the path of the diagram to be annotated, text is the text of the annotation, and [center_x, 0, 0, center_y] is the position of the center of the annotation in pixels relative to the upper left corner of the diagram. For example, the following sequence of commands

```
new_system('test')
open_system('test')
```

```
add_block('built-in/Gain', 'test/Gain', 'Position', [260, 125,
290, 155])
add_block('built-in/Note','test/programmatically created',
'Position', [550 0 0 180])
```

creates the following model:

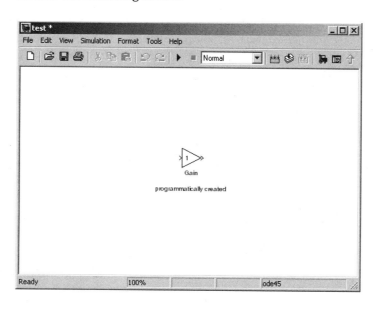

Creating Subsystems

As your model increases in size and complexity, you can simplify it by grouping blocks into subsystems. Using subsystems has these advantages:

- It helps reduce the number of blocks displayed in your model window.
- It allows you to keep functionally related blocks together.
- It enables you to establish a hierarchical block diagram, where a Subsystem block is on one layer and the blocks that make up the subsystem are on another.

You can create a subsystem in two ways:

- Add a Subsystem block to your model, then open that block and add the blocks it contains to the subsystem window.
- Add the blocks that make up the subsystem, then group those blocks into a subsystem.

Creating a Subsystem by Adding the Subsystem Block

To create a subsystem before adding the blocks it contains, add a Subsystem block to the model, then add the blocks that make up the subsystem:

1 Copy the Subsystem block from the Signals & Systems library into your model.

2 Open the Subsystem block by double-clicking it.

   Simulink opens the subsystem in the current or a new model window, depending on the model window reuse mode that you selected (see "Window Reuse" on page 5-23).

3 In the empty Subsystem window, create the subsystem. Use Inport blocks to represent input from outside the subsystem and Outport blocks to represent external output.

For example, the subsystem shown includes a Sum block and Inport and Outport blocks to represent input to and output from the subsystem.

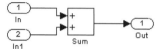

Creating a Subsystem by Grouping Existing Blocks

If your model already contains the blocks you want to convert to a subsystem, you can create the subsystem by grouping those blocks:

1 Enclose the blocks and connecting lines that you want to include in the subsystem within a bounding box. You cannot specify the blocks to be grouped by selecting them individually or by using the **Select All** command. For more information, see "Selecting Multiple Objects Using a Bounding Box" on page 5-3.

For example, this figure shows a model that represents a counter. The Sum and Unit Delay blocks are selected within a bounding box.

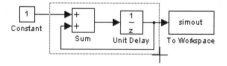

When you release the mouse button, the two blocks and all the connecting lines are selected.

2 Choose **Create Subsystem** from the **Edit** menu. Simulink replaces the selected blocks with a Subsystem block.

This figure shows the model after you choose the **Create Subsystem** command (and resize the Subsystem block so the port labels are readable).

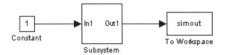

If you open the Subsystem block, Simulink displays the underlying system, as shown below. Notice that Simulink adds Inport and Outport blocks to represent input from and output to blocks outside the subsystem.

As with all blocks, you can change the name of the Subsystem block. You can also use the masking feature to customize the block's appearance and dialog box. See Chapter 10, "Creating Masked Subsystems."

Undoing Subsystem Creation

To undo creation of a subsystem by grouping blocks, select **Undo** from the **Edit** menu. You can undo creation of a subsystem that you have subsequently edited. However, the **Undo** command does not undo any nongraphical changes that you made to the blocks, such as changing the value of a block parameter or the name of a block. Simulink alerts you to this limitation by displaying a warning dialog box before undoing creation of a modified subsystem.

Model Navigation Commands

Subsystems allow you to create a hierarchical model comprising many layers. You can navigate this hierarchy, using the Simulink Model Browser (see "The Model Browser" on page 9-22) and/or the following model navigation commands:

- **Open**

  The **Open** command opens the currently selected subsystem. To execute the command, choose **Open** from the Simulink **Edit** menu, press **Enter**, or double-click the subsystem.

- **Open block in new window**

  Opens the currently selected subsystem regardless of the Simulink window reuse settings (see "Window Reuse" on page 5-23).

- **Go to Parent**

  The **Go to Parent** command displays the parent of the subsystem displayed in the current window. To execute the command, press **Esc** or select **Go to Parent** from the Simulink **View** menu.

Window Reuse

You can specify whether Simulink model navigation commands use the current window or a new window to display a subsystem or its parent. Reusing windows avoids cluttering your screen with windows. Creating a window for each subsystem allows you to view subsystems side by side with their parents or siblings. To specify your preference regarding window reuse, select **Preferences** from the Simulink **File** menu and then select one of the following **Window reuse type** options listed in the Simulink **Preferences** dialog box.

Reuse Type	Open Action	Go to Parent (Esc) Action
none	Subsystem appears in a new window.	Parent window moves to the front.
reuse	Subsystem replaces the parent in the current window.	Parent window replaces subsystem in current window

Reuse Type	Open Action	Go to Parent (Esc) Action
`replace`	Subsystem appears in a new window. Parent window disappears.	Parent window appears. Subsystem window disappears.
`mixed`	Subsystem appears in its own window.	Parent window rises to front. Subsystem window disappears.

Labeling Subsystem Ports

Simulink labels ports on a Subsystem block. The labels are the names of Inport and Outport blocks that connect the subsystem to blocks outside the subsystem through these ports.

You can hide (or show) the port labels by

- Selecting the Subsystem block, then choosing **Hide Port Labels** (or **Show Port Labels**) from the **Format** menu
- Selecting an Inport or Outport block in the subsystem and choosing **Hide Name** (or **Show Name**) from the **Format** menu
- Selecting the **Show port labels** option in the Subsystem block's parameter dialog

This figure shows two models. The subsystem on the left contains two Inport blocks and one Outport block. The Subsystem block on the right shows the labeled ports.

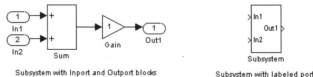

Subsystem with Inport and Outport blocks   Subsystem with labeled ports

Controlling Access to Subsystems

Simulink allows you to control user access to subsystems that reside in libraries. In particular, you can prevent a user from viewing or modifying the contents of a library subsystem while still allowing the user to employ the subsystem in a model.

To control access to a library subsystem, open the subsystem's parameter dialog box and set its Access parameter to either ReadOnly or NoReadOrWrite. The first option allows a user to view the contents of the library subsystem and make local copies but prevents the user from modifying the original library copy. The second option prevents the user from viewing the contents of, creating local copies, or modifying the permissions of the library subsystem. See the Subsystem block for more information on subsystem access options. Note that both options allow a user to use the library system in models by creating links (see "Working with Block Libraries" on page 6-18).

Creating Conditionally Executed Subsystems

A *conditionally executed subsystem* is a subsystem whose execution depends on the value of an input signal. The signal that controls whether a subsystem executes is called the *control signal*. The signal enters the Subsystem block at the *control input*.

Conditionally executed subsystems can be very useful when you are building complex models that contain components whose execution depends on other components.

Simulink supports the following types of conditionally executed subsystems:

- An *enabled subsystem* executes while the control signal is positive. It starts execution at the time step where the control signal crosses zero (from the negative to the positive direction) and continues execution while the control signal remains positive. Enabled subsystems are described in more detail in "Enabled Subsystems" on page 5-26.

- A *triggered subsystem* executes once each time a trigger event occurs. A trigger event can occur on the rising or falling edge of a trigger signal, which can be continuous or discrete. Triggered subsystems are described in more detail in "Triggered Subsystems" on page 5-31.

- A *triggered and enabled subsystem* executes once on the time step when a trigger event occurs if the enable control signal has a positive value at that step. See "Triggered and Enabled Subsystems" on page 5-35 for more information.

- A *control flow subsystem* executes one or more times at the current time step when enabled by a control flow block that implements control logic similar to that expressed by programming language control flow statements (e.g., if-then, while, do, and for. See "Modeling with Control Flow Blocks" in the online documentation for more information.

Enabled Subsystems

Enabled subsystems are subsystems that execute at each simulation step where the control signal has a positive value.

An enabled subsystem has a single control input, which can be scalar or vector valued.

- If the input is a scalar, the subsystem executes if the input value is greater than zero.
- If the input is a vector, the subsystem executes if *any* of the vector elements is greater than zero.

For example, if the control input signal is a sine wave, the subsystem is alternately enabled and disabled, as shown in this figure. An up arrow signifies enable, a down arrow disable.

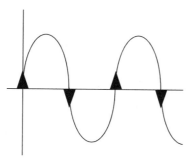

Simulink uses the zero-crossing slope method to determine whether an enable is to occur. If the signal crosses zero and the slope is positive, the subsystem is enabled. If the slope is negative at the zero crossing, the subsystem is disabled.

Creating an Enabled Subsystem

You create an enabled subsystem by copying an Enable block from the Signals & Systems library into a subsystem. Simulink adds an enable symbol and an enable control input port to the Subsystem block.

Subsystem

Setting Output Values While the Subsystem Is Disabled. Although an enabled subsystem does not execute while it is disabled, the output signal is still available to other blocks. While an enabled subsystem is disabled, you can choose to hold the subsystem outputs at their previous values or reset them to their initial conditions.

Open each Outport block's dialog box and select one of the choices for the **Output when disabled** parameter, as shown in the following dialog box:

- Choose held to cause the output to maintain its most recent value.
- Choose reset to cause the output to revert to its initial condition. Set the **Initial output** to the initial value of the output.

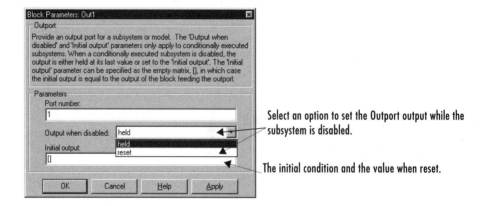

Select an option to set the Outport output while the subsystem is disabled.

The initial condition and the value when reset.

Setting States When the Subsystem Becomes Reenabled. When an enabled subsystem executes, you can choose whether to hold the subsystem states at their previous values or reset them to their initial conditions.

To do this, open the Enable block dialog box and select one of the choices for the **States when enabling** parameter, as shown in the dialog box following:

- Choose held to cause the states to maintain their most recent values.
- Choose reset to cause the states to revert to their initial conditions.

Select an option to set the states when the subsystem is reenabled.

Outputting the Enable Control Signal. An option on the Enable block dialog box lets you output the enable control signal. To output the control signal, select the **Show output port** check box.

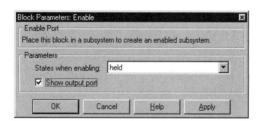

This feature allows you to pass the control signal down into the enabled subsystem, which can be useful where logic within the enabled subsystem is dependent on the value or values contained in the control signal.

Blocks an Enabled Subsystem Can Contain

An enabled subsystem can contain any block, whether continuous or discrete. Discrete blocks in an enabled subsystem execute only when the subsystem executes, and only when their sample times are synchronized with the simulation sample time. Enabled subsystems and the model use a common clock.

Note Enabled subsystems can contain Goto blocks. However, only state ports can connect to Goto blocks in an enabled subsystem. See the Simulink demo model, clutch, for an example of how to use Goto blocks in an enabled subsystem.

For example, this system contains four discrete blocks and a control signal. The discrete blocks are

- Block A, which has a sample time of 0.25 second
- Block B, which has a sample time of 0.5 second
- Block C, within the enabled subsystem, which has a sample time of 0.125 second
- Block D, also within the enabled subsystem, which has a sample time of 0.25 second

The enable control signal is generated by a Pulse Generator block, labeled Signal E, which changes from 0 to 1 at 0.375 second and returns to 0 at 0.875 second.

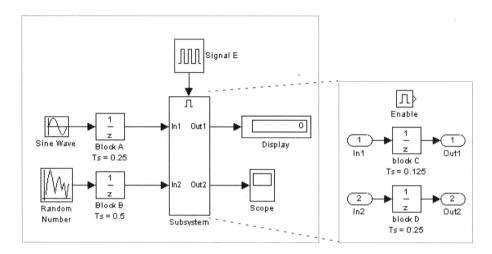

The chart below indicates when the discrete blocks execute.

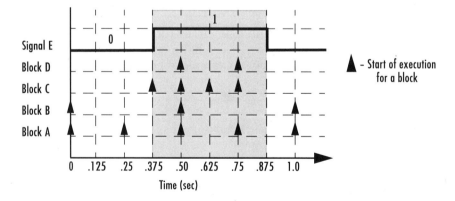

Blocks A and B execute independently of the enable control signal because they are not part of the enabled subsystem. When the enable control signal becomes positive, blocks C and D execute at their assigned sample rates until the enable control signal becomes zero again. Note that block C does not execute at 0.875 second when the enable control signal changes to zero.

Triggered Subsystems

Triggered subsystems are subsystems that execute each time a trigger event occurs.

A triggered subsystem has a single control input, called the *trigger input*, that determines whether the subsystem executes. You can choose from three types of trigger events to force a triggered subsystem to begin execution:

- rising triggers execution of the subsystem when the control signal rises from a negative or zero value to a positive value (or zero if the initial value is negative).

- falling triggers execution of the subsystem when the control signal falls from a positive or a zero value to a negative value (or zero if the initial value is positive).

- either triggers execution of the subsystem when the signal is either rising or falling.

Note In the case of discrete systems, a signal's rising or falling from zero is considered a trigger event only if the signal has remained at zero for more than one time step preceding the rise or fall. This eliminates false triggers caused by control signal sampling.

For example, in the following timing diagram for a discrete system, a rising trigger (R) does not occur at time step 3 because the signal has remained at zero for only one time step when the rise occurs.

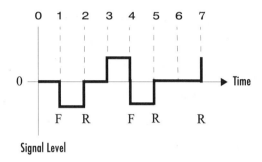

A simple example of a triggered subsystem is illustrated.

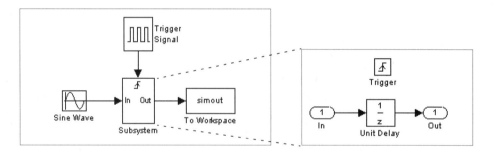

In this example, the subsystem is triggered on the rising edge of the square wave trigger control signal.

Creating a Triggered Subsystem

You create a triggered subsystem by copying the Trigger block from the Signals & Systems library into a subsystem. Simulink adds a trigger symbol and a trigger control input port to the Subsystem block.

To select the trigger type, open the Trigger block dialog box and select one of the choices for the **Trigger type** parameter, as shown in the following dialog box:

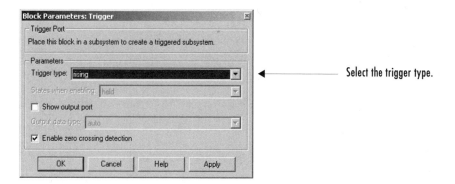

Select the trigger type.

Simulink uses different symbols on the Trigger and Subsystem blocks to indicate rising and falling triggers (or either). This figure shows the trigger symbols on Subsystem blocks.

Subsystem with Rising trigger   Subsystem with Falling trigger   Subsystem with Rising or Falling trigger

Outputs and States Between Trigger Events. Unlike enabled subsystems, triggered subsystems always hold their outputs at the last value between triggering events. Also, triggered subsystems cannot reset their states when triggered; states of any discrete blocks are held between trigger events.

Outputting the Trigger Control Signal. An option on the Trigger block dialog box lets you output the trigger control signal. To output the control signal, select the **Show output port** check box.

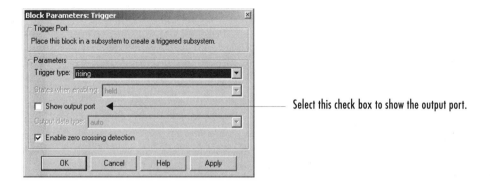

Select this check box to show the output port.

The **Output data type** field allows you to specify the data type of the output signal as auto, int8, or double. The auto option causes the data type of the output signal to be set to the data type (either int8 or double) of the port to which the signal is connected.

Function-Call Subsystems

You can create a triggered subsystem whose execution is determined by logic internal to an S-function instead of by the value of a signal. These subsystems are called *function-call subsystems*. For more information about function-call subsystems, see "Function-Call Subsystems" in the "Implementing Block Features" section of *Writing S-Functions*.

Blocks That a Triggered Subsystem Can Contain

Triggered systems execute only at specific times during a simulation. As a result, the only blocks that are suitable for use in a triggered subsystem are

- Blocks with inherited sample time, such as the Logical Operator block or the Gain block
- Discrete blocks having their sample times set to -1, which indicates that the sample time is inherited from the driving block

Triggered and Enabled Subsystems

A third kind of conditionally executed subsystem combines both types of conditional execution. The behavior of this type of subsystem, called a *triggered and enabled* subsystem, is a combination of the enabled subsystem and the triggered subsystem, as shown by this flow diagram.

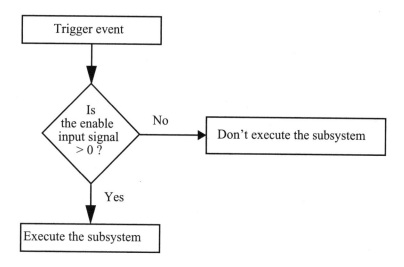

A triggered and enabled subsystem contains both an enable input port and a trigger input port. When the trigger event occurs, Simulink checks the enable input port to evaluate the enable control signal. If its value is greater than zero, Simulink executes the subsystem. If both inputs are vectors, the subsystem executes if at least one element of each vector is nonzero.

The subsystem executes once at the time step at which the trigger event occurs.

Creating a Triggered and Enabled Subsystem

You create a triggered and enabled subsystem by dragging both the Enable and Trigger blocks from the Signals & Systems library into an existing subsystem. Simulink adds enable and trigger symbols and enable and trigger and enable control inputs to the Subsystem block.

Subsystem

You can set output values when a triggered and enabled subsystem is disabled as you would for an enabled subsystem. For more information, see "Setting Output Values While the Subsystem Is Disabled" on page 5-27. Also, you can specify what the values of the states are when the subsystem is reenabled. See "Setting States When the Subsystem Becomes Reenabled" on page 5-28.

Set the parameters for the Enable and Trigger blocks separately. The procedures are the same as those described for the individual blocks.

A Sample Triggered and Enabled Subsystem

A simple example of a triggered and enabled subsystem is illustrated in the model below.

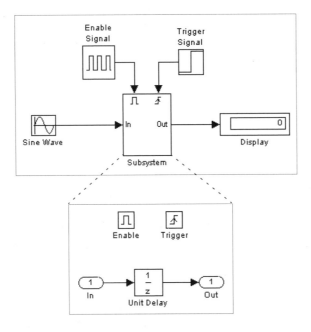

Creating Alternately Executing Subsystems

You can use conditionally executed subsystems in combination with Merge blocks to create sets of subsystems that execute alternately, depending on the current state of the model. For example, the following figure shows a model that uses two enabled blocks and a Merge block to model a full-wave rectifier, that is, a device that converts AC current to pulsating DC current.

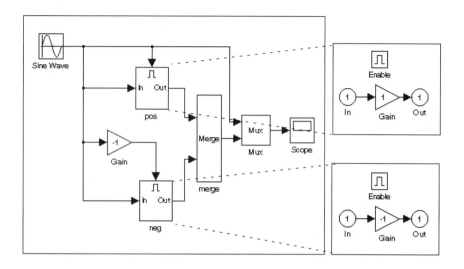

In this example, the block labeled "pos" is enabled when the AC waveform is positive; it passes the waveform unchanged to its output. The block labeled "neg" is enabled when the waveform is negative; it inverts the waveform. The Merge block passes the output of the currently enabled block to the Mux block, which passes the output, along with the original waveform, to the Scope block.

The Scope creates the following display.

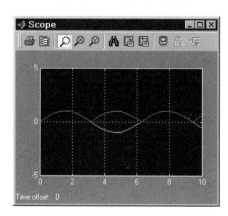

Using Callback Routines

You can define MATLAB expressions that execute when the block diagram or a block is acted upon in a particular way. These expressions, called *callback routines*, are associated with block, port, or model parameters. For example, the callback associated with a block's OpenFcn parameter is executed when the model user double-clicks on that block's name or the path changes.

Tracing Callbacks

Callback tracing allows you to determine the callbacks Simulink invokes and in what order Simulink invokes them when you open or simulate a model. To enable callback tracing, select the **Callback tracing** option on the Simulink **Preferences** dialog box (see "Setting Simulink Preferences" on page 2-18) or execute set_param(0, 'CallbackTracing', 'on'). This option causes Simulink to list callbacks in the MATLAB Command Window as they are invoked.

Creating Model Callback Functions

You can create model callback functions interactively or programmatically. Use the **Callbacks** pane of the model's **Model Properties** dialog box to create model callbacks interactively. To create a callback programmatically, use the set_param command to assign a MATLAB expression that implements the function to the model parameter corresponding to the callback (see "Model Callback Parameters" on page 5-39).

For example, this command evaluates the variable testvar when the user double-clicks the Test block in mymodel.

```
set_param('mymodel/Test', 'OpenFcn', testvar)
```

You can examine the clutch system (clutch.mdl) for routines associated with many model callbacks.

Model Callback Parameters

The following table lists the model parameters used to specify model callback routines and indicates when the corresponding callback routines are executed.

Parameter	When Executed
CloseFcn	Before the block diagram is closed.
PostLoadFcn	After the model is loaded. Defining a callback routine for this parameter might be useful for generating an interface that requires that the model has already been loaded.
InitFcn	Called at start of model simulation.
PostSaveFcn	After the model is saved.
PreLoadFcn	Before the model is loaded. Defining a callback routine for this parameter might be useful for loading variables used by the model.
PreSaveFcn	Before the model is saved.
StartFcn	Before the simulation starts.
StopFcn	After the simulation stops. Output is written to workspace variables and files before the StopFcn is executed.

Note Beware of adverse interactions between callback functions of models referenced by other models. For example, suppose that model A references model B and that model A's OpenFcn creates variables in the MATLAB workspace and model B's CloseFcn clears the MATLAB workspace. Now suppose that simulating model A requires rebuilding model B. Rebuilding B entails opening and closing model B and hence invoking model B's CloseFcn, which clears the MATLAB workspace, including the variables created by A's OpenFcn.

Creating Block Callback Functions

You can create model callback functions interactively or programmatically. Use the **Callbacks** pane of the model's **Block Properties** dialog box (see "Callbacks Pane" on page 6-10) to create model callbacks interactively. To create a callback programmatically, use the set_param command to assign a MATLAB expression that implements the function to the block parameter corresponding to the callback (see "Block Callback Parameters" on page 5-40).

Note A callback for a masked subsystem cannot directly reference the parameters of the masked subsystem (see "About Masks" on page 10-2). The reason? Simulink evaluates block callbacks in a model's base workspace whereas the mask parameters reside in the masked subsystem's private workspace. A block callback, however, can use get_param to obtain the value of a mask parameter, e.g., get_param(gcb, 'gain'), where gain is the name of a mask parameter of the current block.

Block Callback Parameters

This table lists the parameters for which you can define block callback routines, and indicates when those callback routines are executed. Routines that are executed before or after actions take place occur immediately before or after the action.

Parameter	When Executed
ClipboardFcn	When the block is copied or cut to the system clipboard.
CloseFcn	When the block is closed using the close_system command.
CopyFcn	After a block is copied. The callback is recursive for Subsystem blocks (that is, if you copy a Subsystem block that contains a block for which the CopyFcn parameter is defined, the routine is also executed). The routine is also executed if an add_block command is used to copy the block.

Parameter	When Executed
DeleteChildFcn	After a block is deleted from a subsystem.
DeleteFcn	Before a block is deleted, e.g., when the user deletes the block or closes the model containing the block. This callback is recursive for Subsystem blocks.
DestroyFcn	When the block has been destroyed.
InitFcn	Before the block diagram is compiled and before block parameters are evaluated.
LoadFcn	After the block diagram is loaded. This callback is recursive for Subsystem blocks.
ModelCloseFcn	Before the block diagram is closed. This callback is recursive for Subsystem blocks.
MoveFcn	When the block is moved or resized.
NameChangeFcn	After a block's name and/or path changes. When a Subsystem block's path is changed, it recursively calls this function for all blocks it contains after calling its own NameChangeFcn routine.
OpenFcn	When the block is opened. This parameter is generally used with Subsystem blocks. The routine is executed when you double-click the block or when an open_system command is called with the block as an argument. The OpenFcn parameter overrides the normal behavior associated with opening a block, which is to display the block's dialog box or to open the subsystem.
ParentCloseFcn	Before closing a subsystem containing the block or when the block is made part of a new subsystem using the new_system command (see new_system in the "Model Creation Commands" section of the Simulink online Help).

Parameter	When Executed
PreSaveFcn	Before the block diagram is saved. This callback is recursive for Subsystem blocks.
PostSaveFcn	After the block diagram is saved. This callback is recursive for Subsystem blocks.
StartFcn	After the block diagram is compiled and before the simulation starts. In the case of an S-Function block, StartFcn executes immediately before the first execution of the block's mdlProcessParameters function. See "S-Function Callback Methods" in *Writing S-Functions* in the Simulink online Help for more information.
StopFcn	At any termination of the simulation. In the case of an S-Function block, StopFcn executes after the block's mdlTerminate function executes. See "S-Function Callback Methods" in *Writing S-Functions* in the Simulink online Help for more information.
UndoDeleteFcn	When a block delete is undone.

Port Callback Parameters

Block input and output ports have a single callback parameter, ConnectionCallback. This parameter allows you to set callbacks on ports that are triggered every time the connectivity of those ports changes. Examples of connectivity changes include deletion of blocks connected to the port and deletion, disconnection, or connection of branches or lines to the port.

Use get_param to get the port handle of a port and set_param to set the callback on the port. For example, suppose the currently selected block has a single input port. The following code fragment sets foo as the connection callback on the input port.

```
phs = get_param(gcb, 'PortHandles');
set_param(phs.Inport, 'ConnectionCallback', 'foo');
```

The first argument of the callback function must be a port handle. The callback function can have other arguments (and a return value) as well. For example, the following is a valid callback function signature.

```
function foo(port, otherArg1, otherArg2)
```

6

Working with Blocks

This section explores the following block-related topics.

About Blocks

Blocks are the elements from which Simulink models are built. You can model virtually any dynamic system by creating and interconnecting blocks in appropriate ways. This section discusses how to use blocks to build models of dynamic systems.

Block Data Tips

On Microsoft Windows, Simulink displays information about a block in a pop-up window when you allow the pointer to hover over the block in the diagram view. To disable this feature or control what information a data tip includes, select **Block data tips options** from the Simulink **View** menu.

Virtual Blocks

When creating models, you need to be aware that Simulink blocks fall into two basic categories: nonvirtual and virtual blocks. Nonvirtual blocks play an active role in the simulation of a system. If you add or remove a nonvirtual block, you change the model's behavior. Virtual blocks, by contrast, play no active role in the simulation; they help organize a model graphically. Some Simulink blocks are virtual in some circumstances and nonvirtual in others. Such blocks are called conditionally virtual blocks. The following table lists Simulink virtual and conditionally virtual blocks.

Block Name	Condition Under Which Block Is Virtual
Bus Selector	Always virtual.
Demux	Always virtual.
Enable	Virtual unless connected directly to an Outport block.
From	Always virtual.
Goto	Always virtual.
Goto Tag Visibility	Always virtual.
Ground	Always virtual.

Block Name	Condition Under Which Block Is Virtual
Inport	Virtual *unless* the block resides in a conditionally executed subsystem *and* has a direct connection to an outport block.
Mux	Always virtual.
Outport	Virtual when the block resides within any subsystem block (conditional or not), and does *not* reside in the root (top-level) Simulink window.
Selector	Virtual except in matrix mode.
Signal Specification	Always virtual.
Subsystem	Virtual unless the block is conditionally executed and/or the block's **Treat as Atomic Unit** option is selected.
Terminator	Always virtual.
Trigger	Virtual when the outport port is *not* present.

Editing Blocks

The Simulink Editor allows you to cut and paste blocks in and between models.

Copying and Moving Blocks from One Window to Another

As you build your model, you often copy blocks from Simulink block libraries or other libraries or models into your model window. To do this, follow these steps:

1 Open the appropriate block library or model window.

2 Drag the block to copy into the target model window. To drag a block, position the cursor over the block, then press and hold down the mouse button. Move the cursor into the target window, then release the mouse button.

You can also drag blocks from the Simulink Library Browser into a model window. See "Browsing Block Libraries" on page 6-24 for more information.

Note Simulink hides the names of Sum, Mux, Demux, Bus Creator, and Bus Selector blocks when you copy them from the Simulink block library to a model. This is done to avoid unnecessarily cluttering the model diagram. (The shapes of these blocks clearly indicate their respective functions.)

You can also copy blocks by using the **Copy** and **Paste** commands from the **Edit** menu:

1 Select the block you want to copy.

2 Choose **Copy** from the **Edit** menu.

3 Make the target model window the active window.

4 Choose **Paste** from the **Edit** menu.

Simulink assigns a name to each copied block. If it is the first block of its type in the model, its name is the same as its name in the source window. For example, if you copy the Gain block from the Math library into your model window, the name of the new block is Gain. If your model already contains a block named Gain, Simulink adds a sequence number to the block name (for example, Gain1, Gain2). You can rename blocks; see "Manipulating Block Names" on page 6-13.

When you copy a block, the new block inherits all the original block's parameter values.

Simulink uses an invisible five-pixel grid to simplify the alignment of blocks. All blocks within a model snap to a line on the grid. You can move a block slightly up, down, left, or right by selecting the block and pressing the arrow keys.

You can display the grid in the model window by typing the following command in the MATLAB window.

```
set_param('<model name>','showgrid','on')
```

To change the grid spacing, enter

```
set_param('<model name>','gridspacing',<number of pixels>)
```

For example, to change the grid spacing to 20 pixels, enter

```
set_param('<model name>','gridspacing',20)
```

For either of the above commands, you can also select the model, then enter gcs instead of <model name>.

You can copy or move blocks to compatible applications (such as word processing programs) using the **Copy**, **Cut**, and **Paste** commands. These commands copy only the graphic representation of the blocks, not their parameters.

Moving blocks from one window to another is similar to copying blocks, except that you hold down the **Shift** key while you select the blocks.

You can use the **Undo** command from the **Edit** menu to remove an added block.

Moving Blocks in a Model

To move a single block from one place to another in a model window, drag the block to a new location. Simulink automatically repositions lines connected to the moved block.

To move more than one block, including connecting lines:

1 Select the blocks and lines. If you need information about how to select more than one block, see "Selecting More Than One Object" on page 5-3.

2 Drag the objects to their new location and release the mouse button.

Copying Blocks in a Model

You can copy blocks in a model as follows. While holding down the **Ctrl** key, select the block with the left mouse button, then drag it to a new location. You can also do this by dragging the block using the right mouse button. Duplicated blocks have the same parameter values as the original blocks. Sequence numbers are added to the new block names.

Deleting Blocks

To delete one or more blocks, select the blocks to be deleted and press the **Delete** or **Backspace** key. You can also choose **Clear** or **Cut** from the **Edit** menu. The **Cut** command writes the blocks into the clipboard, which enables you to paste them into a model. Using the **Delete** or **Backspace** key or the **Clear** command does not enable you to paste the block later.

You can use the **Undo** command from the **Edit** menu to replace a deleted block.

Setting Block Parameters

All Simulink blocks have a common set of parameters, called block properties, that you can set (see "Common Block Parameters" in the online Simulink Help). See "Block Properties Dialog Box" on page 6-8 for information on setting block properties. In addition, many blocks have one or more block-specific parameters that you can set (see "Block-Specific Parameters" in the online Simulink reference). By setting these parameters, you can customize the behavior of the block to meet the specific requirements of your model.

Setting Block-Specific Parameters

Every block that has block-specific parameters has a dialog box that you can use to view and set the parameters. You can display this dialog by selecting the block in the model window and choosing **BLOCK Parameters** from the model window's **Edit** menu or from the model window's context (right-click) menu, where **BLOCK** is the name of the block you selected, e.g., **Constant Parameters**. You can also display a block's parameter dialog box by double-clicking its icon in the model or library window.

Note This holds true for all blocks with parameter dialog boxes except for the Subsystem block. You must use the model window's **Edit** menu or context menu to display a Subsystem block's parameter dialog.

For information on the parameter dialog of a specific block, see the block's documentation in the "Simulink Blocks" in the online Simulink Help.

You can set any block parameter, using the Simulink set_param command. See set_param in the online Simulink Help for details.

You can use any MATLAB constant, variable, or expression that evaluates to an acceptable result when specifying the value of a parameter in a block parameter dialog or a set_param command.

Tuning Parameters

Simulink lets you change the values of block parameters during simulation. You can use a block's parameter dialog box or the MATLAB Command Line to tune block parameters. To use the block's parameter dialog box, open the block's parameter dialog box, change the value displayed in the dialog box, and click the dialog box's **OK** or **Apply** button. You can use the set_param command to change the value of a variable at the MATLAB Command Line during simulation. Or, if the model uses a MATLAB workspace variable to specify the parameter's value, you can change the parameter's value by assigning a new value to the variable. In either case, you must update the model's block diagram for the change to take effect.

Block Properties Dialog Box

This dialog box lets you set a block's properties. To display this dialog, select the block in the model window and then select **Block Properties** from the **Edit** menu.

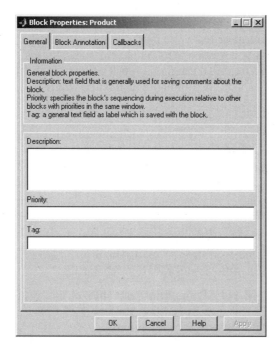

The dialog box contains the following tabbed panes.

General Pane

This pane allows you to set the following properties.

Description. Brief description of the block's purpose.

Priority. Execution priority of this block relative to other blocks in the model. See "Assigning Block Priorities" on page 6-19 for more information.

Tag. Text that is assigned to the block's Tag parameter and saved with the block in the model. You can use the tag to create your own block-specific label for a block.

Block Annotation Pane

The block annotation pane allows you to display the values of selected parameters of a block in an annotation that appears beneath the block's icon.

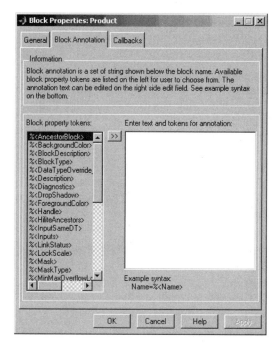

Enter the text of the annotation in the text field that appears on the right side of the pane. The text can include block property tokens, for example

```
%<Name>
Priority = %<priority>
```

of the form %<param> where param is the name of a parameter of the block. When displaying the annotation, Simulink replaces the tokens with the values of the corresponding parameters, e.g.,

The block property tag list on the left side of the pane lists all the tags that are valid for the currently selected block. To include one of the listed tags in the annotation, select the tag and then click the button between the tag list and the annotation field.

You can also create block annotations programmatically. See "Creating Block Annotations Programmatically" on page 6-11.

Callbacks Pane

The **Callbacks Pane** allows you to specify implementations for a block's callbacks (see "Using Callback Routines" on page 5-38).

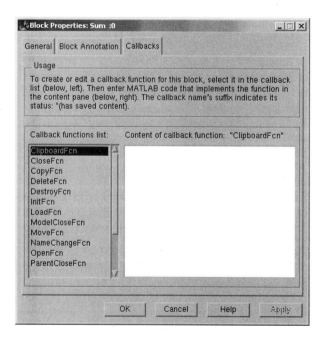

To specify an implementation for a callback, select the callback in the callback list on the left side of the pane. Then enter MATLAB commands that implement the callback in the right-hand field. Click **OK** or **Append** to save the change. Simulink appends an asterisk to the name of the saved callback to indicate that it has been implemented.

Creating Block Annotations Programmatically

You can use a block's `AttributesFormatString` parameter to display selected parameters of a block beneath the block as an "attributes format string," i.e. a string that specifies values of the block's attributes (parameters). The "Model and Block Parameters" section in the online Simulink reference describes the parameters that a block can have. Use the Simulink `set_param` command to set this parameter to the desired attributes format string.

The attributes format string can be any text string that has embedded parameter names. An embedded parameter name is a parameter name preceded by `%<` and followed by `>`, for example, `%<priority>`. Simulink displays the attributes format string beneath the block's icon, replacing each parameter name with the corresponding parameter value. You can use line-feed characters (`\n`) to display each parameter on a separate line. For example, specifying the attributes format string

```
pri=%<priority>\ngain=%<Gain>
```

for a Gain block displays

If a parameter's value is not a string or an integer, Simulink displays `N/S` (not supported) for the parameter's value. If the parameter name is invalid, Simulink displays `???` as the parameter value.

State Properties Dialog Box

The **State Properties** dialog box allows you to specify code generation options for certain blocks with discrete states. To get help on using this dialog box, you must install the Real-Time Workshop documentation. See "Block States: Storing and Interfacing" in the online documentation for Real-Time Workshop for more information.

Changing a Block's Appearance

The Simulink Editor allows you to change the size, orientation, color, and label location of a block in a block diagram.

Changing the Orientation of a Block

By default, signals flow through a block from left to right. Input ports are on the left, and output ports are on the right. You can change the orientation of a block by choosing one of these commands from the **Format** menu:

- The **Flip Block** command rotates the block 180 degrees.
- The **Rotate Block** command rotates a block clockwise 90 degrees.

The figure below shows how Simulink orders ports after changing the orientation of a block using the **Rotate Block** and **Flip Block** menu items. The text in the blocks shows their orientation.

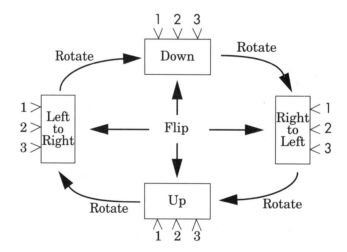

Resizing a Block

To change the size of a block, select it, then drag any of its selection handles. While you hold down the mouse button, a dotted rectangle shows the new block size. When you release the mouse button, the block is resized.

For example, the figure below shows a Signal Generator block being resized. The lower-right handle was selected and dragged to the cursor position. When the mouse button is released, the block takes its new size.

This figure shows a block being resized.

Displaying Parameters Beneath a Block

You can cause Simulink to display one or more of a block's parameters beneath the block. You specify the parameters to be displayed in the following ways:

- By entering an attributes format string in the **Attributes format string** field of the block's **Block Properties** dialog box (see "Block Properties Dialog Box" on page 6-8)
- By setting the value of the block's AttributesFormatString property to the format string, using set_param

Using Drop Shadows

You can add a drop shadow to a block by selecting the block, then choosing **Show Drop Shadow** from the **Format** menu. When you select a block with a drop shadow, the menu item changes to **Hide Drop Shadow**. The figure below shows a Subsystem block with a drop shadow.

Manipulating Block Names

All block names in a model must be unique and must contain at least one character. By default, block names appear below blocks whose ports are on the sides, and to the left of blocks whose ports are on the top and bottom, as the following figure shows.

Left to right   Top to bottom

Note Simulink commands interprets a forward slash, i.e., /, as a block path delimiter. For example, the path vdp/Mu designates a block named Mu in the model named vdp. Therefore, avoid using forward slashes (/) in block names to avoid causing Simulink to interpret the names as paths.

Changing Block Names

You can edit a block name in one of these ways:

- To replace the block name, click the block name, double-click or drag the cursor to select the entire name, then enter the new name.
- To insert characters, click between two characters to position the insertion point, then insert text.
- To replace characters, drag the mouse to select a range of text to replace, then enter the new text.

When you click the pointer anywhere else in the model or take any other action, the name is accepted or rejected. If you try to change the name of a block to a name that already exists or to a name with no characters, Simulink displays an error message.

You can modify the font used in a block name by selecting the block, then choosing the **Font** menu item from the **Format** menu. Select a font from the **Set Font** dialog box. This procedure also changes the font of any text that appears inside the block.

You can cancel edits to a block name by choosing **Undo** from the **Edit** menu.

Note If you change the name of a library block, all links to that block become unresolved.

Changing the Location of a Block Name

You can change the location of the name of a selected block in two ways:

- By dragging the block name to the opposite side of the block.
- By choosing the **Flip Name** command from the **Format** menu. This command changes the location of the block name to the opposite side of the block.

For more information about block orientation, see "Changing the Orientation of a Block" on page 6-12.

Changing Whether a Block Name Appears

To change whether the name of a selected block is displayed, choose a menu item from the **Format** menu:

- The **Hide Name** menu item hides a visible block name. When you select **Hide Name**, it changes to **Show Name** when that block is selected.
- The **Show Name** menu item shows a hidden block name.

Specifying a Block's Color

See "Specifying Block Diagram Colors" on page 5-5 for information on how to set the color of a block.

Displaying Block Outputs

Simulink can display block outputs as data tips on the block diagram while a simulation is running.

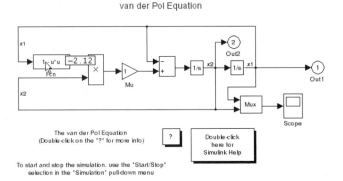

You can specify whether and when to display block outputs (see "Enabling Port Values Display" on page 6-16) and the size and format of the output displays and the rate at which Simulink updates them during a simulation (see "Port Values Display Options" on page 6-17).

Enabling Port Values Display

To turn display of port output values on or off, select **Port Values** from the model editor's **View** menu. A menu of display options appears. Select one of the following display options from the menu:

- **Show none**

  Turns port value displaying off.

- **Show when hovering**

  Displays output port values for the block under the mouse cursor.

- **Toggle when selected**

  Selecting a block displays its outputs. Reselecting the block turns the display off.

When using the Microsoft Windows version of Simulink, you can turn block output display when hovering on or off from the model editor's toolbar. To do this, select the block output display button on the toobar.

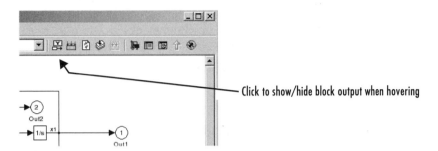

Click to show/hide block output when hovering

Port Values Display Options

To specify other display options, select **Port Values -> Options** from the model editor's **View** menu. The **Block Output Display Options** dialog box appears.

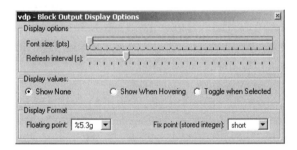

To increase the size of the output display text, move the **Font size** slider to the right. To increase the rate at which Simulink updates the displays, move the **Refresh interval slider** to the left.

Working with Block Libraries

Libraries enable users to copy blocks into their models from external libraries and automatically update the copied blocks when the source blocks change. Using libraries allows users who develop their own block libraries, or who use those provided by others (such as blocksets), to ensure that their models automatically include the most recent versions of these blocks.

Terminology

It is important to understand the terminology used with this feature.

Library – A collection of library blocks. A library must be explicitly created using **New Library** from the **File** menu.

Library block – A block in a library.

Reference block – A copy of a library block.

Link – The connection between the reference block and its library block that allows Simulink to update the reference block when the library block changes.

Copy – The operation that creates a reference block from either a library block or another reference block.

This figure illustrates this terminology.

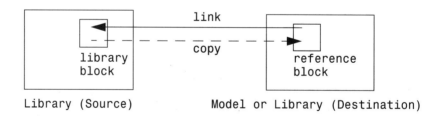

Simulink Block Library

Simulink comes with a library of standard blocks called the Simulink block library. See "Starting Simulink" on page 4-2 for information on displaying and using this library.

Creating a Library Link

To create a link to a library block in a model, copy the block from the library to the model (see "Copying and Moving Blocks from One Window to Another" on page 6-4) or by dragging the block from the Library Browser (see "Browsing Block Libraries" on page 6-24) into the model window.

When you copy a library block into a model or another library, Simulink creates a link to the library block. The reference block is a copy of the library block. You can change the values of the reference block's parameters but you cannot mask the block or, if it is masked, edit the mask. Also, you cannot set callback parameters for a reference block. If the link is to a subsystem, you can modify the contents of the reference subsystem (see "Modifying a Linked Subsystem" on page 6-20).

The library and reference blocks are linked *by name*; that is, the reference block is linked to the specific block and library whose names are in effect at the time the copy is made.

If Simulink is unable to find either the library block or the source library on your MATLAB path when it attempts to update the reference block, the link becomes *unresolved*. Simulink issues an error message and displays these blocks using red dashed lines. The error message is

```
Failed to find block "source-block-name"
in library "source-library-name"
referenced by block
"reference-block-path".
```

The unresolved reference block is displayed like this (colored red).

Reference Block Name

To fix a bad link, you must do one of the following:

- Delete the unlinked reference block and copy the library block back into your model.
- Add the directory that contains the required library to the MATLAB path and select **Update Diagram** from the **Edit** menu.

- Double-click the reference block. On the dialog box that appears, correct the pathname and click **Apply** or **Close**.

Disabling Library Links

Simulink allows you to disable linked blocks in a model. Simulink ignores disabled links when simulating a model. To disable a link, select the link, choose **Link options** from the model window's **Edit** or context menu, then choose **Disable link**. To restore a disabled link, choose **Restore link** from the **Link Options** menu.

Modifying a Linked Subsystem

Simulink allows you to modify subsystems that are library links. If your modifications alter the structure of the subsystem, you must disable the link from the reference block to the library block. If you attempt to modify the structure of a subsystem link, Simulink prompts you to disable the link. Examples of structural modifications include adding or deleting a block or line or changing the number of ports on a block. Examples of nonstructural changes include changes to parameter values that do not affect the structure of the subsystem.

Propagating Link Modifications

Simulink allows a model to have active links with nonstructural but not structural changes. If you restore a link that has structural changes, Simulink prompts you to either propagate or discard the changes. If you choose to propagate the changes, Simulink updates the library block with the changes made in the reference block. If you choose to discard the changes, Simulink replaces the modified reference block with the original library block. In either case, the end result is that the reference block is an exact copy of the library block.

If you restore a link with nonstructural changes, Simulink enables the link without prompting you to propagate or discard the changes. If you want to propagate or discard the changes at a later time, select the reference block, choose **Link options** from the model window's **Edit** or context menu, then choose **Propagate/Discard changes**. If you want to view the nonstructural parameter differences between a reference block and its corresponding library block, choose **View changes** from the **Link options** menu.

Updating a Linked Block

Simulink updates out-of-date reference blocks in a model or library at these times:

- When the model or library is loaded
- When you select **Update Diagram** from the **Edit** menu or run the simulation
- When you query the LinkStatus parameter of a block, using the get_param command (see "Library Link Status" on page 6-23)
- When you use the find_system command

Updating Links to Reflect Block Path Changes

Library forwarding tables enable Simulink to update models to reflect changes in the names or locations of the library blocks that they reference. For example, suppose that you rename a block in a library. You can use a forwarding table for that library to enable Simulink to update models that reference the block under its old name to reference it under its new name.

Simulink allows you to associate a forwarding table with any library. The forwarding table for a library specifies the old locations and new locations of blocks that have moved within the library or to another library. You associate a forwarding table with a library by setting its ForwardingTable parameter to a cell array of two-element cell arrays, each of which specifies the old and new path of a block that has moved. For example, the following command creates a forwarding table and assigns it to a library named Lib1.

```
set_param('Lib1', 'ForwardingTable', {{'Lib1/A', 'Lib2/A'}
{'Lib1/B', 'Lib1/C'}});
```

The forwarding table specifies that block A has moved from Lib1 to Lib2. and that block B is now named C. Suppose that you opens a model that contains links to Lib1/A and Lib1/B. Simulink updates the link to Lib1/A to refer to Lib2/A and the link to Lib1/B to refer to Lib1/C. The changes become permanent when you subsequently save the model.

Breaking a Link to a Library Block

You can break the link between a reference block and its library block to cause the reference block to become a simple copy of the library block, unlinked to the library block. Changes to the library block no longer affect the block. Breaking links to library blocks may enable you to transport a model as a stand-alone model, without the libraries.

To break the link between a reference block and its library block, first disable the block. Then select the block and choose **Break Library Link** from the **Link options** menu. You can also break the link between a reference block and its library block from the command line by changing the value of the LinkStatus parameter to 'none' using this command:

```
set_param('refblock', 'LinkStatus', 'none')
```

You can save a system and break all links between reference blocks and library blocks using this command:

```
save_system('sys', 'newname', 'BreakLinks')
```

Note Breaking library links in a model does not guarantee that you can run the model stand-alone, especially if the model includes blocks from third-party libraries or optional Simulink blocksets. It is possible that a library block invokes functions supplied with the library and hence can run only if the library is installed on the system running the model. Further, breaking a link can cause a model to fail when you install a new version of the library on a system. For example, suppose a block invokes a function that is supplied with the library. Now suppose that a new version of the library eliminates the function. Running a model with an unlinked copy of the block results in invocation of a now nonexistent function, causing the simulation to fail. To avoid such problems, you should generally avoid breaking links to third-party libraries and optional Simulink blocksets.

Finding the Library Block for a Reference Block

To find the source library and block linked to a reference block, select the reference block, then choose **Go To Library Link** from the **Link options** submenu of the model window's **Edit** or context menu. If the library is open, Simulink selects and highlights the library block and makes the source library the active window. If the library is not open, Simulink opens it and selects the library block.

Library Link Status

All blocks have a LinkStatus parameter that indicates whether the block is a reference block. The parameter can have these values.

Status	Description
none	Block is not a reference block.
resolved	Link is resolved.
unresolved	Link is unresolved.
implicit	Block resides in library block and is itself not a link to a library block. For example, suppose that A is a link to a subsystem in a library that contains a Gain block. Further, suppose that you open A and select the Gain block. Then, get_param(gcb, 'LinkStatus') returns implicit.
inactive	Link is disabled.
restore	Restores a broken link to a library block and discards any changes made to the local copy of the library block. For example, set_param(gcb, 'LinkStatus', 'restore') replaces the selected block with a link to a library block of the same type, discarding any changes in the local copy of the library block. Note that this parameter is a "write-only" parameter, i.e., it is usable only with set_param. You cannot use get_param to get it.
propagate	Restores a broken link to a library block and propagates any changes made to the local copy to the library.

Displaying Library Links

Simulink optionally displays an arrow in the bottom left corner of each block that represents a library link in a model.

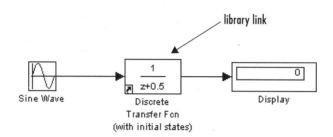

This arrow allows you to tell at a glance whether a block represents a link to a library block or a local instance of a block. To enable display of library links, select **Library Link Display** from the model window's **Format** menu and then select either **User** (displays only links to user libraries) or **All** (displays all links).

The color of the link arrow indicates the status of the link.

Color	Status
Black	Active link
Grey	Inactive link
Red	Active and modified

Getting Information About Library Blocks

Use the `libinfo` command to get information about reference blocks in a system

Browsing Block Libraries

The Library Browser lets you quickly locate and copy library blocks into a model. To display the Library Browser, click the **Library Browser** button in the toolbar of the MATLAB desktop or Simulink model window or enter `simulink` at the MATLAB command line.

Note The Library Browser is available only on Microsoft Windows platforms.

The Library Browser contains three panes.

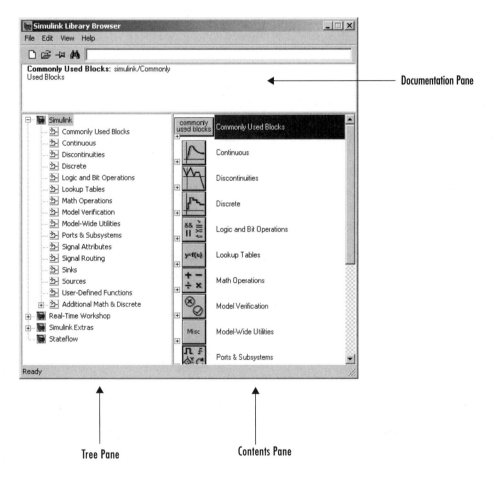

The tree pane displays all the block libraries installed on your system. The contents pane displays the blocks that reside in the library currently selected in the tree pane. The documentation pane displays documentation for the block selected in the contents pane.

You can locate blocks either by navigating the Library Browser's library tree or by using the Library Browser's search facility.

Navigating the Library Tree

The library tree displays a list of all the block libraries installed on the system. You can view or hide the contents of libraries by expanding or collapsing the tree using the mouse or keyboard. To expand/collapse the tree, click the +/- buttons next to library entries or select an entry and press the +/- or right/left arrow key on your keyboard. Use the up/down arrow keys to move up or down the tree.

Searching Libraries

To find a particular block, enter the block's name in the edit field next to the Library Browser's **Find** button, then click the **Find** button.

Opening a Library

To open a library, right-click the library's entry in the browser. Simulink displays an **Open Library** button. Select the **Open Library** button to open the library.

Creating and Opening Models

To create a model, select the **New** button on the Library Browser's toolbar. To open an existing model, select the **Open** button on the toolbar.

Copying Blocks

To copy a block from the Library Browser into a model, select the block in the browser, drag the selected block into the model window, and drop it where you want to create the copy.

Displaying Help on a Block

To display help on a block, right-click the block in the Library Browser and select the button that subsequently pops up.

Pinning the Library Browser

To keep the Library Browser above all other windows on your desktop, select the **PushPin** button on the browser's toolbar.

Adding Libraries to the Library Browser

If you want a library that you have created to appear in the Library Browser, you must create an slblocks.m file that describes the library in the directory that contains it. The easiest way to create an slblocks.m file is to use an existing slblocks.m file as a template. You can find all existing slblocks.m files on your system by typing

```
which('slblocks.m', '-all')
```

at the MATLAB command prompt. Copy any of the displayed files to your library's directory. Then open the copy, edit it, following the instructions included in the file, and save the result. Finally, add your library's directory to the MATLAB path, if necessary. The next time you open the Library Browser, your library should appear among the libraries displayed in the browser.

Working with Signals

This section describes how to create and use Simulink signals.

Signal Basics

This section provides an overview of Simulink signals and explains how to specify, display, and check the validity of signal connections.

About Signals

Simulink defines signals as the outputs of dynamic systems represented by blocks in a Simulink diagram and by the diagram itself. The lines in a block diagram represent mathematical relationships among the signals defined by the block diagram. For example, a line connecting the output of block A to the input of block B indicates that the signal output by B depends on the signal output by A.

Note It is tempting but misleading to think of Simulink signals as traveling along the lines that connect blocks the way electrical signals travel along a telephone wire. This analogy is misleading because it suggests that a block diagram represents physical connections between blocks, which is not the case. Simulink signals are mathematical, not physical, entities and the lines in a block diagram represent mathematical, not physical, relationships among signals.

Creating Signals

You can create signals by creating source blocks in your model. For example, you can create a signal that varies sinusoidally with time by dragging an instance of the Sine block from the Simulink Sources library into the model. See "Sources" in the online "Block Libraries" reference for information on blocks that you can use to create signals in a model. You can also use the Signal & Scope Manager to create signals in your model without using blocks. See "The Signal & Scope Manager" on page 7-16 for more information.

Signal Labels

A signal label is text that appears next to the line that represents a signal that has a name. The signal label displays the signal's name. In addition, if the signal is a virtual signal (see "Virtual Signals" on page 7-4) and its **Show propagated signals** property is on (see "Show propagated signals" in the online Simulink documentation), the label displays the names of the signals that make up the virtual signal.

Simulink creates a label for a signal when you assign it a name in the **Signal Properties** dialog box (see "Signal Properties Dialog Box" in the online Simulink documentation). You can change the signal's name by editing its label on the block diagram. To edit the label, left-click the label. Simulink replaces the label with an edit field. Edit the name in the edit field, the press **Enter** or click outside the label to confirm the change.

Displaying Signal Values

As with creating signals, you can use either blocks or the Signal & Scope Manager to display the values of signals during a simulation. For example, you can use either the Scope block or the Signal & Scope Manager to graph time-varying signals on an oscilloscope-like display during simulation. See "Sinks" in the online "Block Libraries" reference for information on blocks that you can use to display signals in a model.

Signal Dimensions

Simulink blocks can output one- or two-dimensional signals. A one-dimensional (1-D) signal consists of a stream of one-dimensional arrays output at a frequency of one array (vector) per simulation time step. A two-dimensional (2-D) signal consists of a stream of two-dimensional arrays emitted at a frequency of one 2-D array (matrix) per block sample time. The Simulink user interface and documentation generally refer to 1-D signals as *vectors* and 2-D signals as *matrices*. A one-element array is frequently referred to as a *scalar*. A *row vector* is a 2-D array that has one row. A *column vector* is a 2-D array that has one column.

Simulink blocks vary in the dimensionality of the signals they can accept or output during simulation. Some blocks can accept or output signals of any dimensions. Some can accept or output only scalar or vector signals. To determine the signal dimensionality of a particular block, see the block's description in "Simulink Blocks" in the online Simulink Help. See "Determining Output Signal Dimensions" on page 7-12 for information on what determines the dimensions of output signals for blocks that can output nonscalar signals.

Complex Signals

The values of Simulink signals can be complex numbers. A signal whose values are complex numbers is called a complex signal. You can introduce a complex-valued signal into a model in the following ways:

- Load complex-valued signal data from the MATLAB workspace into the model via a root-level inport.
- Create a Constant block in your model and set its value to a complex number.
- Create real signals corresponding to the real and imaginary parts of a complex signal, then combine the parts into a complex signal, using the Real-Imag to Complex conversion block.

You can manipulate complex signals via blocks that accept them. If you are not sure whether a block accepts complex signals, see the documentation for the block in the "Simulink Blocks" section of the Simulink online documentation.

Virtual Signals

A *virtual signal* is a signal that represents another signal graphically. Some blocks, such as Bus Creator, Inport, and Outport blocks (see "Virtual Blocks" on page 6-2), generate virtual signals either exclusively or optionally (see "Virtual Versus Nonvirtual Buses" on page 7-7). Virtual signals are purely graphical entities. They have no mathematical or physical significance. Simulink ignores them when simulating a model.

Whenever you run or update a model, Simulink determines the nonvirtual signal(s) represented by the model's virtual signal(s), using a procedure known as *signal propagation*. When running the model, Simulink uses the corresponding nonvirtual signal(s), determined via signal propagation, to drive the blocks to which the virtual signals are connected. Consider, for example, the following model.

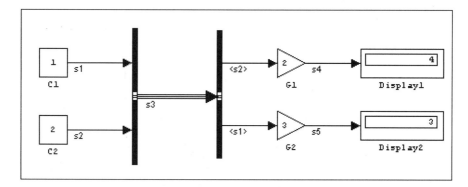

The signals driving Gain blocks G1 and G2 are virtual signals corresponding to signals s2 and s1, respectively. Simulink determines this automatically whenever you update or simulate the model.

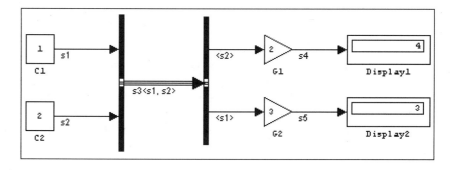

Note Virtual signals can represent virtual as well as nonvirtual signals. For example, you can use a Bus Creator block to combine multiple virtual and nonvirtual signals into a single virtual signal. If during signal propagation Simulink determines that a component of a virtual signal is itself virtual, Simulink determines its nonvirtual components using signal propagation. This process continues until Simulink has determined all nonvirtual components of a virtual signal.

Control Signals

A *control signal* is a signal used by one block to initiate execution of another block, e.g., a function-call or action subsystem. When you update or start simulation of a block diagram, Simulink uses a dash-dot pattern to redraw lines representing the diagram's control signals as illustrated in the following example.

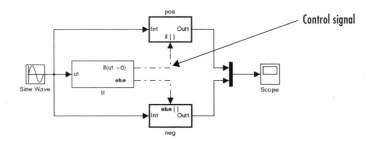

Signal Buses

A bus is a composite signal comprising a set of signals represented graphically by a bundle of lines. It is analogous to a bundle of wires held together by tie wraps. The components of a bus can have different data types and can themselves be composite signals (i.e., buses or muxed signals). You can use Bus Creator and Inport blocks to create signal buses and Bus Selector blocks to access a bus's components.

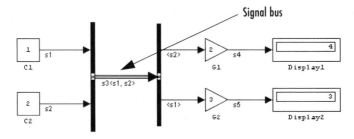

Selecting a bus and then **Signal Dimensions** from the model editor's **Format** menu displays the number of signal components carried by the bus.

Virtual Versus Nonvirtual Buses

Buses may be either virtual or nonvirtual. During simulation, blocks connected to a virtual bus read their inputs from memory allocated to the component signals, which may reside in noncontiguous areas of memory. By contrast, blocks connected to a nonvirtual bus read their inputs from a copy of the component signals maintained by Simulink in a contiguous area of memory allocated to the bus.

Some Simulink features require use of nonvirtual signals. Others require virtual buses. Nonvirtual buses also facilitate code generation by enabling buses to be represented by data structures. On the other hand, nonvirtual buses can save memory where nonvirtual buses are not required.

The Bus Creator and Inport blocks output virtual buses by default. To cause them to output a nonvirtual bus, select the **Output as structure** option on their parameter dialog boxes. You can also use the Signal Conversion block to convert nonvirtual to virtual buses, and vice versa.

Bus-Capable Blocks

A *bus-capable block* is a block through which both virtual and nonvirtual buses can pass. All virtual blocks are bus capable. Further, the following nonvirtual blocks are also bus-capable:

- Memory
- Merge
- Switch
- Multiport Switch
- Rate Transition
- Unit Delay
- Zero-Order Hold

Some bus-capable blocks impose constraints on bus propagation through them. See the documentation for the individual blocks for more information.

Connecting Buses to Subsystem Inports

Generally, an Inport block is a virtual block and hence accepts a bus as input. However, an Inport block is nonvirtual if it resides in a conditionally executed or atomic subsystem and it or any of its components is directly connected to an output of the subsystem. In such a case, the Inport block can accept a bus only if its components have the same data type. If the components are of differing data types, attempting to simulate the model causes Simulink to halt the simulation and display an error message. You can avoid this problem, without changing the semantics of your model, by inserting a Signal Conversion block between the Inport block and the Outport block to which it was originally connected.

Consider, for example, the following model.

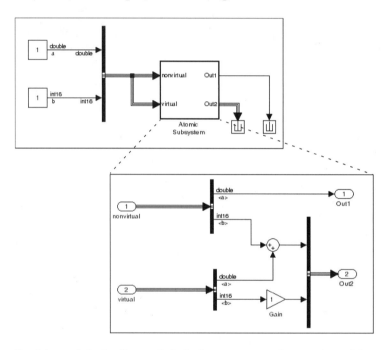

In this model, the Inport labeled nonvirtual is nonvirtual because it resides in an atomic subsystem and one of its components (labeled a) is directly connected to one of the subsystem's outputs. Further, the bus connected to the subsystem's inputs has components of differing data types. As a result, Simulink cannot simulate this model.

Inserting a Signal Conversion block with the bus copy option selected breaks the direct connection to the subsystem's output and hence enables Simulink to simulate the model.

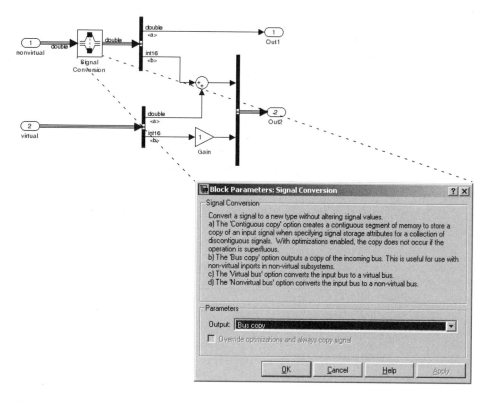

Connecting Buses to Model Inports

If you want a root level Inport of a model to be able to accept a bus signal, you must set the Inport's bus object parameter to the name of a bus object that defines the type of bus that the Inport accepts. See "Working with Data Objects" on page 7-10 and Simulink.Bus class for more information.

Checking Signal Connections

Many Simulink blocks have limitations on the types of signals they can accept. Before simulating a model, Simulink checks all blocks to ensure that they can accommodate the types of signals output by the ports to which they are connected. If any incompatibilities exist, Simulink reports an error and terminates the simulation. To detect such errors before running a simulation, choose **Update Diagram** from the Simulink **Edit** menu. Simulink reports any invalid connections found in the process of updating the diagram.

Signal Glossary

The following table summarizes the terminology used to describe signals in the Simulink user interface and documentation.

Term	Meaning
Complex signal	Signal whose values are complex numbers.
Data type	Format used to represent signal values internally.
Matrix	Two-dimensional signal array.
Real signal	Signal whose values are real (as opposed to complex) numbers.
Scalar	One-element array, i.e., a one-element, 1-D or 2-D array.
Signal bus	A composite signal made up of other signals, including other buses. You can use Bus Creator, Mux, and Inport blocks to create signal buses.
Signal propagation	Process used by Simulink to determine attributes of signals and blocks, such as data types, labels, sample time, dimensionality, and so on, that are determined by connectivity.
Size	Number of elements that a signal contains. The size of a matrix (2-D) signal is generally expressed as M-by-N where M is the number of columns and N is the number of rows making up the signal.
Vector	One-dimensional signal array.

Term	Meaning
Virtual signal	Signal that represents another signal or set of signals.
Width	Size of a vector signal.

Determining Output Signal Dimensions

If a block can emit nonscalar signals, the dimensions of the signals that the block outputs depend on the block's parameters, if the block is a source block; otherwise, the output dimensions depend on the dimensions of the block's input and parameters.

Determining the Output Dimensions of Source Blocks

A *source* block is a block that has no inputs. Examples of source blocks include the Constant block and the Sine Wave block. See the "Sources Library" table in the online Simulink Help for a complete listing of Simulink source blocks. The output dimensions of a source block are the same as those of its output value parameters if the block's **Interpret Vector Parameters as 1-D** parameter is off (i.e., not selected in the block's parameter dialog box). If the **Interpret Vector Parameters as 1-D** parameter is on, the output dimensions equal the output value parameter dimensions unless the parameter dimensions are N-by-1 or 1-by-N. In the latter case, the block outputs a vector signal of width N.

As an example of how a source block's output value parameter(s) and **Interpret Vector Parameters as 1-D** parameter determine the dimensionality of its output, consider the Constant block. This block outputs a constant signal equal to its **Constant value** parameter. The following table illustrates how the dimensionality of the **Constant value** parameter and the setting of the **Interpret Vector Parameters as 1-D** parameter determine the dimensionality of the block's output.

Constant Value	Interpret Vector Parameters as 1-D	Output
2-D scalar	off	2-D scalar
2-D scalar	on	1-D scalar
1-by-N matrix	off	1-by-N matrix
1-by-N matrix	on	N-element vector
N-by-1 matrix	off	N-by-1 matrix
N-by-1 matrix	on	N-element vector

Constant Value	Interpret Vector Parameters as 1-D	Output
M-by-N matrix	off	M-by-N matrix
M-by-N matrix	on	M-by-N matrix

Simulink source blocks allow you to specify the dimensions of the signals that they output. You can therefore use them to introduce signals of various dimensions into your model.

Determining the Output Dimensions of Nonsource Blocks

If a block has inputs, the dimensions of its outputs are, after scalar expansion, the same as those of its inputs. (All inputs must have the same dimensions, as discussed in the next section.)

Signal and Parameter Dimension Rules

When creating a Simulink model, you must observe the following rules regarding signal and parameter dimensions.

Input Signal Dimension Rule

All nonscalar inputs to a block must have the same dimensions.

A block can have a mix of scalar and nonscalar inputs as long as all the nonscalar inputs have the same dimensions. Simulink expands the scalar inputs to have the same dimensions as the nonscalar inputs (see "Scalar Expansion of Inputs" on page 7-14), thus preserving the general rule.

Block Parameter Dimension Rule

In general, a block's parameters must have the same dimensions as the corresponding inputs.

Two seeming exceptions exist to this general rule:

• A block can have scalar parameters corresponding to nonscalar inputs. In this case, Simulink expands a scalar parameter to have the same dimensions as the corresponding input (see "Scalar Expansion of Parameters" on page 7-15), thus preserving the general rule.

- If an input is a vector, the corresponding parameter can be either an N-by-1 or a 1-by-N matrix. In this case, Simulink applies the N matrix elements to the corresponding elements of the input vector. This exception allows use of MATLAB row or column vectors, which are actually 1-by-N or N-by-1 matrices, respectively, to specify parameters that apply to vector inputs.

Vector or Matrix Input Conversion Rules

Simulink converts vectors to row or column matrices and row or column matrices to vectors under the following circumstances:

- If a vector signal is connected to an input that requires a matrix, Simulink converts the vector to a one-row or one-column matrix.
- If a one-column or one-row matrix is connected to an input that requires a vector, Simulink converts the matrix to a vector.
- If the inputs to a block consist of a mixture of vectors and matrices and the matrix inputs all have one column or one row, Simulink converts the vectors to matrices having one column or one row, respectively.

Note You can configure Simulink to display a warning or error message if a vector or matrix conversion occurs during a simulation. See "Vector/matrix block input conversion" on page 8-53 for more information.

Scalar Expansion of Inputs and Parameters

Scalar expansion is the conversion of a scalar value into a nonscalar array of the same dimensions. Many Simulink blocks support scalar expansion of inputs and parameters. Block descriptions in the "Simulink Blocks" section in the online Simulink Help indicate whether Simulink applies scalar expansion to a block's inputs and parameters.

Scalar Expansion of Inputs

Scalar expansion of inputs refers to the expansion of scalar inputs to match the dimensions of other nonscalar inputs or nonscalar parameters. When the input to a block is a mix of scalar and nonscalar signals, Simulink expands the scalar inputs into nonscalar signals having the same dimensions as the other nonscalar inputs. The elements of an expanded signal equal the value of the scalar from which the signal was expanded.

The following model illustrates scalar expansion of inputs. This model adds scalar and vector inputs. The input from block Constant1 is scalar expanded to match the size of the vector input from the Constant block. The input is expanded to the vector [3 3 3].

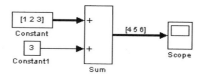

When a block's output is a function of a parameter and the parameter is nonscalar, Simulink expands a scalar input to match the dimensions of the parameter. For example, Simulink expands a scalar input to a Gain block to match the dimensions of a nonscalar gain parameter.

Scalar Expansion of Parameters

If a block has a nonscalar input and a corresponding parameter is a scalar, Simulink expands the scalar parameter to have the same number of elements as the input. Each element of the expanded parameter equals the value of the original scalar. Simulink then applies each element of the expanded parameter to the corresponding input element.

This example shows that a scalar parameter (the Gain) is expanded to a vector of identically valued elements to match the size of the block input, a three-element vector.

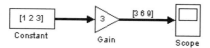

The Signal & Scope Manager

The Signal & Scope Manager lets you globally manage signal generators and viewers.

Note The Signal & Scope Manager requires that you start MATLAB with Java enabled (the default).

To display the Signal & Scope Manager, select **Signal & Scope Manager** from the model editor's **Tools** or context menu. The Signal & Scope Manager appears.

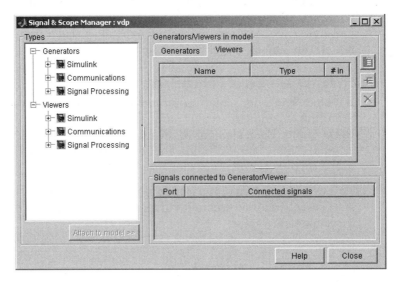

The Signal & Scope Manager contains the following groups of controls.

Generator and Viewer Types

This group of controls lets you create signal generators and viewers of various types and associate them with your model.

The tree control displays a list of the types of generators and viewers installed on your system. The tree's second-level nodes group the generators and viewers by the products that provides them (i.e., Simulink and any MathWorks blocksets installed on your system). Expand a product's nodes to see the generators and viewers that it provides.

For information on the attributes and usage of the generators and viewers, see the documentation for the identically named source (i.e., generator) and sink (i.e., viewer) blocks in the product's documentation. For example, for information on the generators and viewers provided with Simulink, see the documentation for the corresponding blocks in the Simulink Sources and Sinks libraries.

To create an instance of a generator or viewer and associate with the currently selected model, select its type in the type list and then click the **Attach to model** button beneath the list.

Generator and Viewer Objects

This group of controls lets you edit the sources and viewers already associated with your model. It contains the following controls.

Generators

The **Generators** pane displays a table listing the generators associated with your model.

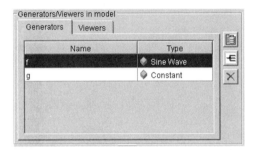

Each row corresponds to a generator. The columns specify each generator's name and type.

Viewers

The **Viewers** pane displays a table listing the viewers associated with your model.

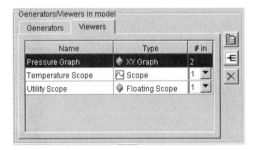

Each row corresponds to a viewer. The columns specify each viewer's name, type, and number of inputs. If a viewer accepts a variable number of inputs, the **#in** entry for the viewer contains a pull-down list that displays the range of inputs that the viewer can accept. To change the number of inputs accepted by the viewer, pull down the list and select the desired value.

Edit Buttons

Selecting the table entry for a generator or viewer enables the following buttons.

Button	Description
	Opens the parameter dialog box for the selected generator or viewer. The parameter dialog box enables you to view and change the current settings of the selected object's parameters. See the documentation for the corresponding source or sink block for more information.
	Opens the Signal Selector for the selected generator or viewer. The Signal Selector lets you connect signal generators to your model's inputs and your model's signals to its signal viewers. **Note** You can also use port or signal context menus to connect signals to input ports and output ports to viewers. For example, to connect a signal to a new viewer, select **Create Viewer** from the signal or output port's context menu, then the type of viewer. To connect a signal to an existing viewer, select **Connect to Viewer**, then the axis to display the signal. Similarly, to connect a new signal generator to a block input port, select **Create Generator** from the input port's context menu, then the type of generator.
	Deletes the selected generator or viewer.

Edit Menu

Selecting a row in the generator or viewer table and pressing the right button on your mouse displays an edit menu containing entries corresponding to the edit buttons described in the preceding section. It also displays a **Rename** command for renaming the selected object (e.g., a viewer). Selecting this command causes Simulink to replace the selected object's name with an edit control. Use the edit control to rename the object.

Note You can also rename a signal generator on a model's block diagram. To do this, select **Edit Source Name** from the context menu of an input port to which the signal generator is connected. Simulink replaces the source's name with an edit field containing the source's name. Edit the name and then click outside the field or press **Enter** to confirm your changes.

Signals connected to Generator/Viewer

This table lists the signals connected to the generator or viewer selected in the Generator/Viewers control panel of the Signal & Scope Manager.

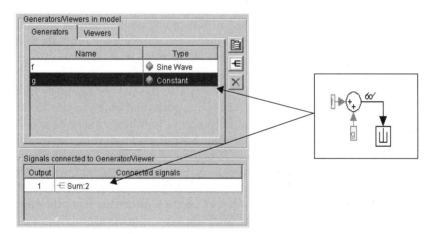

If the selected object is a signal generator, the table lists the block input ports to which each of the generator's outputs is connected. For each connection, the first column of the table specifies the number of the corresponding generator output. The second column specifies the number of the corresponding input port and the name of the block that owns the input port. For example, in the preceding figure, the **Signals connected to Generator/Viewer** table shows that the first (and only output) of the selected Constant generator is connected to the second input port of the block named Sum.

If the selected object is a signal viewer, the **Signals connected to Generator/Viewer** table lists the signals connected to the selected viewer. For each connection, the first column of the table specifies the number of the corresponding viewer axis. The second column specifies the number of the corresponding output port and the name of the block that owns the output port.

For example, in the next figure, the **Signals connected to Generator/Viewer** table shows that the first axis of the selected signal viewer is connected to the first output port of the block named Sum.

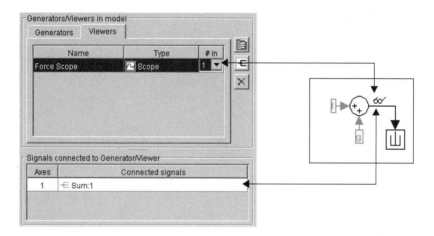

Connection Menu

Selecting a connection in the **Signals connected to Generator/Viewer** table and pressing the right button on your mouse displays a context menu. To highlight the block to which the object is connected, select **Hilight signal in model** from the menu. To open the Signal Selector, select **Edit Signal Connections** from the model.

The Signal Selector

The Signal Selector allows you to connect a signal or viewer object (see "The Signal & Scope Manager" on page 7-16) or the Floating Scope to block inputs and outputs. It appears when you click the signal selection button for a signal or viewer object in the Signal & Scope Manager or on the toolbar of the Floating Scope's window.

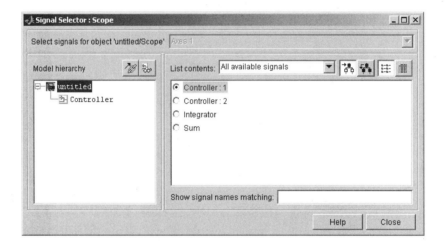

The Signal Selector that appears when you click the signal selection button applies only to the currently selected signal or viewer object (or the Floating Scope). If you want to connect blocks to another signal or viewer object, you must select the object in the Signal & Scope Manager and launch another instance of the Signal Selector. The object used to launch a particular instance of the Signal Selector is called that instance's owner.

The Signal Selector includes the following control panels.

Port/Axis Selector

This list box allows you to select the owner output port (in the case of signal generators) or display axis (in the case of signal viewers) to which you want to connect blocks in your model.

The list box is enabled only if the signal generator has multiple outputs or the signal viewer has multiple axes.

Model Hierarchy

This tree-structured list lets you select any subsystem in your model.

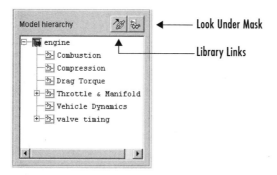

Selecting a subsystem causes the adjacent port list panel to display the ports available for connection in the selected subsystem. To display subsystems included as library links in your model, click the **Library Links** button at the top of the **Model hierarchy** panel. To display subsystems contained by masked subsystems, click the **Look Under Masks** button at the top of the panel.

Inputs/Signals List

The contents of this panel displays input ports available for connection to the Signal Selector's owner if the owner is a signal generator or signals available for connection to the owner if the owner is a signal viewer.

If the Signal Selector's owner is a signal generator, the inputs/signals list by default lists each input port in the system selected in the model hierarchy tree that is either unconnected or connected to a signal generator.

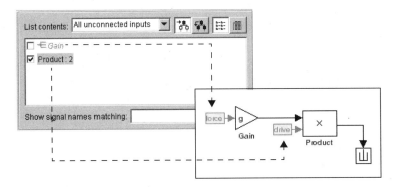

The label for each entry indicates the name of the block of which the port is an input. If the block has more than one input, the label indicates the number of the displayed port. A greyed label indicates that the port is connected to a signal generator other than the Signal Selectors' owner. Checking the checkbox next to a port's entry in the list connects the Signal Selector's owner to the port, replacing, if necessary, the signal generator previously connected to the port.

To display more information on each signal, click the **Detailed view** button at the top of the pane. The detailed view shows the path and data type of each signal and whether the signal is a test point. The controls at the top and bottom of the panel let you restrict the amount of information shown in the ports list.

- To show named signals only, select Named signals only from the **List contents** control at the top of the pane.

- To show test point signals only, select Test point signals only from the **List contents** control.

- To show only signals whose signals match a specified string of characters, enter the characters in the **Show signals matching** control at the bottom of the **Signals** pane and press the **Enter** key.

- To show the selected types of signals for all subsystems below the currently selected subsystem in the model hierarchy, click the **Current and Below** button at the top of the **Signals** pane.

To select or deselect a signal in the **Signals** pane, click its entry or use the arrow keys to move the selection highlight to the signal entry and press the **Enter** key. You can also move the selection highlight to a signal entry by typing the first few characters of its name (enough to uniquely identify it).

Note You can continue to select and deselect signals on the block diagram with the Signal Selector open. For example, shift-clicking a line in the block diagram adds the corresponding signal to the set of signals that you previously selected with the Signal Selector. Simulink updates the Signal Selector to reflect signal selection changes you have made on the block diagram. However, the changes do not appear until you select the Signal Selector window itself.

Displaying Signal Properties

A model window's **Format** menu and its model context (right-click) menu offer the following options for displaying signal properties on the block diagram.

Wide nonscalar lines

Draws lines that carry vector or matrix signals wider than lines that carry scalar signals.

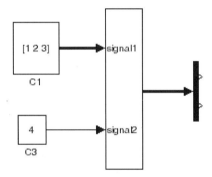

Signal dimensions

Display the dimensions of nonscalar signals next to the line that carries the signal.

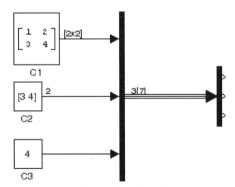

The format of the display depends on whether the line represents a single signal or a bus. If the line represents a single vector signal, Simulink displays the width of the signal. If the line represents a single matrix signal, Simulink displays its dimensions as [N_1xN_2] where N_i is the size of the ith dimension of the signal. If the line represents a bus carrying signals of the same data type, Simulink displays N{M} where N is the number of signals carried by the bus and M is the total number of signal elements carried by the bus. If the bus carries signals of different data types, Simulink displays only the total number of signal elements {M}.

Port data types

Displays the data type of a signal next to the output port that emits the signal.

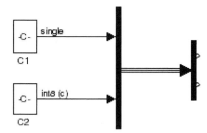

The notation (c) following the data type of a signal indicates that the signal is complex.

Signal Names

You can assign names to signals by

- Editing the signal's label
- Setting the name parameter of the port or line that represents the signal, e.g.,

```
p = get_param(gcb, 'PortHandles')
l = get_param(p.Inport, 'Line')
set_param(l, 'Name', 's9')
```

Signal Labels

A signal's label displays the signal's name. A virtual signal's label optionally displays the signals it represents in angle brackets. You can edit a signal's label, thereby changing the signal's name.

To create a signal label (and thereby name the signal), double-click the line that represents the signal. The text cursor appears. Enter the name and click anywhere outside the label to exit label editing mode.

Note When you create a signal label, take care to double-click the line. If you click in an unoccupied area close to the line, you will create a model annotation instead.

Labels can appear above or below horizontal lines or line segments, and left or right of vertical lines or line segments. Labels can appear at either end, at the center, or in any combination of these locations.

To move a signal label, drag the label to a new location on the line. When you release the mouse button, the label fixes its position near the line.

To copy a signal label, hold down the **Ctrl** key while dragging the label to another location on the line. When you release the mouse button, the label appears in both the original and the new locations.

To edit an existing signal label, select it:

- To replace the label, click the label, double-click or drag the cursor to select the entire label, then enter the new label.
- To insert characters, click between two characters to position the insertion point, then insert text.
- To replace characters, drag the mouse to select a range of text to replace, then enter the new text.

To delete all occurrences of a signal label, delete all the characters in the label. When you click outside the label, the labels are deleted. To delete a single occurrence of the label, hold down the **Shift** key while you select the label, then press the **Delete** or **Backspace** key.

To change the font of a signal label, select the signal, choose **Font** from the **Format** menu, then select a font from the **Set Font** dialog box.

Displaying Signals Represented by Virtual Signals

To display the signal(s) represented by a virtual signal, click the signal's label and enter an angle bracket (<) after the signal's name. (If the signal has no name, simply enter the angle bracket.) Click anywhere outside the signal's label. Simulink exits label editing mode and displays the signals represented by the virtual signal in brackets in the label.

Running Simulations

The following sections explain how to use Simulink to simulate a dynamic system.

Simulation Basics

Simulating a Simulink model requires only that you start the simulation (see "Starting a Simulation" on page 8-3). However, before starting the simulation, you may want to specify various simulation options, such as the simulation's start and stop time and the type of solver used to solve the model at each simulation time step. Specifying simulation options is called configuring a simulation. Simulink enables you to create multiple simulation configurations, called configuration sets, for a model, modify existing configuration sets, and switch configuration sets with a click of a mouse button (see "Configuration Sets" on page 8-26 for information on creating and selecting configuration sets).

Once you have defined or selected a simulation configuration set that meets your needs, you can start the simulation. Simulink then runs the simulation from the specified start time to the specified stop time. While the simulation is running, you can interact with the simulation in various ways, stop or pause the simulation (see "Pausing or Stopping a Simulation" on page 8-4), and launch simulations of other models. If an error occurs during a simulation, Simulink halts the simulation and pops up a diagnostic viewer that helps you to determine the cause of the error.

Controlling Execution of a Simulation

The Simulink graphical interface includes menu commands and toolbar buttons that enable you to start, stop, and pause a simulation.

Starting a Simulation

To start execution of a model, select **Start** from the model editor's **Simulation** menu or click the **Start** button on the model's toolbar.

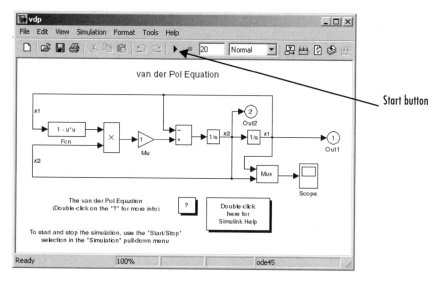

You can also use the keyboard shortcut, **Ctrl+T**, to start the simulation.

Note A common mistake that new Simulink users make is to start a simulation while the Simulink block library is the active window. Make sure your model window is the active window before starting a simulation.

Simulink starts executing the model at the start time specified on the **Configuration Parameters** dialog box. Execution continues until the simulation reaches the final time step specified on the **Configuration Parameters** dialog box, an error occurs, or you pause or terminate the simulation (see "The Configuration Parameters Dialog Box" on page 8-29).

While the simulation is running, a progress bar at the bottom of the model window shows how far the simulation has progressed. A **Stop** command replaces the **Start** command on the **Simulation** menu. A **Pause** command appears on the menu and replaces the **Start** button on the model toolbar.

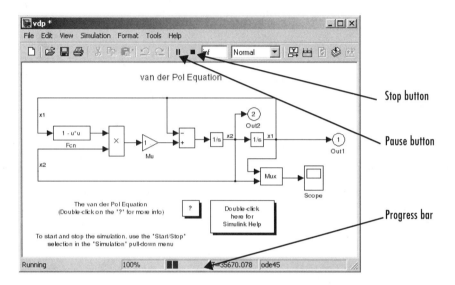

Your computer beeps to signal the completion of the simulation.

Pausing or Stopping a Simulation

Select the **Pause** command or button to pause the simulation. Simulink completes execution of the current time step and suspends execution of the simulation. When you select **Pause**, the menu item and button change to **Continue**. (The button has the same appearance as the **Start** button). You can resume a suspended simulation at the next time step by choosing **Continue**.

To terminate execution of the model, select the **Stop** command or button. The keyboard shortcut for stopping a simulation is **Ctrl+T**, the same as for starting a simulation. Simulink completes execution of the current time step before terminating the model. Subsequently selecting the **Start** command or button restarts the simulation at the first time step specified on the **Configuration Parameters** dialog box.

If the model includes any blocks that write output to a file or to the workspace, or if you select output options on the **Configuration Parameters** dialog box, Simulink writes the data when the simulation is terminated or suspended.

Interacting with a Running Simulation

You can perform certain operations interactively while a simulation is running. You can

- Modify some configuration parameters, including the stop time and the maximum step size
- Click a line to see the signal carried on that line on a floating (unconnected) Scope or Display block
- Modify the parameters of a block, as long as you do not cause a change in
  - Number of states, inputs, or outputs
  - Sample time
  - Number of zero crossings
  - Vector length of any block parameters
  - Length of the internal block work vectors

You cannot make changes to the structure of the model, such as adding or deleting lines or blocks, during a simulation. If you need to make these kinds of changes, you need to stop the simulation, make the change, then start the simulation again to see the results of the change.

Specifying a Simulation Start and Stop Time

Simulink simulations start by default at 0.0 seconds and end at 10.0 seconds. The **Solver** configuration pane allows you to specify other start and stop times for the currently selected simulation configuration. See "The Solver Pane" on page 8-30 for more information.

Note Simulation time and actual clock time are not the same. For example, running a simulation for 10 seconds usually does not take 10 seconds. The amount of time it takes to run a simulation depends on many factors, including the model's complexity, the solver's step sizes, and the computer's speed.

Choosing a Solver

A solver is a Simulink software component that determines the next time step that a simulation needs to take to meet target accuracy requirements that you specify. Simulink provides an extensive set of solvers, each adept at choosing the next time step for specific types of applications. The following sections explain how to choose the solver best suited to your application. For information on tailoring the selected solver to your model, see "Improving Simulation Accuracy" on page 8-73.

Choosing a Solver Type

Simulink divides solvers into two types: fixed-step and variable-step. Both types of solvers compute the next simulation time as the sum of the current simulation time and a quantity known as the step size. With a fixed-step solver, the step size remains constant throughout the simulation. By contrast, with a variable-step solver, the step size can vary from step to step, depending on the model's dynamics. In particular, a variable-step solver reduces the step size when a model's states are changing rapidly to maintain accuracy and increases the step size when the system's states are changing slowly in order to avoid taking unnecessary steps. The **Type** control on the Simulink **Solver** configuration pane allows you to select either of these two types of solvers (see "The Solver Pane" on page 8-30).

The choice between the two types depends on how you plan to deploy your model and the model's dynamics. If you plan to generate code from your model and run the code on a real-time computer system, you should choose a fixed-step solver to simulate the model. This is because real-time computer systems operate at fixed-size signal sample rates. A variable-step solver may cause the simulation to miss error conditions that can occur on a real-time computer system.

If you do not plan to deploy your model as generated code, the choice between a variable-step and a fixed-step solver depends on the dynamics of your model. If your model's states change rapidly or contain discontinuities, a variable-step solver can shorten the time required to simulate your model significantly. This is because, for such a model, a variable-step solver can require fewer time steps than a fixed-step solver to achieve a comparable level of accuracy.

The following model illustrates how a variable-step solver can shorten simulation time for a multirate discrete model.

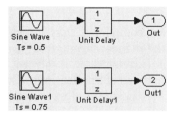

This model generates outputs at two different rates, every 0.5 second and every 0.75 second. To capture both outputs, the fixed-step solver must take a time step every 0.25 second (the *fundamental sample time* for the model).

```
[0.0 0.25 0.5 0.75 1.0 1.25 ...]
```

By contrast, the variable-step solver need take a step only when the model actually generates an output.

```
[0.0 0.5 0.75 1.0 1.5 2.0 2.25 ...]
```

This significantly reduces the number of time steps required to simulate the model.

The variable-step discrete solver uses zero-crossing detection (see "Zero-Crossing Detection" on page 3-19) to handle continuous signals. Simulink uses this solver by default if you specify a continuous solver and your model has no continuous states.

Choosing a Fixed-Step Solver

When the **Type** control of the **Solver** configuration pane is set to `fixed-step`, the configuration pane's **Solver** control allows you to choose one of the set of fixed-step solvers that Simulink provides. The set of fixed-step solvers comprises two types of solvers: discrete and continuous.

About the Fixed-Step Discrete Solver

The fixed-step discrete solver computes the time of the next time step by adding a fixed step size to the time of the current time. The accuracy and length of time of the resulting simulation depends on the size of the steps taken by the simulation: the smaller the step size, the more accurate the results but the longer the simulation takes. You can allow Simulink to choose the size of the step size (the default) or you can choose the step size yourself. If you allow Simulink to choose the step size, Simulink sets the step size to the fundamental sample time of the model if the model has discrete states or to the result of dividing the difference between the simulation start and stop time by 50 if the model has no discrete states. This choice assures that the simulation will hit every simulation time required to update the model's discrete states at the model's specified sample times

The fixed-step discrete solver has a fundamental limitation. It cannot be used to simulate models that have continuous states. That's because the fixed-step discrete solver relies on a model's blocks to compute the values of the states that they define. Blocks that define discrete states compute the values of those states at each time step taken by the solver. Blocks that define continuous states, on the other hand, rely on the solver to compute the states. Continuous solvers perform this task. You should thus select a continuous solver if your model contains continuous states.

Note If you attempt to use the fixed-step discrete solver to update or simulate a model that has continuous states, Simulink displays an error message. Thus, updating or simulating a model is a quick way to determine whether it has continuous states.

About Fixed-Step Continuous Solvers

Simulink provides a set of fixed-step continuous solvers that, like the fixed-step discrete solver, compute the simulation's next time by adding a fixed-size time step to the current time. In addition, the continuous solvers employ numerical integration to compute the values of a model's continuous states at the current step from the values at the previous step and the values of the state derivatives. This allows the fixed-step continuous solvers to handle models that contain both continuous and discrete states.

Note In theory, a fixed-step continuous solver can handle models that contain no continuous states. However, that would impose an unnecessary computational burden on the simulation. Consequently, Simulink always uses the fixed-step discrete solver for a model that contains no states or only discrete states, even if you specify a fixed-step continuous solver for the model.

Simulink provides two distinct types of fixed-step continuous solvers: explicit and implicit solvers. Explicit solvers (see "Explicit Fixed-Step Continuous Solvers" on page 8-10) compute the value of a state at the next time step as an explicit function of the current value of the state and the state derivative, e.g.,

```
X(n+1) = X(n) + h * DX(n)
```

where X is the state, DX is the state derivative, and h is the step size. An implicit solver (see "Implicit Fixed-Step Continuous Solvers" on page 8-11) computes the state at the next time step as an implicit function of the state and the state derivative at the next time step, e.g.,

```
X(n+1) - X(n) - h*DX(n+1) = 0
```

This type of solver requires more computation per step than an explicit solver but is also more accurate for a given step size. This solver thus can be faster than explicit fixed-step solvers for certain types of stiff systems.

Explicit Fixed-Step Continuous Solvers. Simulink provides a set of explicit fixed-step continuous solvers. The solvers differ in the specific integration technique used to compute the model's state derivatives. The following table lists the available solvers and the integration techniques they use.

Solver	Integration Technique
ode1	Euler's Method
ode2	Heun's Method
ode3	Bogacki-Shampine Formula
ode4	Fourth-Order Runge-Kutta (RK4) Formula
ode5	Dormand-Prince Formula

The integration techniques used by the fixed-step continuous solvers trade accuracy for computational effort. The table lists the solvers in order of the computational complexity of the integration methods they use from least complex (ode1) to most complex (ode5).

As with the fixed-step discrete solver, the accuracy and length of time of a simulation driven by a fixed-step continuous solver depends on the size of the steps taken by the solver: the smaller the step size, the more accurate the results but the longer the simulation takes. For any given step size, the more computationally complex the solver, the more accurate the simulation.

If you specify a fixed-step solver type for a model, Simulink sets the solver's model to ode3, i.e., it chooses a solver capable of handling both continuous and discrete states with moderate computational effort. As with the discrete solver, Simulink by default sets the step size to the fundamental sample time of the model if the model has discrete states or to the result of dividing the difference between the simulation start and stop time by 50 if the model has no discrete states. This assures that the solver will take a step at every simulation time required to update the model's discrete states at the model's specified sample rates. However, it does not guarantee that the default solver will accurately compute a model's continuous states or that the model cannot be simulated in less time with a less complex solver. Depending on the dynamics of your model, you may need to choose another solver and/or sample time to achieve acceptable accuracy or to shorten the simulation time.

Implicit Fixed-Step Continuous Solvers. Simulink provides one solver in this category: ode14x. This solver uses a combination of Newton's method and extrapolation from the current value to compute the value of a model state at the next time step. Simulink allows you to specify the number of Newton's method iterations and the extrapolation order that the solver uses to compute the next value of a model state (see "Fixed-Step Solver Options" on page 8-34). The more iterations and the higher the extrapolation order that you select, the greater the accuracy but also the greater the computational burden per step size.

Choosing a Fixed-Step Continuous Solver

Any of the fixed-step continuous solvers in Simulink can simulate a model to any desired level of accuracy, given enough time and a small enough step size. Unfortunately, in general, it is not possible, or at least not practical, to decide *a priori* which solver and step size combination will yield acceptable results for a model's continuous states in the shortest time. Determining the best solver for a particular model thus generally requires experimentation.

Here is the most efficient way to choose the best fixed-step solver for your model experimentally. First, use one of the variable-step solvers to simulate your model to the level of accuracy that you desire. This will give you an idea of what the simulation results should be. Next, use ode1 to simulate your model at the default step size for your model. Compare the results of simulating your model with ode1 with the results of simulating with the variable-step solver. If the results are the same within the specified level of accuracy, you have found the best fixed-step solver for your model, namely ode1. That's because ode1 is the simplest of the Simulink fixed-step solvers and hence yields the shorted simulation time for the current step size.

If ode1 does not give accurate results, repeat the preceding steps with the other fixed-step solvers until you find the one that gives accurate results with the least computational effort. The most efficient way to do this is to use a binary search technique. First, try ode3. If it gives accurate results, try ode2. If ode2 gives accurate results, it is the best solver for your model; otherwise, ode3 is the best. If ode3 does not give accurate results, try ode5. If ode5 gives accurate results, try ode4. If ode4 gives accurate results, select it as the solver for your model; otherwise, select ode5.

If ode5 does not give accurate results, reduce the simulation step size and repeat the preceding process. Continue in this way until you find a solver that solves your model accurately with the least computational effort.

Choosing a Variable-Step Solver

When the **Type** control of the **Solver** configuration pane is set to variable-step, the configuration pane's **Solver** control allows you to choose one of the set of variable-step solvers that Simulink provides. As with fixed-step solvers in Simulink, the set of variable-step solvers comprises a discrete solver and a subset of continuous solvers. Both types compute the time of the next time step by adding a step size to the time of the current time that varies depending on the rate of change of the model's states. The continuous solvers, in addition, use numerical integration to compute the values of the model's continuous states at the next time step. Both types of solvers rely on blocks that define the model's discrete states to compute the values of the discrete states that each defines.

The choice between the two types of solvers depends on whether the blocks in your model defines states and, if so, the kind of states that they define. If your model defines no states or defines only discrete states, you should select the discrete solver. In fact, if a model has no states or only discrete states, Simulink will use the discrete solver to simulate the model even if the model specifies a continuous solver.

About Variable-Step Continuous Solvers

Simulink variable-step solvers vary the step size during the simulation, reducing the step size to increase accuracy when a model's states are changing rapidly and increasing the step size to avoid taking unnecessary steps when the model's states are changing slowly. Computing the step size adds to the computational overhead at each step but can reduce the total number of steps, and hence simulation time, required to maintain a specified level of accuracy for models with rapidly changing or piecewise continuous states.

Simulink provides the following variable-step continuous solvers:

- ode45 is based on an explicit Runge-Kutta (4,5) formula, the Dormand-Prince pair. It is a *one-step* solver; that is, in computing $y(t_n)$, it needs only the solution at the immediately preceding time point, $y(t_{n-1})$. In general, ode45 is the best solver to apply as a first try for most problems. For this reason, ode45 is the default solver used by Simulink for models with continuous states.

- ode23 is also based on an explicit Runge-Kutta (2,3) pair of Bogacki and Shampine. It can be more efficient than ode45 at crude tolerances and in the presence of mild stiffness. ode23 is a one-step solver.

- ode113 is a variable-order Adams-Bashforth-Moulton PECE solver. It can be more efficient than ode45 at stringent tolerances. ode113 is a *multistep* solver; that is, it normally needs the solutions at several preceding time points to compute the current solution.

- ode15s is a variable-order solver based on the numerical differentiation formulas (NDFs). These are related to but are more efficient than the backward differentiation formulas, BDFs (also known as Gear's method). Like ode113, ode15s is a multistep method solver. If you suspect that a problem is stiff, or if ode45 failed or was very inefficient, try ode15s.

- ode23s is based on a modified Rosenbrock formula of order 2. Because it is a one-step solver, it can be more efficient than ode15s at crude tolerances. It can solve some kinds of stiff problems for which ode15s is not effective.

- ode23t is an implementation of the trapezoidal rule using a "free" interpolant. Use this solver if the problem is only moderately stiff and you need a solution without numerical damping.

- ode23tb is an implementation of TR-BDF2, an implicit Runge-Kutta formula with a first stage that is a trapezoidal rule step and a second stage that is a backward differentiation formula of order two. By construction, the same iteration matrix is used in evaluating both stages. Like ode23s, this solver can be more efficient than ode15s at crude tolerances.

Note For a *stiff* problem, solutions can change on a time scale that is very short compared to the interval of integration, but the solution of interest changes on a much longer time scale. Methods not designed for stiff problems are ineffective on intervals where the solution changes slowly because they use time steps small enough to resolve the fastest possible change. Jacobian matrices are generated numerically for ode15s and ode23s. For more information, see Shampine, L. F., *Numerical Solution of Ordinary Differential Equations*, Chapman & Hall, 1994.

Specifying Variable-Step Solver Error Tolerances

The solvers use standard local error control techniques to monitor the error at each time step. During each time step, the solvers compute the state values at the end of the step and also determine the *local error*, the estimated error of these state values. They then compare the local error to the *acceptable error*, which is a function of the relative tolerance (*rtol*) and absolute tolerance (*atol*). If the error is greater than the acceptable error for *any* state, the solver reduces the step size and tries again:

- *Relative tolerance* measures the error relative to the size of each state. The relative tolerance represents a percentage of the state's value. The default, 1e-3, means that the computed state is accurate to within 0.1%.

- *Absolute tolerance* is a threshold error value. This tolerance represents the acceptable error as the value of the measured state approaches zero.

The error for the ith state, e_i, is required to satisfy

$$e_i \leq max(rtol \times |x_i|, atol_i)$$

The following figure shows a plot of a state and the regions in which the acceptable error is determined by the relative tolerance and the absolute tolerance.

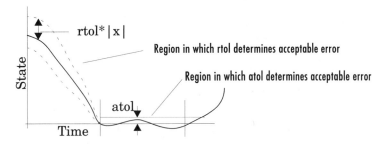

If you specify auto (the default), Simulink sets the absolute tolerance for each state initially to 1e-6. As the simulation progresses, Simulink resets the absolute tolerance for each state to the maximum value that the state has assumed thus far times the relative tolerance for that state. Thus, if a state goes from 0 to 1 and reltol is 1e-3, then by the end of the simulation the abstol is set to 1e-3 also. If a state goes from 0 to 1000, then the abstol is set to 1.

If the computed setting is not suitable, you can determine an appropriate setting yourself. You might have to run a simulation more than once to determine an appropriate value for the absolute tolerance.

The Integrator, Transfer Fcn, State-Space, and Zero-Pole blocks allow you to specify absolute tolerance values for solving the model states that they compute or that determine their output. The absolute tolerance values that you specify for these blocks override the global settings in the **Configuration Parameters** dialog box. You might want to override the global setting in this way, if the global setting does not provide sufficient error control for all of your model's states, for example, because they vary widely in magnitude.

Importing and Exporting Simulation Data

Simulink allows you to import input signal and initial state data from the MATLAB workspace and export output signal and state data to the MATLAB workspace during simulation. This capability allows you to use standard or custom MATLAB functions to generate a simulated system's input signals and to graph, analyze, or otherwise postprocess the system's outputs. See the following sections for more information:

- "Importing Input Data from the MATLAB Workspace" on page 8-16
- "Exporting Output Data to the MATLAB Workspace" on page 8-20
- "Importing and Exporting States" on page 8-22

Importing Input Data from the MATLAB Workspace

Simulink can apply input from a model's base workspace to the model's top-level inports during a simulation run. To specify this option, select the **Input** box in the **Load from workspace** area of the **Data Import/Export** pane (see "Data Import/Export Pane" on page 8-38). Then, enter an external input specification (see below) in the adjacent edit box and click **Apply**.

The input data can take any of the following forms.

Importing Data Arrays

To use this format, select **Input** in the **Load from workspace** pane and select the Array option from the **Format** list on the **Data Import/Export** pane. Selecting this option causes Simulink to evaluate the expression next to the **Input** check box and use the result as the input to the model.

The expression must evaluate to a real (noncomplex) matrix of data type double. The first column of the matrix must be a vector of times in ascending order. The remaining columns specify input values. In particular, each column represents the input for a different Inport block signal (in sequential order) and each row is the input value for the corresponding time point. Simulink linearly interpolates or extrapolates input values as necessary if the **Interpolate data** option is selected for the corresponding Inport.

The total number of columns of the input matrix must equal n + 1, where n is the total number of signals entering the model's inports.

The default input expression for a model is [t,u] and the default input format is Array. So if you define t and u in the base workspace, you need only select the **Input** option to input data from the model's base workspace. For example, suppose that a model has two inports, one of which accepts two signals and the other of which accepts one signal. Also, suppose that the base workspace defines u and t as follows:

```
t = (0:0.1:1)';
u = [sin(t), cos(t), 4*cos(t)];
```

Note The array input format allows you to load only real (noncomplex) scalar or vector data of type double. Use the structure format to input complex data, matrix (2-D) data, and/or data types other than double.

Using a MATLAB Time Expression to Import Data

You can use a MATLAB time expression to import data from the MATLAB workspace. To use a time expression, enter the expression as a string (i.e., enclosed in single quotes) in the **Input** field of the **Data Import/Export** pane. The time expression can be any MATLAB expression that evaluates to a row vector equal in length to the number of signals entering the model's inports. For example, suppose that a model has one vector Inport that accepts two signals. Furthermore, suppose that timefcn is a user-defined function that returns a row vector two elements long. The following are valid input time expressions for such a model:

```
'[3*sin(t), cos(2*t)]'
```

```
'4*timefcn(w*t)+7'
```

Simulink evaluates the expression at each step of the simulation, applying the resulting values to the model's inports. Note that Simulink defines the variable t when it runs the simulation. Also, you can omit the time variable in expressions for functions of one variable. For example, Simulink interprets the expression sin as sin(t).

Importing Data Structures

Simulink can read data from the workspace in the form of a structure whose name is specified in the **Input** text field. You can import structures that include only signal data or both signal and time data.

Importing signal-and-time data structures. To import structures that include both signal and time data, select the Structure with time option on from the **Format** list on the **Data Import/Export** pane. The input structure must have two top-level fields: time and signals. The time field contains a column vector of the simulation times. The signals field contains an array of substructures, each of which corresponds to a model input port.

Each signals substructure must contain two fields named values and dimensions, respectively. The values field must contain an array of inputs for the corresponding input port where each input corresponds to a time point specified by the time field. The dimensions field specifies the dimensions of the input. If each input is a scalar or vector (1-D array) value, the dimensions field must be a scalar value that specifies the length of the vector (1 for a scalar). If each input is a matrix (2-D array), the dimensions field must be a two-element vector whose first element specifies the number of rows in the matrix and whose second element specifies the number of columns.

Note You must set the **Port dimensions** parameter of the Inport to be the same value as the dimensions field of the corresponding input structure. If the values differ, Simulink stops and displays an error message when you try to simulate the model.

If the inputs for a port are scalar or vector values, the values field must be an M-by-N array where M is the number of time points specified by the time field and N is the length of each vector value. For example, the following code creates an input structure for loading 11 time samples of a two-element signal vector of type int8 into a model with a single input port:

```
a.time = (0:0.1:1)';
c1 = int8([0:1:10]');
c2 = int8([0:10:100]');
a.signals(1).values = [c1 c2];
a.signals(1).dimensions = 2;
```

To load this data into the model's inport, you would select the **Input** option on the **Data Import/Export** pane and enter a in the input expression field.

If the inputs for a port are matrices (2-D arrays), the values field must be an M-by-N-by-T array where M and N are the dimensions of each matrix input and T is the number of time points. For example, suppose that you want to input 51 time samples of a 4-by-5 matrix signal into one of your model's input ports. Then, the corresponding dimensions field of the workspace structure must equal [4 5] and the values array must have the dimensions 4-by-5-by-51.

As another example, consider the following model, which has two inputs.

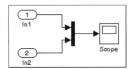

Suppose that you want to input a sine wave into the first port and a cosine wave into the second port. To do this, define a vector, a, as follows, in the base workspace:

```
a.time = (0:0.1:1)';
a.signals(1).values = sin(a.time);
a.signals(1).dimensions = 1;
a.signals(2).values = cos(a.time);
a.signals(2).dimensions = 1;
```

Select the **Input** box for this model, enter a in the adjacent text field, and select StructureWithTime as the I/O format.

Importing Signal-Only Structures. The Structure format is the same as the Structure with time format except that the time field is empty. For example, in the preceding example, you could set the time field as follows:

```
a.time = []
```

In this case, Simulink reads the input for the first time step from the first element of an inport's value array, the value for the second time step from the second element of the value array, etc.

Per-Port Structures. This format consists of a separate structure-with-time or structure-without-time for each port. Each port's input data structure has only one signals field. To specify this option, enter the names of the structures in the **Input** text field as a comma-separated list, in1, in2, ..., inN, where in1 is the data for your model's first port, in2 for the second inport, and so on.

Exporting Output Data to the MATLAB Workspace

You can specify return variables by selecting the **Time**, **States**, and/or **Output** check boxes in the **Save to workspace** area of this dialog box pane. Specifying return variables causes Simulink to write values for the time, state, and output trajectories (as many as are selected) into the workspace.

To assign values to different variables, specify those variable names in the fields to the right of the check boxes. To write output to more than one variable, specify the variable names in a comma-separated list. Simulink saves the simulation times in the vector specified in the **Save to workspace** area.

Note Simulink saves the output to the workspace at the base sample rate of the model. Use a To Workspace block if you want to save output at a different sample rate.

The **Save options** area enables you to specify the format and restrict the amount of output saved.

Format options for model states and outputs are listed below.

Array. If you select this option, Simulink saves a model's states and outputs in a state and output array, respectively.

The state matrix has the name specified in the **Save to workspace** area (for example, xout). Each row of the state matrix corresponds to a time sample of the model's states. Each column corresponds to an element of a state. For example, suppose that your model has two continuous states, each of which is a two-element vector. Then the first two elements of each row of the state matrix contains a time sample of the first state vector. The last two elements of each row contain a time sample of the second state vector.

The model output matrix has the name specified in the **Save to workspace** area (for example, yout). Each column corresponds to a model outport, each row to the outputs at a specific time.

Note You can use array format to save your model's outputs and states only if the outputs are either all scalars or all vectors (or all matrices for states), are either all real or all complex, and are all of the same data type. Use the Structure or StructureWithTime output formats (see the following) if your model's outputs and states do not meet these conditions.

Structure with time. If you select this format, Simulink saves the model's states and outputs in structures having the names specified in the **Save to workspace** area (for example, xout and yout).

The structure used to save outputs has two top-level fields: time and signals. The time field contains a vector of the simulation times. The signals field contains an array of substructures, each of which corresponds to a model outport. Each substructure has four fields: values, dimensions, label, and blockName. The values field contains the outputs for the corresponding outport. If the outputs are scalars or vectors, the values field is a matrix each of whose rows represents an output at the time specified by the corresponding element of the time vector. If the outputs are matrix (2-D) values, the values field is a 3-D array of dimensions M-by-N-by-T where M-by-N is the dimensions of the output signal and T is the number of output samples. If T = 1, MATLAB drops the last dimension. Therefore, the values field is an M-by-N matrix. The dimensions field specifies the dimensions of the output signal. The label field specifies the label of the signal connected to the outport or the type of state (continuous or discrete). The blockName field specifies the name of the corresponding outport or block with states.

The structure used to save states has a similar organization. The states structure has two top-level fields: time and signals. The time field contains a vector of the simulation times. The signals field contains an array of substructures, each of which corresponds to one of the model's states. Each signals structure has four fields: values, dimensions, label, and blockName. The values field contains time samples of a state of the block specified by the blockName field. The label field for built-in blocks indicates the type of state: either CSTATE (continuous state) or DSTATE (discrete state). For S-Function blocks, the label contains whatever name is assigned to the state by the S-Function block.

The time samples of a state are stored in the values field as a matrix of values. Each row corresponds to a time sample. Each element of a row corresponds to an element of the state. If the state is a matrix, the matrix is stored in the values array in column-major order. For example, suppose that the model includes a 2-by-2 matrix state and that Simulink logs 51 samples of the state during a simulation run. The values field for this state would contain a 51-by-4 matrix where each row corresponds to a time sample of the state and where the first two elements of each row correspond to the first column of the sample and the last two elements correspond to the second column of the sample.

Simulink can read back simulation data saved to the workspace in the Structure with time output format. See "Importing signal-and-time data structures" on page 8-18 for more information.

Structure. This format is the same as the preceding except that Simulink does not store simulation times in the time field of the saved structure.

Per-Port Structures. This format consists of a separate structure-with-time or structure-without-time for each output port. Each output data structure has only one signals field. To specify this option, enter the names of the structures in the **Output** text field as a comma-separated list, out1, out2, ..., outN, where out1 is the data for your model's first port, out2 for the second inport, and so on.

Importing and Exporting States

Initial conditions, which are applied to the system at the start of the simulation, are generally set in the blocks. You can override initial conditions set in the blocks by specifying them in the **Initial state** field of the **Load from workspace** area of the **Data Import/Export** pane.

You can also save the final states for the current simulation run and apply them to a subsequent simulation run. This feature can be useful when you want to save a steady-state solution and restart the simulation at that known state. The states are saved in the format that you select in the **Save options** area of the **Data Import/Export** pane.

Saving Final States

To save the final states (the values of the states at the termination of the simulation), select the **Final states** check box and enter a variable in the adjacent edit field.

Loading Initial States

To load states, select the **Initial state** check box and specify the name of a variable that contains the initial state values. This variable can be a matrix or a structure of the same form as is used to save final states. This allows Simulink to set the initial states for the current session to the final states saved in a previous session, using the Structure or Structure with time format.

Model Reference Limitations On Loading Initial States. Simulink imposes the following limitations on loading the states of models that reference other models or that are referenced by other models.

- You cannot initialize the states of a referenced model from the workspace. Simulink ignores the **Initial state** setting for such models.

- You can use the array format to initialize the states of a top model only if the models that the top model references do not themselves have states.

- You can use the structure format to initialize the states of a top model but not those of the models that it references.

Limiting Output

Saving data to the workspace can slow down the simulation and consume memory. To avoid this, you can limit the number of samples saved to the most recent samples or you can skip samples by applying a decimation factor. To set a limit on the number of data samples saved, select the check box labeled **Limit data points to last** and specify the number of samples to save. To apply a decimation factor, enter a value in the field to the right of the **Decimation** label. For example, a value of 2 saves every other point generated.

Specifying Output Options

The **Output options** list on the **Data Import/Export** configuration pane ("Data Import/Export Pane" on page 8-38) enables you to control how much output the simulation generates. You can choose from three options:

- Refine output

- Produce additional output
- Produce specified output only

Refining Output

The Refine output choice provides additional output points when the simulation output is too coarse. This parameter provides an integer number of output points between time steps; for example, a refine factor of 2 provides output midway between the time steps, as well as at the steps. The default refine factor is 1.

To get smoother output, it is much faster to change the refine factor instead of reducing the step size. When the refine factor is changed, the solvers generate additional points by evaluating a continuous extension formula at those points. Changing the refine factor does not change the steps used by the solver.

The refine factor applies to variable-step solvers and is most useful when you are using ode45. The ode45 solver is capable of taking large steps; when graphing simulation output, you might find that output from this solver is not sufficiently smooth. If this is the case, run the simulation again with a larger refine factor. A value of 4 should provide much smoother results.

Note This option does not help the solver to locate zero crossings (see "Zero-Crossing Detection" on page 3-19).

Producing Additional Output

The Produce additional output choice enables you to specify directly those additional times at which the solver generates output. When you select this option, Simulink displays an **Output times** field on the **Data Import/Export** pane. Enter a MATLAB expression in this field that evaluates to an additional time or a vector of additional times. The additional output is produced using a continuous extension formula at the additional times. Unlike the refine factor, this option changes the simulation step size so that time steps coincide with the times that you have specified for additional output.

Producing Specified Output Only

The Produce specified output only choice provides simulation output *only* at the specified output times. This option changes the simulation step size so that time steps coincide with the times that you have specified for producing output. This choice is useful when you are comparing different simulations to ensure that the simulations produce output at the same times.

Comparing Output Options

A sample simulation generates output at these times:

```
0, 2.5, 5, 8.5, 10
```

Choosing Refine output and specifying a refine factor of 2 generates output at these times:

```
0, 1.25, 2.5, 3.75, 5, 6.75, 8.5, 9.25, 10
```

Choosing the Produce additional output option and specifying [0:10] generates output at these times

```
0, 1, 2, 3, 4, 5, 6, 7, 8, 9, 10
```

and perhaps at additional times, depending on the step size chosen by the variable-step solver.

Choosing the Produce specified output only option and specifying [0:10] generates output at these times:

```
0, 1, 2, 3, 4, 5, 6, 7, 8, 9, 10
```

In general, you should specify output points as integers times a fundamental step size. For example,

```
[1:100]*0.01
```

is more accurate than

```
[1:0.01:100]
```

Configuration Sets

A configuration set is a named set of values for a model's parameters, such as solver type and simulation start or stop time. Every new model is created with a default configuration set, called Configuration, that initially specifies default values for the model's parameters. You can subsequently create and modify additional configuration sets and associate them with the model. The sets associated with a model can each specify different values for any given model parameter.

The Active Set

Only one of the configuration sets associated with a model is active at any given time. The active set determines the current values of the model's model parameters. Changing the value of a parameter in the Model Explorer changes its value in the active set. Simulink allows you to change the active set at any time (except when executing the model). In this way, you can quickly reconfigure a model for different purposes, e.g., testing and production, or apply standard configuration settings to new models.

To determine the configuration sets associated with a model, open the Model Explorer (see "The Model Explorer" on page 9-2). The configuration sets associated with the model appear as gear-shaped nodes in the Model Explorer's **Model Hierarchy** pane.

Activating a Configuration Set

To activate a configuration set, right-click the configuration set's node to display the node's context menu, then select **Activate** from the context menu.

Copying and Moving Configuration Sets

You can copy or move a configuration set by dragging its node and dropping it on any model node in the **Model Hierarchy** pane. To move a configuration set from one model to another, hold the **Ctrl** key and the left mouse button down and drag the configuration set's node to the node of the destination model; to copy a configuration, hold the **Ctrl** key and the right mouse button down and drag the configuration set's node to the node of the same or a different model.

Creating Configuration Sets

To create a new configuration set, copy an existing configuration set.

Setting Values in Configuration Sets

To set the value of a parameter in a configuration set, select the configuration set in the Model Explorer and then edit the value of the parameter on the corresponding dialog in the Model Explorer's dialog view.

The Model Configuration Dialog Box

The Model Configuration dialog box appears when you select a model configuration in the Model Explorer.

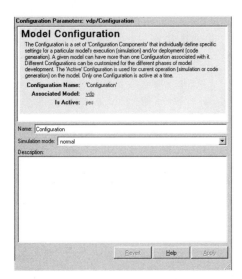

The dialog box has the following fields.

Name

Name of the configuration. You can change the name of the configuration by editing this field.

Simulation mode

The simulation mode used to simulate the model in this configuration. The options are normal ("Simulation Basics" on page 8-2), accelerator (see "The Simulink Accelerator" on page 14-2), or external mode (see the Real-Time Workshop documentation).

Description

A description of this configuration. You can use this field to enter information pertinent to using this configuration.

The Configuration Parameters Dialog Box

The **Configuration Parameters** dialog box allows you to modify settings for a model's active configuration set (see "Configuration Sets" on page 8-26).

Note You can also use the Model Explorer to modify settings for the active configuration set as well as for any other configuration set. See "The Model Explorer" on page 9-2 for more information.

To display the dialog box, select **Configuration Parameters** from the model editor's **Simulation** or context menu. The dialog box appears.

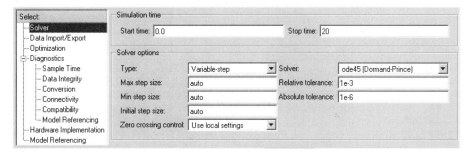

The dialog box groups the controls used to set the configuration parameters into various categories. To display the controls for a specific category, click the category in the **Select** tree on the left side of the dialog box. See the following sections for information on how to use the various categories of controls to set configuration parameters for the active configuration set.

- "The Solver Pane" on page 8-30
- "Data Import/Export Pane" on page 8-38
- "The Optimization Pane" on page 8-42
- "The Diagnostics Pane" on page 8-47
- "Hardware Implementation Pane" on page 8-60
- "Model Referencing Pane" on page 8-63

In most cases, Simulink does not immediately apply a change that you have made with a control. To apply a change, you must click either the **OK** or the

Apply button at the bottom of the dialog box. The **OK** button applies all the changes you made and dismisses the dialog box. The **Apply** button applies the changes but leaves the dialog box open so that you can continue to make changes.

Note Each of the controls on the **Configuration Parameters** dialog box correspond to a configuration parameter that you can set via the sim and simset commands. The "Model Parameters" subsection of the "Model and Block Parameters" section of the Simulink Reference documentation lists these parameters. This section also specifies for each configuration parameter the **Configuration Parameters** dialog box prompt of the control that sets it. This allows you to determine the model parameter corresponding to a control on the **Configuration Parameters** dialog box.

The Solver Pane

The **Solver** configuration parameters pane allows you to specify a simulation start and stop time and select and configure a solver for a particular simulation configuration.

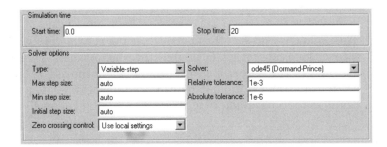

The **Solver** pane contains the following control groups.

Simulation time

This control group enables you to specify the simulation start and stop time. It contains the following controls.

Start time. Specifies the simulation start time. The default start time is 0.0 seconds.

Stop time. Specifies the simulation stop time. The default stop time is 10.0 seconds. Specify `inf` to cause the simulation to run until you pause or stop it.

Simulation time and actual clock time are not the same. For example, running a simulation for 10 seconds usually does not take 10 seconds. The amount of time it takes to run a simulation depends on many factors, including the model's complexity, the solver's step sizes, and the computer's speed.

Solver Options

The **Solver options** controls group allows you to specify the type of solver to be used and simulation options specific to that solver.

The contents of the group depends on the solver type.

General Solver Options

The follow options always appear.

Type. Specifies the type of solver to be used to solve the currently selected model, either `Fixed-step` or `Variable-step`. See "Choosing a Solver Type" on page 8-7 and "Improving Simulation Performance and Accuracy" on page 8-72 for information on how to choose the solver type that best suits your application.

Solver. Specifies the solver used to simulate this configuration of the current model. The associated pull-down list displays available solvers of the type specified by the **Type** control. To specify another solver of the specified type, select the solver from the pull-down list. See "Choosing a Fixed-Step Solver" on page 8-8 and "Choosing a Variable-Step Solver" on page 8-12 for information on how to choose the solvers listed in the **Solver** list.

The other controls that appear in this group depend on the type of solver you have selected.

Variable-Step Discrete Solver Options

The following options appear when you select the Simulink variable-step discrete solver.

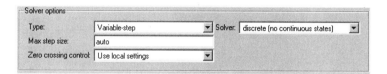

Max step size. Appears only if the solver **Type** is Variable-step. Specifies the largest time step the selected variable-step solver can take. The default auto causes Simulink to choose the model's shortest sample time as the maximum step size.

Zero crossing control. Enables zero-crossing detection during variable-step simulation of the model. For most models, this speeds up simulation by enabling the solver to take larger time steps. If a model has extreme dynamic changes, disabling this option can speed up the simulation but can also decrease the accuracy of simulation results. See "Zero-Crossing Detection" on page 3-19 for more information.

You can override this optimization on a block-by-block basis for the following types of blocks:

Abs	Integrator	Step
Backlash	MinMax	Switch
Dead Zone	Relay	Switch Case
Enable	Relational Operator	Trigger
Hit Crossing	Saturation	
If	Sign	

To override zero-crossing detection for an instance of one of these blocks, open the block's parameter dialog box and uncheck the **Enable zero crossing detection** option. You can enable or disable zero-crossing selectively for these blocks only if you have selected the Use local settings setting of the **Zero** crossing control control on the **Solver** pane of the **Configuration Parameters** dialog box.

Variable-Step Continuous Solver Options

The following options appear when you select any of the Simulink variable-step continuous solvers.

Max step size. Specifies the largest time step the solver can take. The default is determined from the start and stop times. If the stop time equals the start time or is `inf`, Simulink chooses `0.2` sec. as the maximum step size. Otherwise, it sets the maximum step size to

$$h_{max} = \frac{t_{stop} - t_{start}}{50}$$

Generally, the default maximum step size is sufficient. If you are concerned about the solver's missing significant behavior, change the parameter to prevent the solver from taking too large a step. If the time span of the simulation is very long, the default step size might be too large for the solver to find the solution. Also, if your model contains periodic or nearly periodic behavior and you know the period, set the maximum step size to some fraction (such as 1/4) of that period.

In general, for more output points, change the refine factor, not the maximum step size. For more information, see "Output options" on page 8-41.

Initial step size. By default, the solver selects an initial step size by examining the derivatives of the states at the start time. If the first step size is too large, the solver might step over important behavior. The initial step size parameter is a *suggested* first step size. The solver tries this step size but reduces it if error criteria are not satisfied.

Min step size. This option appears only for variable-step continuous solvers. Specifies the smallest time step the selected variable-step solver can take. If the solver needs to take a smaller step to meet error tolerances, it issues a warning indicating the current effective relative tolerance. This parameter can be either a real number greater than zero or a two-element vector where the first element is the minimum step size and the second element is the maximum number of minimum step size warnings to be issued before issuing an error. Setting the second element to zero results in an error the first time the solver must take a step smaller than the specified minimum. This is equivalent to changing the minimum step size violation diagnostic to error on the **Diagnostics** pane. Setting the second element to -1 results in an unlimited number of warnings. This is also the default if the input is a scalar. The default values for this parameter are a minimum step size on the order of machine precision and an unlimited number of warnings.

Relative tolerance. Relative tolerance for this solver (see "Specifying Variable-Step Solver Error Tolerances" on page 8-14).

Absolute tolerance. Absolute tolerance for this solver (see "Specifying Variable-Step Solver Error Tolerances" on page 8-14).

Maximum order. This option appears only if you select the ode15s solver, which is based on NDF formulas of orders one through five. Although the higher order formulas are more accurate, they are less stable. If your model is stiff and requires more stability, reduce the maximum order to 2 (the highest order for which the NDF formula is A-stable). As an alternative, you can try using the ode23s solver, which is a lower order (and A-stable) solver.

Fixed-Step Solver Options

The following options appear when you choose one of the Simulink fixed-step solvers.

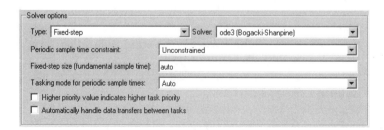

Periodic sample time constraint. Allows you to specify constraints on the sample times defined by this model. During simulation, Simulink checks to ensure that the model satisfies the constraints. If the model does not satisfy the specified constraint, Simulink displays an error message. The contents of the **Solver options** group changes depending on the options selected. The options are

- Unconstrained

  No constraints. Selecting this option causes Simulink to display a field for entering the solver step size.

  See "Fixed step size (fundamental sample time)" on page 8-35 for a description of this field.

- Ensure sample time independent

  Check to ensure that this model can inherit its sample times from a model that references it without altering its behavior. Models that specify a step size (i.e., a base sample time) cannot satisfy this constraint. For this reason, selecting this option causes Simulink to hide the group's step size field (see "Fixed step size (fundamental sample time)" on page 8-35.

- Specified

  Check to ensure that this model operates at a specified set of prioritized periodic sample times.

  Selecting this option causes Simulink to display additional controls for specifying prioritized sample times and sample time priority options.

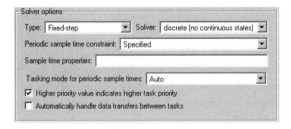

See below for a description of these additional controls.

Fixed step size (fundamental sample time). Specifies the step size used by the selected fixed-step solver. Entering auto (the default) in this field causes Simulink to choose the step size. If the model specifies one or more periodic sample times, Simulink chooses a step size equal to the least common denominator of the specified sample times. This step size, known as the fundamental sample time of the model, ensures that the solver will take a step at every sample time defined by the model. If the model does not define any periodic sample times, Simulink chooses a step size that divides the total simulation time into 50 equal steps.

Sample time properties. Specifies and assigns priorities to the sample times that this model implements. Enter an Nx3 matrix in this field whose rows specify the sample times specified by this model in order from fastest rate to slowest rate.

Note If the model's fundamental rate differs from the fastest rate specified by the model (see "Determining Step Size for Discrete Systems" on page 3-36), you should specify the fundamental rate as the first entry in the matrix followed by the specified rates in order from fastest to slowest.

The row for each sample time should have the form

```
[period, offset, priority]
```

where period is the sample time's period of a sample time, offset is the sample time's offset, and priority is the execution priority of the real-time task associated with the sample rate, with faster rates receiving higher priorities. For example, the following entry

```
[[0.1, 0, 10]; [0.2, 0, 11]; [0.3, 0, 12]]
```

declares that this model should specify two sample rates, whose fundamental sample time is 0.1 second, and assigns priorities of 10, 11, and 12 to the sample times. This example assumes that for this model, higher priority values indicate lower priorities, i.e., the **Higher priority value indicates higher task priority** option is not selected (see "Higher priority value indicates higher task priority" on page 8-38).

Note If your model operates at only one rate, you can enter the rate as a three-element vector in this field, e.g., [0.1, 0, 10].

When updating a model, Simulink checks the sample times defined by the model against this field. If the model defines more or fewer sample times than this field specifies, Simulink displays an error message.

Note If you select Unconstrained as the **Periodic sample time constraint**, Simulink assigns a priority of 40 to the model's base sample rate. If the **Higher priority value indicates higher task priority** option is selected (see "Higher priority value indicates higher task priority" on page 8-38), Simulink assigns priorities 39, 38, etc., to subrates of the base rate; otherwise, it assigns priorities 41, 42, 43, etc., to the subrates. Continuous rate is assigned a higher priority than is the discrete base rate no matter whether you select Specified or Unconstrained as the **Periodic sample time constraint**.

Tasking mode for periodic sample times. Specifies one of the following options:

- MultiTasking

  This mode issues an error if it detects an illegal sample rate transition between blocks, that is, a direct connection between blocks operating at different sample rates. In real-time multitasking systems, illegal sample rate transitions between tasks can result in a task's output not being available when needed by another task. By checking for such transitions, multitasking mode helps you to create valid models of real-world multitasking systems, where sections of your model represent concurrent tasks.

  Use the Rate Transition block to eliminate illegal rate transitions from your model. For more information, see "Models with Multiple Sample Rates" in the Real-Time Workshop documentation for more information.

- SingleTasking

  This mode does not check for sample rate transitions among blocks. This mode is useful when you are modeling a single-tasking system. In such systems, task synchronization is not an issue.

- Auto

  This option causes Simulink to use single-tasking mode if all blocks operate at the same rate and multitasking mode if the model contains blocks operating at different rates.

Higher priority value indicates higher task priority. If checked, this option indicates that the real-time system targeted by this model assigns a higher priority to tasks with higher priority values. This in turn causes Simulink Rate Transition blocks to treat asynchronous transitions between rates with lower priority values to rates with higher priority values as low-to-high rate transitions. If unchecked (the default), this option indicates that the real-time system targeted by this model assigns a higher priority to tasks with lower priority values. This in turn causes Simulink Rate Transition blocks to treat asynchronous transitions between rates with lower priority values to rates with higher priority values as high-to-low rate transitions. See the Real-Time Workshop documentation for more information on this option.

Automatically handle data transfers between tasks. If checked, this option causes Simulink to insert hidden Rate Transition blocks where rate transitions occur between blocks.

The next two options appear only if you select the ode14x solver (see "Implicit Fixed-Step Continuous Solvers" on page 8-11).

Extrapolation Order. Extrapolation order used by the ode14x solver to compute a model's states at the next time step from the states at the current time step. The higher the order, the more accurate but the more computationally intensive is the solution per step size.

Number Newton's iterations. Number of Newton's method iterations used by the ode14x solver to compute a model's states at the next time step from the states at the current time step. The more iterations, the more accurate but the more computationally intensive is the solution per step size.

Data Import/Export Pane

The **Data Import/Export** pane allows you to import and export data to the MATLAB workspace. To display the pane, select **Data Import/Export** from the **Select** tree of the **Configuration Parameters** dialog box or select a configuration set (see "Configuration Sets" on page 8-26) in the Model Explorer and display the configuration's **Data Import/Export** subset.

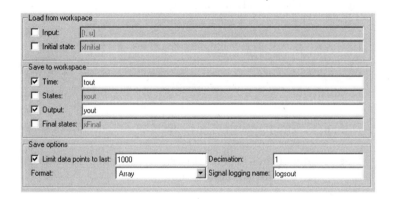

Load from workspace

This group contains controls that enable you to specify options for importing data from the MATLAB workspace.

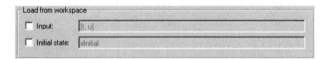

It includes the following controls.

Input. A MATLAB expression that specifies the data to be imported from the MATLAB workspace. See "Importing Input Data from the MATLAB Workspace" on page 8-16 for information on how to use this field.

Initial state. A MATLAB expression that specifies the initial values of a model's states. See "Importing and Exporting States" on page 8-22 for more information.

Save to workspace

This group contains controls that enable you to specify options for exporting data to the MATLAB workspace.

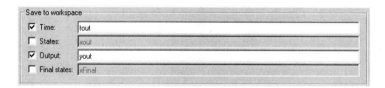

It includes the following controls.

Time. Name of the MATLAB variable to be used to store simulation time data to be exported during simulation.

States. Specifies the name of a MATLAB variable to be used to store state data exported during a simulation. See "Importing and Exporting States" on page 8-22 for more information.

Ouput. Name of the MATLAB variable to be used to store signal data exported during this simulation. See "Exporting Output Data to the MATLAB Workspace" on page 8-20 for more information.

Final states. Specifies the name of a MATLAB variable to be used to store the values of this model's states at the end of a simulation. See "Importing and Exporting States" on page 8-22 for more information.

Save options

This group contains controls that allow you to specify options for saving (and reloading) data from the MATLAB workspace.

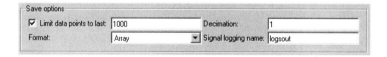

It includes the following controls.

Limit data points to last. Limits the number of data points exported to the MATLAB workspace to N, the number specified in the adjacent edit field. At the end of the simulation, the MATLAB workspace contains the last N points generated by the simulation.

Decimation. If specified, Simulink outputs only every N points, where N is the specified decimation factor.

Format. Specifies the format of state and output data saved to or loaded from the MATLAB workspace. The options are

- Array

  The format of the data is a matrix each row of which corresponds to a simulation time step.

- Structure with time

  The format of the data is a structure that has two fields: a time field and a signals field. The time field contains a vector of simulation times. The signals field contains a substructure for each model input port (for imported data) or output port (for exported data). Each port substructure contains signal data for the corresponding port.

- Structure

  The format of the data is a structure that contains substructures for each port. Each port substructure contains signal data for the corresponding port.

See "Importing and Exporting Simulation Data" on page 8-16 for more information on these formats.

Signal logging name. Variable name used to store signals logged during a simulation (see "Logging Signals" in the online Simulink documentation).

Output options. Options for generating additional output signal data.

Note These options appear only if the model specifies a variable-step solver (see "The Solver Pane" on page 8-30).

The options are

- Refine output

  Output data between as well as at simulation times steps. Selecting this option causes the **Refine factor** edit field to appear below this control (see

"Refine factor" on page 8-42). Use this field to specify the number of points to generate between simulation time steps. For more information, see "Refining Output" on page 8-24.

- `Produce additional output`

  Produce additional output at specified times. Selecting this option causes the **Output times** field to appear. Use this field to specify the simulation times at which Simulink should generate additional output.

- `Produce specified output`

  Produce output only at specified times. Selecting this option causes the **Output times** field to appear. Use this field to specify the simulation times at which Simulink should generate additional output.

Refine factor. This field appears when you select `Refine output` as the value of **Output options**. It specifies how many points to generate between time steps. For example, a refine factor of 2 provides output midway between the time steps, as well as at the steps. The default refine factor is 1. For more information, see "Refining Output" on page 8-24.

Output times. This field appears when you select `Produce additional output` or `Produce specified output` as the value of **Output options**. Use this field to specify times at which Simulink should generate output in addition to or instead of at the simulation steps taken by the solver used to simulate the model.

The Optimization Pane

The **Optimization** pane allows you to select various options that improve simulation performance and the performance of code generated from this model.

The pane contains the following controls.

Block reduction optimization. Replaces a group of blocks with a synthesized block, thereby speeding up execution of the model.

Conditional input branch execution. This optimization applies to models containing Switch and Multiport Switch blocks. When enabled, this optimization executes only the blocks required to compute the control input and the data input selected by the control input at each time step for each Switch or Multiport Switch block in the model. Similarly, code generated from the model by Real-Time Workshop executes only the code needed to compute the control input and the selected data input. This optimization speeds simulation and execution of code generated from the model.

At the beginning of the simulation or code generation, Simulink examines each signal path feeding a switch block data input to determine the portion of the path that can be optimized. The optimizable portion of the path is that part of the signal path that stretches from the corresponding data input back to the first block that is a nonvirtual subsystem, has continuous or discrete states, or detects zero crossings.

Simulink encloses the optimizable portion of the signal path in an invisible atomic subsystem. During simulation, if a switch data input is not selected, Simulink executes only the nonoptimizable portion of the signal path feeding the input. If the data input is selected, Simulink executes both the nonoptimizable and the optimizable portion of the input signal path.

Inline parameters. By default you can modify ("tune") many block parameters during simulation (see "Tunable Parameters" on page 3-8). Selecting this option makes all parameters nontunable by default. Making parameters nontunable allows Simulink to move blocks whose outputs depend only on block parameter values outside the simulation loop, thereby speeding up simulation of the model and execution of code generated from the model. When this option is selected, Simulink disables the parameter controls of the block dialog boxes for the blocks in your model to prevent you from accidentally modifying the block parameters.

Simulink allows you to override the **Inline parameters** option for parameters whose values are defined by variables in the MATLAB workspace. To specify that such a parameter remain tunable, specify the parameter as global in the **Model Parameter Configuration** dialog box (see "Model Parameter Configuration Dialog Box" on page 8-46). To display the dialog box, click the adjacent **Configure** button. To tune a global parameter, change the value of the corresponding workspace variable and choose **Update Diagram** (**Ctrl+D**) from the Simulink **Edit** menu.

Note You cannot tune inlined parameters in code generated from a model. However, when simulating a model, you can tune an inlined parameter if its value derives from a workspace variable. For example, suppose that a model has a Gain block whose **Gain** parameter is inlined and equals a, where a is a variable defined in the model's workspace. When simulating the model, Simulink disables the **Gain** parameter field, thereby preventing you from using the block's dialog box to change the gain. However, you can still tune the gain by changing the value of a at the MATLAB command line and updating the diagram.

Implement logic signals as boolean data (vs. double). Causes blocks that accept Boolean signals to require Boolean signals. If this option is off, blocks that accept inputs of type boolean also accept inputs of type double. For example, consider the following model.

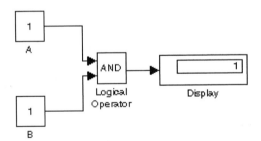

This model connects signals of type double to a Logical Operator block, which accepts inputs of type boolean. If the Boolean logic signals option is on, this model generates an error when executed. If the Boolean logic signals option is off, this model runs without error.

Note This option allows the current version of Simulink to run models that were created by earlier versions of Simulink that supported only signals of type `double`.

Signal storage reuse. Causes Simulink to reuse memory buffers allocated to store block input and output signals. If this option is off, Simulink allocates a separate memory buffer for each block's outputs. This can substantially increase the amount of memory required to simulate large models, so you should select this option only when you need to debug a model. In particular, you should disable signal storage reuse if you need to

- Debug a C-MEX S-function
- Use a Floating Scope or a Display block with the **Floating display** option selected to inspect signals in a model that you are debugging

Simulink opens an error dialog if `Signal storage reuse` is enabled and you attempt to use a Floating Scope or floating Display block to display a signal whose buffer has been reused.

Application lifespan (days). Specifies the lifespan in days of the system represented by this model. This value and the simulation step size determine the data type used by fixed-point blocks to store absolute time values.

Model Parameter Configuration Dialog Box

The **Model Parameter Configuration** dialog box allows you to override the **Inline parameters** option (see "Inline parameters" on page 8-43) for selected parameters.

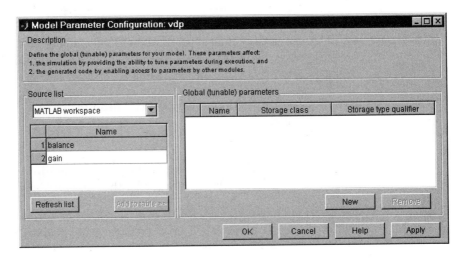

The dialog box has the following controls.

Source list. Displays a list of workspace variables. The options are

- MATLAB workspace

  List all variables in the MATLAB workspace that have numeric values.

- Referenced workspace variables

  List only those variables referenced by the model.

Refresh list. Updates the source list. Click this button if you have added a variable to the workspace since the last time the list was displayed.

Add to table. Adds the variables selected in the source list to the adjacent table of tunable parameters.

New. Defines a new parameter and adds it to the list of tunable parameters. Use this button to create tunable parameters that are not yet defined in the MATLAB workspace.

Note This option does not create the corresponding variable in the MATLAB workspace. You must create the variable yourself.

Storage class. Used for code generation. See the Real-Time Workshop documentation for more information.

Storage type qualifier. Used for code generation. See the Real-Time Workshop documentation for more information.

The Diagnostics Pane

The **Diagnostics** configuration parameters pane enables you to specify what diagnostic action Simulink should take, if any, when it detects an abnormal condition during compilation or simulation of a model.

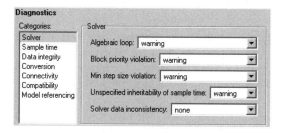

The options are typically to do nothing or to display a warning or an error message (see "Diagnosing Simulation Errors" on page 8-68). A warning message does not terminate a simulation, but an error message does.

The pane displays groups of controls corresponding to various categories of abnormal conditions that can occur during a solution. To display controls for a specific category, left-click the category in the **Categories** list on the left side of the **Diagnostics** pane. To display controls for additional categories, left-click the categories while pressing the **Ctrl** key on your keyboard. See the following sections for information on using the controls on the **Diagnostics** pane:

- "Solver Diagnostics" on page 8-48
- "Sample Time Diagnostics" on page 8-50
- "Data Integrity Diagnostics" on page 8-51

Solver Diagnostics

This control group enables you to specify the diagnostic action that Simulink should take when it detects a solver-related error.

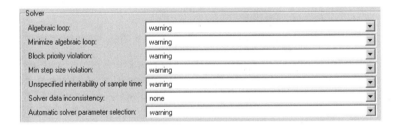

Algebraic loop. Simulink detected an algebraic loop while compiling the model. See "Algebraic Loops" on page 3-24 for more information. If you set this option to Error, Simulink displays an error message and highlights the portion of the block diagram that comprises the loop (see "Highlighting Algebraic Loops" on page 3-26).

Minimize algebraic loop. Specifies diagnostic action to take if you have requested that Simulink attempt to remove algebraic loops involving a specified subsystem (see "Eliminating Algebraic Loops" on page 3-27) and an input port of that subsystem has direct feedthrough. If the port is involved in an algebraic loop, Simulink can remove the loop only if at least one other input port in the loop lacks direct feedthrough.

Block priority violation. Simulink detected a block priority specification error while compiling the model.

Min step size violation. The next simulation step is smaller than the minimum step size specified for the model. This can occur if the specified error tolerance for the model requires a step size smaller than the specified minimum step size. See "Min step size" on page 8-34 and "Maximum order" on page 8-34 for more information.

Unspecified inheritability of sample time. Specifies diagnostic action to be taken if this model contains S-functions that do not specify whether they preclude this model from inheriting their sample times from a parent model. Simulink checks for this condition only if the solver used to simulate this model is a fixed-step discrete solver and the periodic sample time constraint for the solver is set to ensure sample time independence (see "Periodic sample time constraint" on page 8-35).

Solver data inconsistency. Consistency checking is a debugging tool that validates certain assumptions made by Simulink ODE solvers. Its main use is to make sure that S-functions adhere to the same rules as Simulink built-in blocks. Because consistency checking results in a significant decrease in performance (up to 40%), it should generally be set to none. Use consistency checking to validate your S-functions and to help you determine the cause of unexpected simulation results.

To perform efficient integration, Simulink saves (caches) certain values from one time step for use in the next time step. For example, the derivatives at the end of a time step can generally be reused at the start of the next time step. The solvers take advantage of this to avoid redundant derivative calculations.

Another purpose of consistency checking is to ensure that blocks produce constant output when called with a given value of t (time). This is important for the stiff solvers (ode23s and ode15s) because, while calculating the Jacobian matrix, the block's output functions can be called many times at the same value of t.

When consistency checking is enabled, Simulink recomputes the appropriate values and compares them to the cached values. If the values are not the same, a consistency error occurs. Simulink compares computed values for these quantities:

- Outputs
- Zero crossings
- Derivatives
- States

Automatic solver parameter selection. Specifies diagnostic action to take if Simulink changes a solver parameter setting. For example, suppose that you simulate a discrete model that specifies a continuous solver and warning as the setting for this diagnostic. In this case, Simulink changes the solver type to discrete and displays a warning message about this change at the MATLAB command line.

Sample Time Diagnostics

This control group enables you to specify the diagnostic action that Simulink should take when it detects a compilation error related to model sample times.

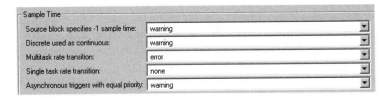

Source block specifies -1 sample time. A source block (e.g., a Sine Wave block) specifies a sample time of -1.

Discrete used as continuous. The Unit Delay block, which is a discrete block, inherits a continuous sample time from the block connected to its input.

Multitask rate transition. An invalid rate transition occurred between two blocks operating in multitasking mode (see "Tasking mode for periodic sample times" on page 8-37).

Single task rate transition. A rate transition occurred between two blocks operating in single-tasking mode (see "Tasking mode for periodic sample times" on page 8-37).

Asynchronous triggers with equal priority. One asynchronous task of the target represented by this model has the same priority as another of the target's asynchronous tasks. This option must be set to Error if the target allows tasks having the same priority to preempt each other.

Data Integrity Diagnostics

This control group enables you to specify the diagnostic action that Simulink should take when it detects a condition that could compromise the integrity of data defined by the model.

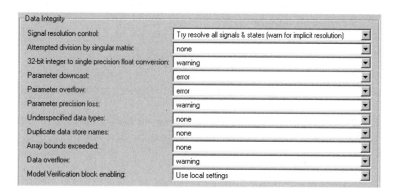

Signal resolution control. Specifies how Simulink resolves signals to `Simulink.Signal` objects in the MATLAB workspace. The options are

- `Try resolve all signals & states (warn for implicit resolution)`

  Try to resolve every signal or discrete state that has a name to a `Simulink.Signal` object having the same name. Display a warning message if a signal or state resolves implicitly to a signal object, i.e., a signal object with the same name as the signal or state exists in the MATLAB workspace but the model does not specify that the signal or state should resolve to a signal object.

- `Try resolve all signals & states`

  Try to resolve every signal or discrete state that has a name to a `Simulink.Signal` object having the same name regardless of whether the model specifies that the signal or state should resolve to a signal object.

- `Use local settings`

  Try to resolve every signal or discrete state that the model specifies should resolve to a `Simulink.Signal` object in the MATLAB workspace.

Note Use the Signal Properties dialog box (see "Signal Properties Dialog Box" in the online Simulink documentation) to specify explicit resolution for signals. Use the **State Properties** dialog boxes of blocks that have discrete states, e.g., the Discrete-Time Integrator block, to specify explicit resolution for discrete states.

Attempted division by singular matrix. The Product block detected a singular matrix while inverting one of its inputs in matrix multiplication mode.

32-bit integer to single precision float conversion. A 32-bit integer value was converted to a floating-point value. Such a conversion can result in a loss of precision.

Parameter downcast. Computation of the output of the block required converting the parameter's specified type to a type having a smaller range of values (e.g., from uint32 to uint8). This diagnostic applies only to named tunable parameters.

Parameter overflow. The data type of the parameter could not accommodate the parameter's value.

Parameter precision loss. Computation of the output of the block required converting the specified data type of the parameter to a less precise data type (e.g., from double to uint8).

Underspecified data types. Simulink could not infer the data type of a signal during data type propagation.

Duplicate data store names. The model contains multiple Data Store Memory blocks that specify the same data store name.

Array bounds exceeded. This option causes Simulink to check whether a block writes outside the memory allocated to it during simulation. Typically this can happen only if your model includes a user-written S-function that has a bug. If enabled, this check is performed for every block in the model every time the block is executed. As a result, enabling this option slows down model execution considerably. Thus, to avoid slowing down model execution needlessly, you should enable the option only if you suspect that your model contains a user-written S-function that has a bug. See *Writing S-Functions* for more information on using this option.

Data overflow. The value of a signal or parameter is too large to be represented by the signal or parameter's data type.

Model Verification block enabling. This parameter allows you to enable or disable model verification blocks in the current model either globally or locally. Select one of the following options:

• `Use local settings`

  Enables or disables blocks based on the value of the **Enable assertion** parameter of each block. If a block's **Enable assertion** parameter is on, the block is enabled; otherwise, the block is disabled.

• `Enable all`

  Enables all model verification blocks in the model regardless of the settings of their **Enable assertion** parameters.

• `Disable all`

  Disables all model verification blocks in the model regardless of the settings of their **Enable assertion** parameters.

Conversion Diagnostics

This control group enables you to specify the diagnostic action that Simulink should take when it detects a data type conversion problem while compiling the model.

Unnecessary type conversions. A Data Type Conversion block is used where no type conversion is necessary.

Vector/matrix block input conversion. A vector-to-matrix or matrix-to-vector conversion occurred at a block input (see "Vector or Matrix Input Conversion Rules" on page 7-14).

Connectivity Diagnostics

This control group enables you to specify the diagnostic action that Simulink should take when it detects a problem with block connections while compiling the model.

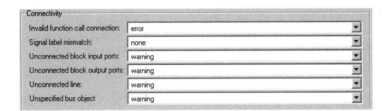

Invalid function call connection. Simulink has detected an incorrect use of a function-call subsystem in your model (see the "Function-call systems" examples in the Simulink "Subsystem Semantics" library for examples of invalid uses of function-call subsystems. Disabling this error message can lead to invalid simulation results.

Signal label mismatch. The simulation encountered virtual signals that have a common source signal but different labels (see "Virtual Signals" on page 7-4).

Unconnected block input ports. Model contains a block with an unconnected input.

Unconnected block output ports. Model contains a block with an unconnected output.

Unconnected line. Model contains an unconnected line.

Unspecified bus object. Specifies diagnostic action to take while generating a simulation target for a referenced model if any of the model's root Outport blocks is connected to a bus but does not specify a bus object (see Simulink.Bus).

Compatibility Diagnostics

This control group enables you to specify the diagnostic action that Simulink should take when it detects an incompatibility between this version of Simulink and the model when updating or simulating the model.

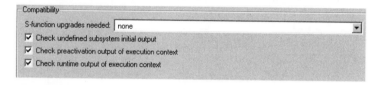

S-function upgrade needed. A block was encountered that has not been upgraded to use features of the current release.

Check undefined subsystem initial output. Display a warning if the model contains a conditionally executed subsystem in which a block with a specified initial condition (e.g., a Constant, Initial Condition, or Delay block) drives an Outport block with an undefined initial condition, i.e., the Outport block's **Initial output** parameter is set to [].

Models with such subsystems can produce initial results (i.e., before initial activation of the conditionally executed subsystem) in the current release that differ from initial results produced in Release 13 or earlier releases.

Consider for example the following model.

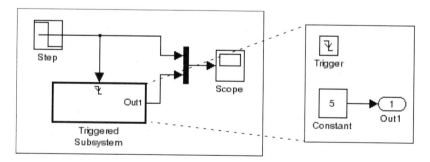

This model does not define the initial condition of the triggered subsystem's output port.

The following figure compares the superimposed output of this model's Step block and the triggered subsystem in Release 13 and the current release.

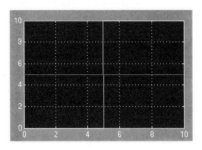 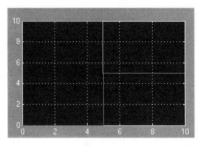

Release 13   Current Release

Notice that the initial output of the triggered subsystem differs between the two releases. This is because Release 13 and earlier releases use the initial output of the block connected to the output port (i.e., the Constant block) as the triggered subsystem's initial output. By contrast, this release outputs 0 as the initial output of the triggered subsystem because the model does not specify the port's initial output.

Check preactivation output of execution context. Display a warning if the model contains a block that meets the following conditions:

• The block produces nonzero output for zero input (e.g., a Cosine block).

• The block is connected to an output of a conditionally executed subsystem.

• The block inherits its execution context from that subsystem.

• The Outport to which it is connected has an undefined initial condition, i.e., the Outport block's **Initial output** parameter is set to [].

Models with blocks that meet these criteria can produce initial results (i.e., before the conditionally executed subsystem is first activated in the current release that differ from initial results produced in Release 13 or earlier releases.

Consider for example the following model.

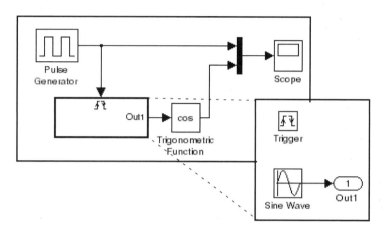

The following figure compares the superimposed output of the Pulse Generator and cos block in Release 13 and the current release.

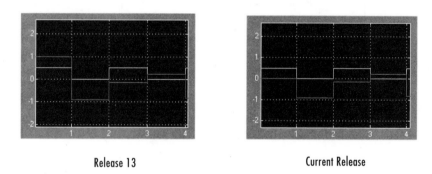

Release 13   Current Release

Note that the initial output of the cos block differs between the two releases. This is because in Release 13, the cos block belongs to the execution context of the root system and hence executes at every time step whereas in the current release, the cos block belongs to the execution context of the triggered subsystem and hence executes only when the triggered subsystem executes.

Check runtime output of execution context. Display a warning if the model contains a block that meets the following conditions:

• The block has a tunable parameter.

- The block is connected to an output of a conditionally executed subsystem.
- The block inherits its execution context from that subsystem.
- The Outport to which it is connected has an undefined initial condition, i.e., the Outport block's **Initial output** parameter is set to [].

Models with blocks that meet these criteria can produce results when the parameter is tuned in the current release that differ from results produced in Release 13 or earlier releases.

Consider for example the following model.

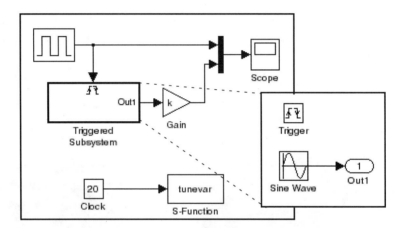

In this model, the tunevar S-function changes the value of the Gain block's k parameter and updates the diagram at simulation time 7 (i.e., it simulates interactively tuning the parameter).

The following figure compares the superimposed output of the model's Pulse Generator block and its Gain block in Release 13 and the current release.

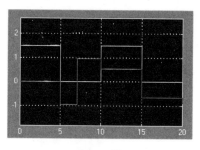

Release 13

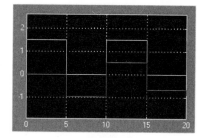

Current Release

Note that the output of the Gain block changes at time 7 in Release 13 but does not change in the current release. This is because in Release 13, the Gain block belongs to the execution context of the root system and hence executes at every time step whereas in the current release, the Gain block belongs to the execution context of the triggered subsystem and hence executes only when the triggered subsystem executes, i.e., at times 5, 10, 15, and 20.

Model Reference Diagnostics

This control group enables you to specify the diagnostic action that Simulink should take when it detects in incompatibility between this version of Simulink and the model while when updating or simulating the model.

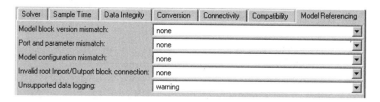

Model block version mismatch. Specifies the diagnostic action to take during loading or updating of this model when Simulink detects a mismatch between the version of the model used to create or refresh a Model block in this model and the referenced model's current version. See the online Simulink documentation for more information.

Hardware Implementation Pane

This pane applies to models of computer-based systems, such as embedded controllers. It allows you to specify the characteristics of the hardware to be used to implement the system represented by this model. This in turn enables simulation of the model to detect error conditions that could arise on the target hardware, such as hardware overflow.

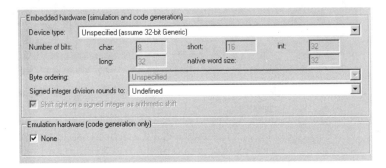

This pane contains the following groups of controls.

Embedded hardware

This group of controls enables you to specify the characteristics of the hardware that will be used to implement the production version of the system represented by this model. (See "Emulation hardware" on page 8-62 for information on specifying the characteristics of hardware used to emulate the production hardware.) This group includes the following controls.

Device type. Specifies the type of hardware that will be used to implement the production version of the system represented by this model. The adjacent list lists types of hardware that Simulink knows about and hence does not require you to enter their characteristics. If your production hardware does not match any of the listed types, select Unspecified (assume 32-bit Generic) if it has the characteristics of a generic 32-bit microprocessor; otherwise, Custom.

Number of bits. This group of controls specifies the length in bits of C data types supported by the selected device type. Simulink disables these controls if it knows the data type lengths for the selected device type.

Native word size. Specifies the word length in bits of the selected production hardware device type. Simulink disables this field if it knows the word length of the selected device type.

Signed integer division rounds to. Specifies how an ANSI C conforming compiler used to compile code for the production hardware rounds the result of dividing one signed integer by another to produce a signed integer quotient. The options are

- Zero

  If the ideal quotient is between two integers, the compiler chooses the integer that is closest to zero as the result.

- Floor

  If the ideal quotient is between two integers, the compiler chooses the integer that is closest to negative infinity as the result.

- Undefined

  The compiler's rounding behavior is undefined if either or both operands are negative.

The following table illustrates the compiler behavior specified by these options.

N	D	Ideal N/D	Zero	Floor	Undefined
33	4	8.25	8	8	8
-33	4	-8.25	-8	-9	-8 or -9
33	-4	-8.25	-8	-9	-8 or -9
-33	-4	8.25	8	8	-8 or -9

The setting of this option affects only generation of code from the model (see the Real-Time Workshop documentation for information on how this option affects code generation). Use the **Round integer calculations toward** parameter settings on your model's blocks to simulate the rounding behavior of the C compiler that you intend to use to compile code generated from the model. This setting appears on the **Signal data type** pane of the parameter dialog boxes of blocks that can perform signed integer arithmetic, such as the Product and Sum blocks.

Shift right on a signed integer as arithmetic shift. Select this option if the C compiler implements a signed integer right shift as an arithmetic right shift. An arithmetic right shift fills bits vacated by the right shift with the value of the most significant bit, which indicates the sign of the number in twos complement notation. It is equivalent to dividing the number by 2. This setting affects only code generation.

Byte ordering. Specifies the significance of the first byte of a data word of the target hardware. Select Big Endian if the first byte is the most significant, Little Endian if it is the least significant, or Unspecified if the significance is unknown. This setting affects only code generation. See the Real-Time Workshop documentation for more information.

Emulation hardware

This group of controls allows you to specify the characteristics of hardware used to test code generated from this model.

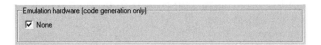

Initially, this group of controls has only one control.

None. If checked, this check box specifies that the hardware used to test the code generated from this model is the same as the production hardware or has the same characteristics. If you plan to use emulation hardware that has different characteristics, unselect this check box. This causes Simulink to expand the group to display controls that allow you to specify the characteristics of the emulation hardware.

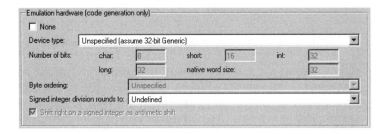

The additional controls are identical to the ones used to specify the characteristics of the target hardware for your system. See "Embedded hardware" on page 8-60 for information on using these controls.

Model Referencing Pane

The **Model Referencing** pane allows you to specify options for including other models in this model and this model in other models and for building simulation and code generation targets.

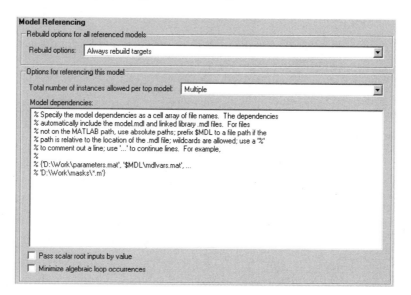

Note The option descriptions use the term *this model* to refer to the model that you are configuring and the term *referenced model* to designate models referenced by *this model*.

The pane includes controls for specifying options for

- Including other models in this model (see "Rebuild options for all referenced models" on page 8-64)
- Including the current model in other models (see "Options for referencing this model" on page 8-65)

Rebuild options for all referenced models

This group allows you to specify rebuild options for models directly or indirectly referenced by this model. It includes the following controls.

Rebuild targets. This control specifies whether to rebuild simulation and Real-Time Workshop targets for referenced models before updating, simulating, or generating code from this model. This includes models indirectly referenced by this model. The options, in order from safe and slow to fast and risky, are

- `Always rebuild targets`

  Always rebuild all targets referenced by this model before simulating, updating, or generating code from it.

- `If any changes detected` (the default)

  Rebuild the target for a referenced model if Simulink detects any changes of any kind in the target's dependencies. The dependencies include

  - The referenced model's model file
  - Block library files used by the referenced model
  - Targets of models referenced by the referenced model
  - S-functions and associated TLC files used by the referenced model
  - User-specified dependencies (see "Model dependencies" on page 8-66)
  - Workspace variables used by the referenced model

  This also checks for changes in the compiled form of the referenced model. Checking the compiled model can detect some changes that occur even in dependencies that you do not specify.

- `If any changes in known dependencies detected`

  Rebuild a target if Simulink detects any changes in known target dependencies (see above) since the target was last built. This option ignores cosmetic changes, such as annotation changes, in the referenced model and in any block library dependencies, thus preventing unnecessary rebuilds. However, before selecting it, you should be certain that you have specified every user-created dependency (e.g., M-files or MAT-files) for this model to ensure that all targets that need to be rebuilt are rebuilt. Otherwise, invalid simulation results may occur.

  Note that this option cannot detect changes in unspecified dependencies, such as M-files used to initialize block masks. If you suspect that a model has such unknown dependencies, you can still guarantee valid simulation by selecting the Always rebuild targets or the If any changes detected option.

- Never rebuild targets

Never rebuild targets before simulating or generating code from this model. If you are certain that your targets are up-to-date, you can use this option to avoid time-consuming target dependency checking when simulating, updating, or generating code from a model. Use this option with caution because it may lead to invalid results if referenced model targets are not in fact up-to-date.

Note It is a good idea to use the Always rebuild targets option before deployment of a model to assure that all the model reference targets are up-to-date.

Never rebuild targets diagnostic. This control appears only if you select the Never rebuild targets option. It allows you to specify the diagnostic action that Simulink should take if it detects a target that needs to be rebuilt. The options are

- Error if targets require rebuild (the default)
- Warn if targets require rebuild
- None

Selecting None bypasses dependency checking, and thus enables faster updating, simulation, and code generation, but can cause models that are not up-to-date to malfunction or generate incorrect results.

Options for referencing this model

This group of controls specifies options for including this model in other models. It includes the following controls.

Total number of instances allowed per top model. This option allows you to specify how many references to this model (i.e., the model you are configuring) can safely occur in another model. The options are

- One

- `Multiple` (the default)
- `None`

If you specify `None`, and a reference to this model occurs in another model (including its model references), Simulink displays an error when you try to simulate or update the root model. Simulink similarly displays an error, if you specify `One` and multiple references to this model occur in a root model (including its model references). If you specify multiple and Simulink determines that for some reason this model cannot be multiply referenced, Simulink displays an error when the model that references it is compiled or simulated. This occurs even if the model is referenced only once.

Model dependencies. Specifies files on which this model relies. They are typically MAT-files and M-files used to initialize parameters and to provide data.

Specify the dependencies as a cell array of strings, where each cell array entry is the filename or path of a dependent file. These filenames may include spaces and must include file extensions (e.g., `.m`, `.mat`, etc.).

Prefix the token `$MDL` to a dependency to indicate that the path to the dependency is relative to the location of this model file.

If Simulink cannot find a specified dependent file when you update or simulate a model that references this model, Simulink displays an error.

Pass scalar root inputs by value. Checking this option causes a model that calls (i.e., references) this model to pass this model's scalar inputs by value. Otherwise, the calling model passes the inputs by reference, i.e., it passes the addresses of the inputs rather than the input values.

Passing roots by value allows this model to read its scalar inputs from register or local memory which is faster than reading the inputs from their original locations. However, this option can lead to incorrect results if the model's root scalar inputs can change within a time step. This can happen, for instance, if this model's inputs and outputs share memory locations (e.g., as a result of a feedback loop) and the model is invoked multiple times in a time step (i.e., by a Function-Call Subsystem). In such cases, this model sees scalar input changes that occur in the same time step only if the inputs are passed by reference. That is why this option is off by default. If you are certain that this model is not referenced in contexts where its inputs can change within a time step, select this option to generate more efficient code for this model.

Note Selecting this option can affect reuse of code generated for subsystems. See the Real-Time Workshop documentation for more information.

Minimize algebraic loop occurrences. Checking this option causes Simulink to try to eliminate algebraic loops involving this model from models that reference it. Enabling this option disables conditional input branch optimization for simulation and the Real-Time Workshop single update/output function optimization for code generation. See "Eliminating Algebraic Loops" on page 3-27 for more information.

Diagnosing Simulation Errors

If errors occur during a simulation, Simulink halts the simulation, opens the subsystems that caused the error (if necessary), and displays the errors in the Simulation Diagnostics Viewer. The following section explains how to use the viewer to determine the cause of the errors.

Simulation Diagnostics Viewer

The viewer comprises an Error Summary pane and an Error Message pane.

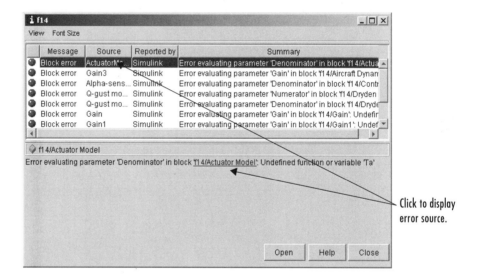

Click to display error source.

Error Summary Pane

The upper pane lists the errors that caused Simulink to terminate the simulation. The pane displays the following information for each error.

Message. Message type (for example, block error, warning, log)

Source. Name of the model element (for example, a block) that caused the error

Reported by. Component that reported the error (for example, Simulink, Stateflow, Real-Time Workshop, etc.)

Summary. Error message, abbreviated to fit in the column

You can remove any of these columns of information to make more room for the others. To remove a column, select the viewer's **View** menu and uncheck the corresponding item.

Error Message Pane

The lower pane initially contains the contents of the first error message listed in the top pane. You can display the contents of other messages by clicking their entries in the upper pane.

In addition to displaying the viewer, Simulink opens (if necessary) the subsystem that contains the first error source and highlights the source.

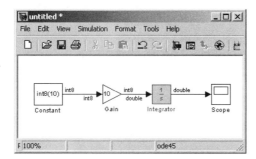

You can display the sources of other errors by clicking anywhere in the error message in the upper pane, by clicking the name of the error source in the error message (highlighted in blue), or by clicking the **Open** button on the viewer.

Changing Font Size

To change the size of the font used to display errors, select **Font Size** from the viewer's menu bar. A menu of font sizes appears. Select the desired font size from the menu.

Creating Custom Simulation Error Messages

The Simulation Diagnostics Viewer displays the output of any instance of the MATLAB error function executed during a simulation, including instances invoked by block or model callbacks or S-functions that you create or that are executed by the MATLAB Fcn block. Thus, you can use the MATLAB error function in callbacks and S-functions or in the MATLAB Fcn block to create simulation error messages specific to your application.

For example, in the following model,

the MATLAB Fcn block invokes the following function:

```
function y=check_signal(x)
  if x<0
    error('Signal is negative.');
  else
    y=x;
  end
```

Executing this model displays an error message in the Simulation Diagnostics Viewer.

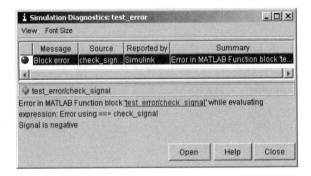

Including Hyperlinks in Error Messages

You can include hyperlinks to blocks, text files, and directories.

To include a hyperlink to a block, path, or directory, include the item's path in the error message enclosed in quotation marks, e.g.,

- `error ('Error evaluating parameter in block "mymodel/Mu"')`

  displays a text hyperlink to the block Mu in the current model in the error message. Clicking the hyperlink displays the block in the model window.

- `error ('Error reading data from "c:/work/test.data"')`

  displays a text hyperlink to the file `test.data` in the error message. Clicking the link displays the file in your preferred MATLAB editor.
- `error ('Could not find data in directory "c:/work"')`

  displays a text hyperlink to the c:/work directory. Clicking the link opens a system command window (shell) and sets its working directory to `c:/work`.

Note The text hyperlink is enabled only if the corresponding block exists in the current model or if the corresponding file or directory exists on the user's system.

Improving Simulation Performance and Accuracy

Simulation performance and accuracy can be affected by many things, including the model design and choice of configuration parameters.

The solvers handle most model simulations accurately and efficiently with their default parameter values. However, some models yield better results if you adjust solver parameters. Also, if you know information about your model's behavior, your simulation results can be improved if you provide this information to the solver.

Speeding Up the Simulation

Slow simulation speed can have many causes. Here are a few:

- Your model includes a MATLAB Fcn block. When a model includes a MATLAB Fcn block, the MATLAB interpreter is called at each time step, drastically slowing down the simulation. Use the built-in Fcn block or Math Function block whenever possible.

- Your model includes an M-file S-function. M-file S-functions also cause the MATLAB interpreter to be called at each time step. Consider either converting the S-function to a subsystem or to a C-MEX file S-function.

- Your model includes a Memory block. Using a Memory block causes the variable-order solvers (ode15s and ode113) to be reset back to order 1 at each time step.

- The maximum step size is too small. If you changed the maximum step size, try running the simulation again with the default value (auto).

- Did you ask for too much accuracy? The default relative tolerance (0.1% accuracy) is usually sufficient. For models with states that go to zero, if the absolute tolerance parameter is too small, the simulation can take too many steps around the near-zero state values. See the discussion of error in "Maximum order" on page 8-34.

- The time scale might be too long. Reduce the time interval.

- The problem might be stiff, but you are using a nonstiff solver. Try using ode15s.

- The model uses sample times that are not multiples of each other. Mixing sample times that are not multiples of each other causes the solver to take small enough steps to ensure sample time hits for all sample times.

- The model contains an algebraic loop. The solutions to algebraic loops are iteratively computed at every time step. Therefore, they severely degrade performance. For more information, see "Algebraic Loops" on page 3-24.
- Your model feeds a Random Number block into an Integrator block. For continuous systems, use the Band-Limited White Noise block in the Sources library.

Improving Simulation Accuracy

To check your simulation accuracy, run the simulation over a reasonable time span. Then, either reduce the relative tolerance to 1e-4 (the default is 1e-3) or reduce the absolute tolerance and run it again. Compare the results of both simulations. If the results are not significantly different, you can feel confident that the solution has converged.

If the simulation misses significant behavior at its start, reduce the initial step size to ensure that the simulation does not step over the significant behavior.

If the simulation results become unstable over time,

- Your system might be unstable.
- If you are using ode15s, you might need to restrict the maximum order to 2 (the maximum order for which the solver is A-stable) or try using the ode23s solver.

If the simulation results do not appear to be accurate,

- For a model that has states whose values approach zero, if the absolute tolerance parameter is too large, the simulation takes too few steps around areas of near-zero state values. Reduce this parameter value or adjust it for individual states in the Integrator dialog box.
- If reducing the absolute tolerances does not sufficiently improve the accuracy, reduce the size of the relative tolerance parameter to reduce the acceptable error and force smaller step sizes and more steps.

Exploring, Searching, and Browsing Models

The following sections describe tools that enable you to quickly navigate to any point in a model and find and modify objects in a model.

The Model Explorer

The Model Explorer allows you to quickly locate, view, and change elements of a Simulink model or Stateflow chart. To display the Model Explorer, select **Model Explorer** from the Simulink **View** menu or select an object in the block diagram and select **Explore** from its context menu. The Model Explorer appears.

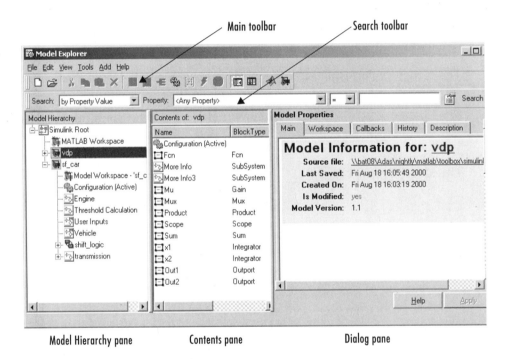

The Model Explorer includes the following components:

- **Model Hierarchy** pane (see "Model Hierarchy Pane" on page 9-3)
- **Contents** pane (see "Contents Pane" on page 9-4)
- **Dialog** pane (see "Dialog Pane" on page 9-9)
- **Main** toolbar (see "Main Toolbar" on page 9-9)
- **Search** bar (see "Search Bar" on page 9-11)

You can use the Model Explorer's **View** menu to hide the **Dialog** pane and the toolbars, thereby making more room for the other panes.

Model Hierarchy Pane

The **Model Hierarchy** pane displays a tree-structured view of the Simulink model hierarchy.

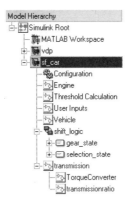

Simulink Root

The first node in the view represents the Simulink root. Expanding the root node displays nodes representing the MATLAB workspace (Simulink's base workspace) and each model and library loaded in the current session.

Base Workspace

This node represents the MATLAB workspace. The MATLAB workspace is the base workspace for Simulink models. Variables defined in this workspace are visible to all open Simulink models, i.e., to all models whose nodes appear beneath the **Base Workspace** node in the **Model Hierarchy** pane.

Model Nodes

Expanding a model node displays nodes representing the model's configuration sets (see "Configuration Sets" on page 8-26), top-level subsystems, model references, and Stateflow charts. Expanding a node representing a subsystem displays its subsystems, if any. Expanding a node representing a Stateflow chart displays the chart's top-level states. Expanding a node representing a state shows its substates.

Displaying Node Contents

To display the contents of an object displayed in the **Model Hierarchy** pane (e.g., a model or configuration set) in the adjacent **Contents** pane, select the object. To open a graphical object (e.g., a model, subsystem, or chart) in an editor window, right-click the object. A context menu appears. Select **Open** from the context menu. To open an object's properties dialog, select **Properties** from the object's context menu or from the **Edit** menu. See "Configuration Sets" on page 8-26 for information on using the **Model Hierarchy** pane to delete, move, and copy configuration sets from one model to another.

Contents Pane

The **Contents** pane displays a tabular view of the contents of the object selected in the **Model Hierarchy** pane or the results of a search operation (see "Search Bar" on page 9-11).

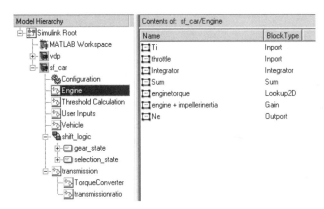

The table rows correspond to objects (e.g., blocks or states); the table columns, to object properties (e.g., name and type). The table cells display the values of the properties of the objects contained by the object selected in the **Model Hierarchy** pane.

The objects and properties displayed in the **Contents** pane depend on the type of object (e.g., subsystem, chart, or configuration set) selected in the **Model Hierarchy** pane. For example, if the object selected in the **Model Hierarchy** pane is a model or subsystem, the **Contents** pane by default displays the name and type of the top-level blocks contained by that model or subsystem. If the selected object is a Stateflow chart or state, the **Contents** pane by default shows the name, scope, and other properties of the events and data that make up the chart or state.

Customizing the Contents Pane

The Model Explorer's **View** menu allows you to control the type of objects and properties displayed in the **Contents** pane.

- To display only object names in the **Contents** pane, uncheck the **Show Properties in List View** item on the **View** menu.

- To customize the set or properties displayed in the **Contents** pane, select **Customize Contents** from the **View** menu or click the **Customize Contents** button on the Model Explorer's main toolbar (see "Main Toolbar" on page 9-9). The **Customize Contents** pane appears. Use the pane to select the properties you want the **Contents** pane to display.

- To specify the types of subsystem or chart contents displayed in the **Contents** pane, select **List View Options** from the **View** menu. A menu of object types appears. Check the types that you want to be displayed (e.g., **Blocks** and **Named Signals/Connections** or **All Simulink Objects** for models and subsystems).

Reordering the Contents Pane

The **Contents** pane by default displays its contents in ascending order by name. To order the contents in ascending order by any other displayed property, click the head of the column that displays the property. To change the order from ascending to descending, or vice versa, click the head of the property column that determines the current order.

Customize Contents Pane

The **Customize Contents** pane allows you to select the properties that the **Contents** pane displays for the object selected in the **Model Hierarchy** pane. When visible, the pane appears in the lower left corner of the Model Explorer window.

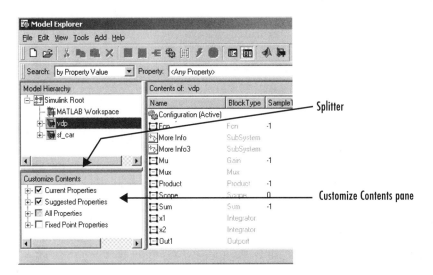

A splitter divides the **Customize Contents** pane from the **Model Hierarchy** pane above it. Drag the splitter up or down to adjust the relative size of the two panes.

The **Customize Contents** pane contains a tree-structured property list. The list's top-level nodes group object properties into the following categories:

- Current Properties

  Properties that the **Contents** pane currently displays.

- Suggested Properties

  Properties that Simulink suggests that the **Contents** pane should display, based on the type of object selected in the **Model Hierarchy** pane and the contents of the selected object.

- All Properties

  Properties of the contents of all models displayed in the Model Explorer thus far in this session.

- Fixed Point Properties

  Fixed-point properties of blocks.

By default, the properties currently displayed in the **Contents** pane are the suggested properties for the currently selected model. The **Customize Contents** pane allows you to perform the following customizations:

- To display additional properties of the selected model, expand the `All Properties` node, if necessary, and check the desired properties.

- To delete some but not all properties from the **Contents** pane, expand the `Current Properties` node, if necessary, and uncheck the properties that you do not want to appear in the **Contents** pane.

- To delete all properties from the **Contents** pane (except the selected object's name), uncheck `Current Properties`.

- To restore the properties suggested for the current model, uncheck `Current Properties` and check `Suggested Properties`.

- To add or remove fixed-point block properties from the **Contents** pane, check or uncheck `Fixed Point Properties`.

Marking Nonexistent Properties

Some of the properties that the Contents pane is configured to display may not apply to all the objects currently listed in the Contents pane. You can configure the Model Explorer to indicate the inapplicable properties.

To do this, select **Mark Nonexistent Properties** from the Model Explorer's **View** menu. The Model Explorer now displays dashes for the values of properties that do not apply to the objects displayed in the **Contents** pane.

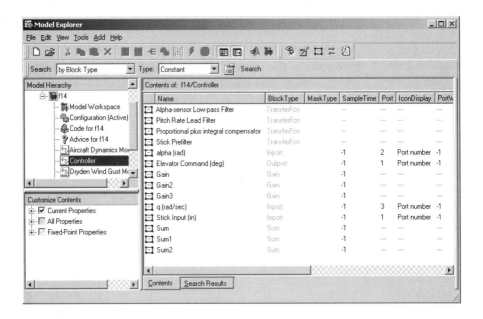

Changing Property Values

You can change modifiable properties displayed in the **Contents** pane (e.g., a block's name) by editing the displayed value. To edit a displayed value, first select the row that contains it. Then click the value. An edit control replaces the displayed value (e.g., an edit field for text values or a pull-down list for a range of values). Use the edit control to change the value of the selected property.

To assign the same property value to multiple objects displayed in the **Contents** pane, select the objects and then change one of the selected objects to have the new property value. The Model Explorer assigns the new property value to the other selected objects as well.

Dialog Pane

The **Dialog** pane displays the dialog view of the object selected in the **Contents** pane, e.g., a block or a configuration subset. You can use the **Dialog** pane to view and change the selected object's properties. To show or hide this pane, select the **Show Dialog View** menu from the Model Explorer's **View** menu or the **Show Dialog View** button on the Model Explorer's main toolbar (see "Main Toolbar" on page 9-9).

Main Toolbar

The Model Explorer's main toolbar appears near the top of the Model Explorer window under the Model Explorer's menu.

Main toolbar

The toolbar contains buttons that select commonly used Model Explorer commands:

Button	Usage
	Create a new model.
	Open an existing model.
	Cut the objects (e.g., variables) selected in the **Contents** pane from the object (e.g., a workspace) selected in the **Model Hierarchy** pane. Save a copy of the object on the system clipboard.

Button	Usage
	Copy the objects selected in the **Contents** pane to the system clipboard.
	Paste objects from the clipboard into the object selected in the Model Explorer's **Model Hierarchy** pane.
	Delete the objects selected in the **Contents** pane from the object selected in the **Model Hierarchy** pane.
	Add a MATLAB variable to the workspace selected in the **Model Hierarchy** pane.
	Add a Simulink.Parameter object to the workspace selected in the **Model Hierarchy** pane.
	Add a Simulink.Signal object to the workspace selected in the **Model Hierarchy** pane.
	Add a configuration set to the model selected in the **Model Hierarchy** pane.
	Add a Stateflow datum to the machine or chart selected in the **Model Hierarchy** pane.
	Add a Stateflow event to the machine or chart selected in the **Model Hierarchy** pane or to the state selected in the Model Explorer.
	Add a code generation target to the model selected in the **Model Hierarchy** pane.
	Turn the Model Explorer's **Dialog** pane on or off.
	Customize the Model Explorer's **Contents** pane.

Button	Usage
	Bring the MATLAB desktop to the front.
	Display the Simulink Library Browser.

To show or hide the main toolbar, select **Main Toolbar** from the Model Explorer's **View** menu.

Search Bar

The Model Explorer's search bar allows you to select, configure, and initiate searches of the object selected in the **Model Hierarchy** pane. It appears at the top of the Model Explorer window.

Search bar

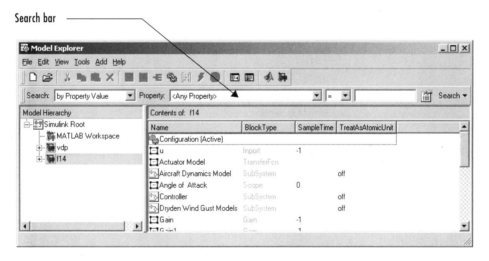

To show or hide the search bar, check or uncheck **Search Bar** in the Model Explorer's **View** menu.

The search bar includes the following controls:

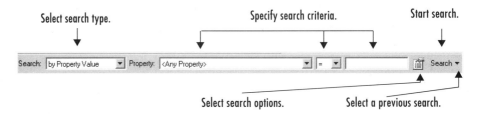

Select search type.   Specify search criteria.   Start search.

Select search options.   Select a previous search.

Search Type

Specifies the type of search to be performed. Options include:

- by Property Value

  Search for objects whose property matches a specified value. Selecting this search type causes the search bar to display controls that allow you to specify the name of the property, the value to be matched, and the type of match (equals, less than, greater than, etc.).

- by Property Name

  Search for objects that have a specified property. Selecting this search type causes the search bar to display a control that allows you to specify the target property's name by selecting from a list of properties that objects in the search domain can have.

- by Block Type

  Search for blocks of a specified block type. Selecting this search type causes the search bar to display a block type list control that allows you to select the target block type from the types contained by the currently selected model.

- for Library Links

  Searches for library links in the current model.

- by Class

  Searches for Simulink objects of a specified class.

- for Model References

  Searches a model for references to other models.

- for Fixed Point

  Searches a model for all blocks that support fixed-point computations.

- by Dialog Prompt

  Searches a model for all objects whose dialogs contain a specified prompt.
- by String

  Searches a model for all objects in which a specified string occurs.

Search Options

Specifies options that apply to the current search. The options include:

- Search All Descendants

  Search the descendants of the currently selected object as well as the selected object itself.
- Look Inside Masked Subsystems

  Search includes masked subsystems.
- Look Inside Linked Subsystems

  Search includes linked subsystems.
- Match Whole String

  Do not allow partial string matches, e.g., do not allow sub to match substring.
- Match Case

  Consider case when matching strings, e.g., Gain does not match gain.
- Regular Expression

  The Model Explorer considers a string to be matched as a regular expression.
- Refine Search Uses Boolean 'AND'

  When refining a search, search for objects that meet both the original and the new search criteria.
- Refine Search Uses Boolean 'OR'

  When refining a search, search for objects that meet either the original or the new search criteria. (Not yet implemented.)
- Clear Search History

  Not yet implemented.

Search Button

Initiates the search specified by the current settings of the search bar on the object selected in the Model Explorer's **Model Hierarchy** pane. The Model

Explorer displays the results of the search in its **Contents** pane and enters search mode.

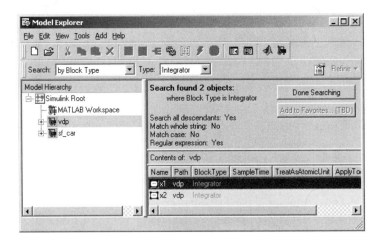

In search mode, you can perform the following tasks:

- Refine the previous search.

  In search mode, a **Refine** button replaces the **Search** button on the search bar. To refine the search results, use the search bar to define new search criteria and then click the **Refine** button. The Model Explorer searches for objects that match the previous search criteria and/or the new criteria, depending on the setting of the refine search options.

- Apply the previous search to another object.

  To apply the previous search to another object, select the object in the Model Explorer's **Model Hierarchy** pane. The Model Explorer repeats the search on the new object and displays the results.

- Edit search results.

  In search mode, you can edit the results displayed in the **Contents** pane just as you can edit them in explore mode. For example, to change all objects found by a search to have the same property value, select the objects in the **Contents** pane and change one of them to have the new property value.

To exit search mode, click the **Done Searching** button at the top of the search results.

Search History

The down arrow control adjacent to the **Search** button displays a list of searches previously executed in the current Simulink session. To reexecute a search, select it from the history and click the **Search** button. (Note this feature is not yet implemented.)

The Finder

The Finder locates blocks, signals, states, or other objects in a model. To display the Finder, select **Find** from the **Edit** menu. The **Find** dialog box appears.

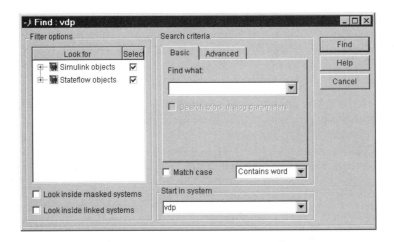

Use the **Filter options** (see "Filter Options" on page 9-18) and **Search criteria** (see "Search Criteria" on page 9-18) panels to specify the characteristics of the object you want to find. Next, if you have more than one system or subsystem open, select the system or subsystem where you want the search to begin from the **Start in system** list. Finally, click the **Find** button. Simulink searches the selected system for objects that meet the criteria you have specified.

Any objects that satisfy the criteria appear in the results panel at the bottom of the dialog box.

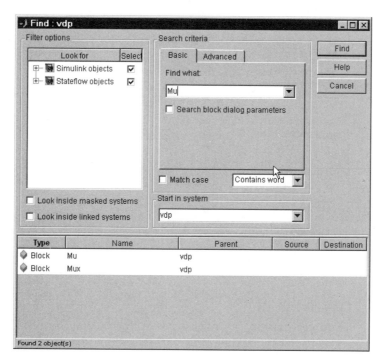

You can display an object by double-clicking its entry in the search results list. Simulink opens the system or subsystem that contains the object (if necessary) and highlights and selects the object. To sort the results list, click any of the buttons at the top of each column. For example, to sort the results by object type, click the **Type** button. Clicking a button once sorts the list in ascending order, clicking it twice sorts it in descending order. To display an object's parameters or properties, select the object in the list. Then press the right mouse button and select **Parameter** or **Properties** from the resulting context menu.

Filter Options

The **Filter options** panel allows you to specify the kinds of objects to look for and where to search for them.

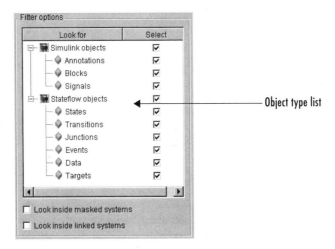

Object type list

The object type list lists the types of objects that Simulink can find. By clearing a type, you can exclude it from the Finder's search.

Look inside masked subsystem

Selecting this option causes Simulink to look for objects inside masked subsystems.

Look inside linked systems

Selecting this option causes Simulink to look for objects inside subsystems linked to libraries.

Search Criteria

The **Search criteria** panel allows you to specify the criteria that objects must meet to satisfy your search request.

Basic

The **Basic** panel allows you to search for an object whose name and, optionally, dialog parameters match a specified text string. Enter the search text in the panel's **Find what** field. To display previous search text, select the drop-down list button next to the **Find what** field. To reenter text, click it in the drop-down list. Select **Search block dialog parameters** if you want dialog parameters to be included in the search.

Advanced

The **Advanced** panel allows you to specify a set of as many as seven properties that an object must have to satisfy your search request.

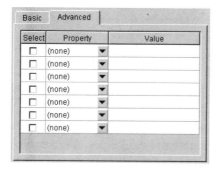

To specify a property, enter its name in one of the cells in the **Property** column of the **Advanced** pane or select the property from the cell's property list. To display the list, select the down arrow button next to the cell. Next enter the value of the property in the **Value** column next to the property name. When you enter a property name, the Finder checks the check box next to the property name in the **Select** column. This indicates that the property is to be included in the search. If you want to exclude the property, clear the check box.

Match case

Select this option if you want Simulink to consider case when matching search text against the value of an object property.

Other match options

Next to the **Match case** option is a list that specifies other match options that you can select.

- Match whole word

  Specifies a match if the property value and the search text are identical except possibly for case.

- Contains word

  Specifies a match if a property value includes the search text.

- Regular expression

  Specifies that the search text should be treated as a regular expression when matched against property values. The following characters have special meanings when they appear in a regular expression.

Character	Meaning
^	Matches start of string.
$	Matches end of string.
.	Matches any character.
\	Escape character. Causes the next character to have its ordinary meaning. For example, the regular expression \.. matches .a and .2 and any other two-character string that begins with a period.
*	Matches zero or more instances of the preceding character. For example, ba* matches b, ba, baa, etc.
+	Matches one or more instances of the preceding character. For example, ba+ matches ba, baa, etc.
[ ]	Indicates a set of characters that can match the current character. A hyphen can be used to indicate a range of characters. For example, [a-zA-Z0-9_]+ matches foo_bar1 but not foo$bar. A ^ indicates a match when the current character is not one of the following characters. For example, [^0-9] matches any character that is not a digit.
\w	Matches a word character (same as [a-z_A-Z0-9]).
\W	Matches a nonword character (same as [^a-z_A-Z0-9]).

Character	Meaning
\d	Matches a digit (same as [0-9]).
\D	Matches a nondigit (same as [^0-9]).
\s	Matches white space (same as [\t\r\n\f]).
\S	Matches nonwhite space (same as [^ \t\r\n\f]).
\<WORD\>	Matches WORD where WORD is any string of word characters surrounded by white space.

The Model Browser

The Model Browser enables you to

- Navigate a model hierarchically
- Open systems in a model
- Determine the blocks contained in a model

The browser operates differently on Microsoft Windows and Linux platforms.

Using the Model Browser on Windows

To display the Model Browser, select **Model Browser** from the Simulink **View** menu.

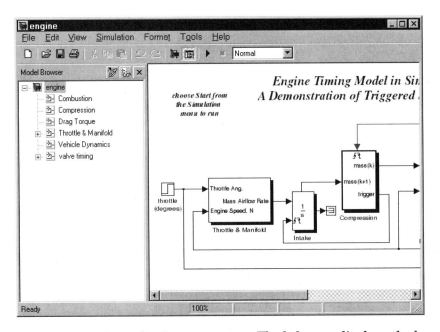

The model window splits into two panes. The left pane displays the browser, a tree-structured view of the block diagram displayed in the right pane.

Note The **Browser initially visible** preference causes Simulink to open models by default in the Model Browser. To set this preference, select **Preferences** from the Simulink **File** menu.

The top entry in the tree view corresponds to your model. A button next to the model name allows you to expand or contract the tree view. The expanded view shows the model's subsystems. A button next to a subsystem indicates that the subsystem itself contains subsystems. You can use the button to list the subsystem's children. To view the block diagram of the model or any subsystem displayed in the tree view, select the subsystem. You can use either the mouse or the keyboard to navigate quickly to any subsystem in the tree view.

Navigating with the Mouse

Click any subsystem visible in the tree view to select it. Click the + button next to any subsystem to list the subsystems that it contains. Click the button again to contract the entry.

Navigating with the Keyboard

Use the up/down arrows to move the current selection up or down the tree view. Use the left/right arrow or +/- keys on your numeric keypad to expand an entry that contains subsystems.

Showing Library Links

The Model Browser can include or omit library links from the tree view of a model. Use the Simulink **Preferences** dialog box to specify whether to display library links by default. To toggle display of library links, select **Show library links** from the **Model browser options** submenu of the Simulink **View** menu.

Showing Masked Subsystems

The Model Browser can include or omit masked subsystems from the tree view. If the tree view includes masked subsystems, selecting a masked subsystem in the tree view displays its block diagram in the diagram view. Use the Simulink **Preferences** dialog box to specify whether to display masked subsystems by default. To toggle display of masked subsystems, select **Look under masks** from the **Model browser options** submenu of the Simulink **View** menu.

Using the Model Browser on Linux

To open the Model Browser, select **Show Browser** from the **File** menu. The Model Browser window appears, displaying information about the current model. This figure shows the Model Browser window displaying the contents of the clutch system.

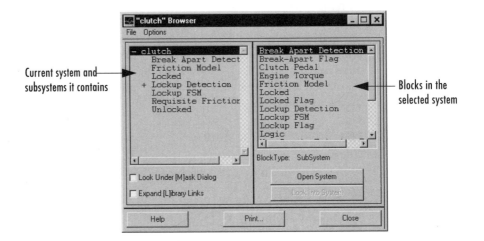

Contents of the Browser Window

The Model Browser window consists of

- The systems list. The list on the left contains the current system and the subsystems it contains, with the current system selected.

- The blocks list. The list on the right contains the names of blocks in the selected system. Initially, this window displays blocks in the top-level system.

- The **File** menu, which contains the **Print**, **Close Model**, and **Close Browser** menu items.

- The **Options** menu, which contains the menu items **Open System**, **Look Into System**, **Display Alphabetical/Hierarchical List**, **Expand All**, **Look Under Mask Dialog**, and **Expand Library Links**.

- The **Options** check boxes and buttons **Look Under [M]ask Dialog** and **Expand [L]ibrary Links** check boxes, and **Open System** and **Look Into System** buttons. By default, Simulink does not display the contents of masked blocks and blocks that are library links. These check boxes enable you to override the default.

- The block type of the selected block.
- Dialog box buttons **Help**, **Print**, and **Close**.

Interpreting List Contents

Simulink identifies masked blocks, reference blocks, blocks with defined OpenFcn parameters, and systems that contain subsystems using these symbols before a block or system name:

- A plus sign (+) before a system name in the systems list indicates that the system is expandable, which means that it has systems beneath it. Double-click the system name to expand the list and display its contents in the blocks list. When a system is expanded, a minus sign (-) appears before its name.
- [M] indicates that the block is masked, having either a mask dialog box or a mask workspace. For more information about masking, see Chapter 10, "Creating Masked Subsystems."
- [L] indicates that the block is a reference block. For more information, see "Connecting Blocks" on page 5-9.
- [O] indicates that an open function (OpenFcn) callback is defined for the block. For more information about block callbacks, see "Using Callback Routines" on page 5-38.
- [S] indicates that the system is a Stateflow block.

Opening a System

You can open any block or system whose name appears in the blocks list. To open a system:

1 In the systems list, select by single-clicking the name of the parent system that contains the system you want to open. The parent system's contents appear in the blocks list.

2 Depending on whether the system is masked, linked to a library block, or has an open function callback, you open it as follows:

- If the system has no symbol to its left, double-click its name or select its name and click the **Open System** button.

- If the system has an [M] or [O] before its name, select the system name and click the **Look Into System** button.

Looking into a Masked System or a Linked Block

By default, the Model Browser considers masked systems (identified by [M]) and linked blocks (identified by [L]) as blocks and not subsystems. If you click **Open System** while a masked system or linked block is selected, the Model Browser displays the system or block's dialog box (**Open System** works the same way as double-clicking the block in a block diagram). Similarly, if the block's OpenFcn callback parameter is defined, clicking **Open System** while that block is selected executes the callback function.

You can direct the Model Browser to look beyond the dialog box or callback function by selecting the block in the blocks list, then clicking **Look Into System**. The Model Browser displays the underlying system or block.

Displaying List Contents Alphabetically

By default, the systems list indicates the hierarchy of the model. Systems that contain systems are preceded with a plus sign (+). When those systems are expanded, the Model Browser displays a minus sign (-) before their names. To display systems alphabetically, select the **Display Alphabetical List** menu item on the **Options** menu.

Creating Masked Subsystems

This section explains how to create custom user interfaces (masks) for Simulink subsystems.

About Masks

A mask is a custom user interface for a subsystem that hides the subsystem's contents, making it appear to the user as an atomic block with its own icon and parameter dialog box. The Simulink Mask Editor enables you to create a mask for any subsystem. Masking a subsystem allows you to

- Replace the parameter dialogs of a subsystem and its contents with a single parameter dialog with its own block description, parameter prompts, and help text
- Replace a subsystem's standard icon with a custom icon that depicts its purpose
- Prevent unintended modification of subsystems by hiding their contents behind a mask
- Create a custom block by encapsulating a block diagram that defines the block's behavior in a masked subsystem and then placing the masked subsystem in a library

---

Note You can also mask S-Function and Model blocks. The instructions for masking Subsystem blocks apply to S-Function and Model blocks as well except where noted.

Mask Features

Masks can include any of the following features.

Mask Icon

The mask icon replaces a subsystem's standard icon, i.e., it appears in a block diagram in place of the standard icon for a subsystem block. Simulink uses MATLAB code that you supply to draw the custom icon. You can use any MATLAB drawing command in the icon code. This gives you great flexibility in designing an icon for a masked subsystem.

Mask Parameters

Simulink allows you to define a set of user-settable parameters for a masked subsystem. Simulink stores the value of a parameter in the mask workspace (see "Mask Workspace" on page 10-4) as the value of a variable whose name you specify. These associated variables allow you to link mask parameters to specific parameters of blocks inside a masked subsystem (internal parameters) such that setting a mask parameter sets the associated block parameter (see "Linking Mask Parameters to Block Parameters" on page 10-27).

Note If you intend to allow the user to specify the model referenced by a masked Model block or a Model block in a masked subsystem, you must ensure that the mask requires that the user specify the model name as a literal value rather than as a workspace variable. This is because Simulink updates model reference targets before evaluating block parameters. The recommended way to force the user to specify the model name as a literal is to use a pop-up control on the mask to specify the model name. See "Pop-Up Control" on page 10-22 for more information.

Mask Parameter Dialog Box

The mask parameter dialog box contains controls that enable a user to set the values of the masks parameters and hence the values of any internal parameters linked to the mask parameters.

The mask parameter dialog box replaces the subsystem's standard parameter dialog box, i.e., clicking on the masked subsystem's icon causes the mask dialog box to appear instead of the standard parameter dialog box for a Subsystem block. You can customize every feature of the mask dialog box, including which parameters appear on the dialog box, the order in which they appear, parameter prompts, the controls used to edit the parameters, and the parameter callbacks (code used to process parameter values entered by the user).

Mask Initialization Code

The initialization code is MATLAB code that you specify and that Simulink runs to initialize the masked subsystem at the start of a simulation run. You can use the initialization code to set the initial values of the masked subsystem's mask parameters.

Mask Workspace

Simulink associates a workspace with each masked subsystem that you create. Simulink stores the current values of the subsystem's parameters in the workspace as well as any variables created by the block's initialization code and parameter callbacks. You can use model and mask workspace variables to initialize a masked subsystem and to set the values of blocks inside the masked subsystem, subject to the following rules.

- A block parameter expression can refer only to variables defined in the mask workspaces of the subsystem or nested subsystems that contain the block or in the model's workspace.

- A valid reference to a variable defined on more than one level in the model hierarchy resolves to the most local definition.

  For example, suppose that model M contains masked subsystem A, which contains masked subsystem B. Further suppose that B refers to a variable x that exists in both A's and M's workspaces. In this case, the reference resolves to the value in A's workspace.

- A masked subsystem's initialization code can refer only to variables in its local workspace.

- The mask workspace of a Model block is not visible to the model that it references. Any variables used by the referenced model must resolve to workspaces defined in the referenced model or to the base (i.e., the MATLAB) workspace.

Creating Masks

See "Masking a Subsystem" on page 10-10 for an overview of the process of creating a masked subsystem. See "Masked Subsystem Example" on page 10-5 for an example of the process.

Masked Subsystem Example

This simple subsystem models the equation for a line, y = mx + b.

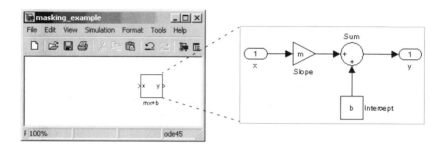

Ordinarily, when you double-click a Subsystem block, the Subsystem block opens, displaying its blocks in a separate window. The mx + b subsystem contains a Gain block, named Slope, whose **Gain** parameter is specified as m, and a Constant block, named Intercept, whose **Constant value** parameter is specified as b. These parameters represent the slope and intercept of a line.

This example creates a custom dialog box and icon for the subsystem. One dialog box contains prompts for both the slope and the intercept. After you create the mask, double-click the Subsystem block to open the mask dialog box. The mask dialog box and icon look like this:

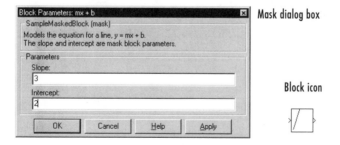

Mask dialog box

Block icon

A user enters values for **Slope** and **Intercept** in the mask dialog box. Simulink makes these values available to all the blocks in the underlying subsystem. Masking this subsystem creates a self-contained functional unit with its own application-specific parameters, **Slope** and **Intercept**. The mask maps these *mask parameters* to the generic parameters of the underlying blocks. The complexity of the subsystem is encapsulated by a new interface that has the look and feel of a built-in Simulink block.

To create a mask for this subsystem, you need to

- Specify the prompts for the mask dialog box parameters. In this example, the mask dialog box has prompts for the slope and intercept.
- Specify the variable name used to store the value of each parameter.
- Enter the documentation of the block, consisting of the block description and the block help text.
- Specify the drawing command that creates the block icon.
- Specify the commands that provide the variables needed by the drawing command (there are none in this example).

Creating Mask Dialog Box Prompts

To create the mask for this subsystem, select the Subsystem block and choose **Mask Subsystem** from the **Edit** menu.

This example primarily uses the Mask Editor's **Parameters** pane to create the masked subsystem's dialog box.

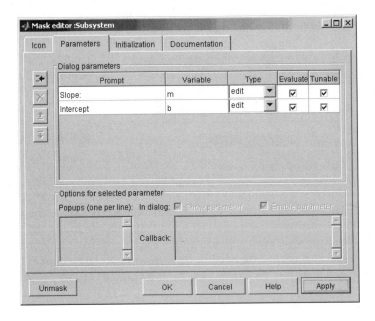

The Mask Editor enables you to specify these attributes of a mask parameter:

- Prompt, the text label that describes the parameter
- Control type, the style of user interface control that determines how parameter values are entered or selected
- Variable, the name of the variable that stores the parameter value

Generally, it is convenient to refer to masked parameters by their prompts. In this example, the parameter associated with slope is referred to as the **Slope** parameter, and the parameter associated with intercept is referred to as the **Intercept** parameter.

The slope and intercept are defined as edit controls. This means that the user types values into edit fields in the mask dialog box. These values are stored in variables in the *mask workspace*. Masked blocks can access variables only in the mask workspace. In this example, the value entered for the slope is assigned to the variable m. The Slope block in the masked subsystem gets the value for the slope parameter from the mask workspace. This figure shows how the slope parameter definitions in the Mask Editor map to the actual mask dialog box parameters.

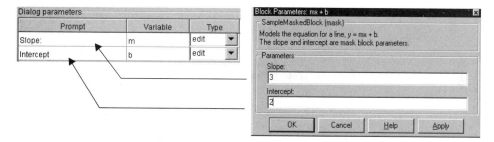

After you create the mask parameters for slope and intercept, click the **OK** button. Then double-click the Subsystem block to open the newly constructed dialog box. Enter 3 for the **Slope** and 2 for the **Intercept** parameter.

Creating the Block Description and Help Text

The mask type, block description, and help text are defined on the **Documentation** pane. For this sample masked block, the pane looks like this.

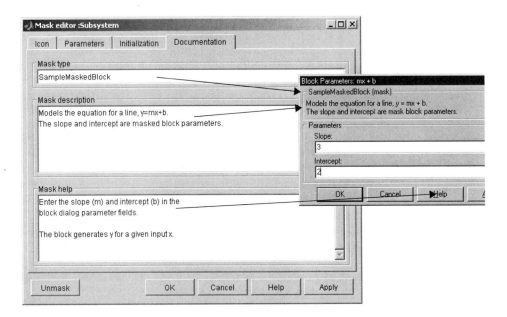

Creating the Block Icon

So far, we have created a customized dialog box for the mx + b subsystem. However, the Subsystem block still displays the generic Simulink subsystem icon. An appropriate icon for this masked block is a plot that indicates the slope of the line. For a slope of 3, that icon looks like this.

The block icon is defined on the **Icon** pane. For this block, the **Icon** pane looks like this.

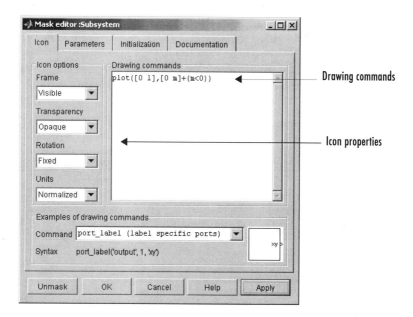

The drawing command plots a line from (0,0) to (1,m). If the slope is negative, Simulink shifts the line up by 1 to keep it within the visible drawing area of the block.

The drawing commands have access to all the variables in the mask workspace. As you enter different values of slope, the icon updates the slope of the plotted line.

Select **Normalized** as the **Drawing coordinates** parameter, located at the bottom of the list of icon properties, to specify that the icon be drawn in a frame whose bottom left corner is (0,0) and whose top right corner is (1,1). See "The Icon Pane" on page 10-14 for more information.

Masking a Subsystem

To mask a subsystem,

1 Select the subsystem.

2 Select **Edit mask** from the **Edit** menu of the model window or from the block's context menu. (Right-click the subsystem block to display its context menu.)

The Mask Editor appears.

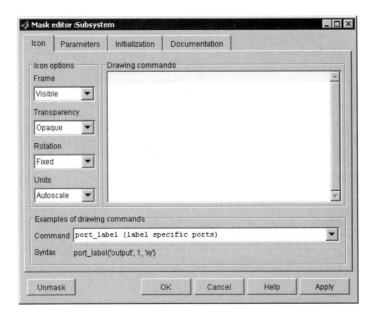

See "The Mask Editor" on page 10-12 for a detailed description of the Mask Editor.

3 Use the Mask Editor's tabbed panes to perform any of the following tasks.

- Create a custom icon for the masked subsystem (see "The Icon Pane" on page 10-14)

- Create parameters that allow a user to set subsystem options (see "The Mask Editor" on page 10-12)

- Initialize the masked subsystem's parameters
- Create online user documentation for the subsystem

4 Click **Apply** to apply the mask to the subsystem or **OK** to apply the mask and dismiss the Mask Editor.

The Mask Editor

The Mask Editor allows you to create or edit a subsystem's mask. To open the Mask Editor, select the subsystem's block icon and then select **Edit Mask** from the **Edit** menu of the model window containing the subsystem's block. The Mask Editor appears.

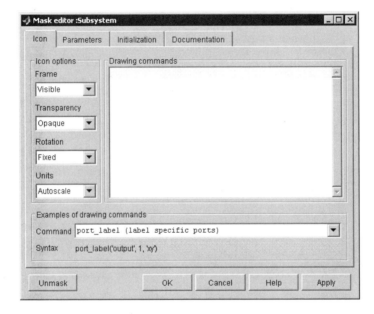

The Mask Editor contains a set of tabbed panes, each of which enables you to define a feature of the mask:

- The **Icon** pane enables you to define the block icon (see "The Icon Pane" on page 10-14).

- The **Parameters** pane enables you to define and describe mask dialog box parameter prompts and name the variables associated with the parameters (see "The Parameters Pane" on page 10-17).

- The **Initialization** pane enables you to specify initialization commands (see "The Initialization Pane" on page 10-23).

- The **Documentation** pane enables you to define the mask type and specify the block description and the block help (see "The Documentation Pane" on page 10-25).

Five buttons appear along the bottom of the Mask Editor:

- The **Unmask** button deactivates the mask and closes the Mask Editor. The mask information is retained so that the mask can be reactivated. To reactivate the mask, select the block and choose **Create Mask**. The Mask Editor opens, displaying the previous settings. The inactive mask information is discarded when the model is closed and cannot be recovered.

- The **OK** button applies the mask settings on all panes and closes the Mask Editor.

- The **Cancel** button closes the Mask Editor without applying any changes made since you last clicked the **Apply** button.

- The **Help** button displays the contents of this chapter.

- The **Apply** button creates or changes the mask using the information that appears on all masking panes. The Mask Editor remains open.

To see the system under the mask without unmasking it, select the Subsystem block, then choose **Look Under Mask** from the **Edit** menu. This command opens the subsystem. The block's mask is not affected.

The Icon Pane

The Mask Editor's **Icon** pane enables you to create icons that can contain descriptive text, state equations, images, and graphics.

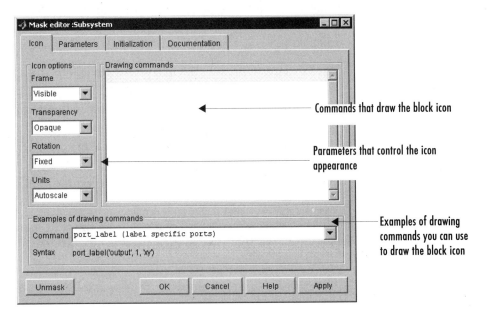

The **Icon** pane contains the following controls.

Drawing commands

This field allows you to enter commands that draw the block's icon. Simulink provides a set of commands that can display text, one or more plots, or show a transfer function (see "Mask Icon Drawing Commands") in the online Simulink reference). You must use these commands to draw your icon. Simulink executes the drawing commands in the order in which they appear in this field. Drawing commands have access to all variables in the mask workspace.

This example demonstrates how to create an improved icon for the mx + b sample masked subsystem discussed earlier in this chapter.

```
pos = get_param(gcb, 'Position');
width = pos(3) - pos(1); height = pos(4) - pos(2);
x = [0, width];
if (m >= 0), y = [0, (m*width)]; end
```

```
if (m < 0),  y = [height, (height + (m*width))]; end
```

These initialization commands define the data that enables the drawing command to produce an accurate icon regardless of the shape of the block. The drawing command that generates this icon is plot(x,y).

Examples of drawing commands

This panel illustrates the usage of the various icon drawing commands supported by Simulink. To determine the syntax of a command, select the command from the **Command** list. Simulink displays an example of the selected command at the bottom of the panel and the icon produced by the command to the right of the list.

Icon options

These controls allow you to specify the following attributes of the block icon.

Frame. The icon frame is the rectangle that encloses the block. You can choose to show or hide the frame by setting the **Frame** parameter to Visible or Invisible. The default is to make the icon frame visible. For example, this figure shows visible and invisible icon frames for an AND gate block.

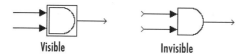

Transparency. The icon can be set to Opaque or Transparent, either hiding or showing what is underneath the icon. Opaque, the default, covers information Simulink draws, such as port labels. This figure shows opaque and transparent icons for an AND gate block. Notice the text on the transparent icon.

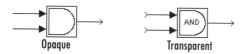

Rotation. When the block is rotated or flipped, you can choose whether to rotate or flip the icon or to have it remain fixed in its original orientation. The default is not to rotate the icon. The icon rotation is consistent with block port rotation. This figure shows the results of choosing Fixed and Rotates icon rotation when the AND gate block is rotated.

Fixed   Rotates

Units. This option controls the coordinate system used by the drawing commands. It applies only to `plot` and `text` drawing commands. You can select from among these choices: `Autoscale`, `Normalized`, and `Pixel`.

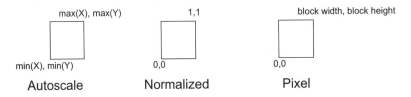

Autoscale   Normalized   Pixel

- `Autoscale` scales the icon to fit the block frame. When the block is resized, the icon is also resized. For example, this figure shows the icon drawn using these vectors:

  `X = [0 2 3 4 9]; Y = [4 6 3 5 8];`

  The lower left corner of the block frame is (0,3) and the upper right corner is (9,8). The range of the x-axis is 9 (from 0 to 9), while the range of the y-axis is 5 (from 3 to 8).

- `Normalized` draws the icon within a block frame whose bottom left corner is (0,0) and whose top right corner is (1,1). Only X and Y values between 0 and 1 appear. When the block is resized, the icon is also resized. For example, this figure shows the icon drawn using these vectors:

  `X = [.0 .2 .3 .4 .9]; Y = [.4 .6 .3 .5 .8];`

- Pixel draws the icon with X and Y values expressed in pixels. The icon is not automatically resized when the block is resized. To force the icon to resize with the block, define the drawing commands in terms of the block size.

The Parameters Pane

The **Parameters** pane allows you to create and modify masked subsystem parameters (mask parameters, for short) that determine the behavior of the masked subsystem.

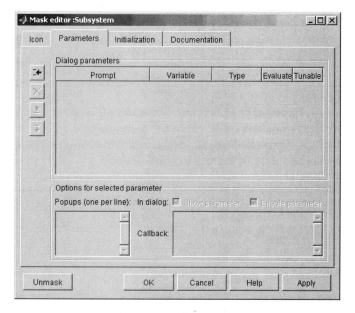

The **Parameters** pane contains the following elements:

- The **Dialog parameters** panel allows you to select and change the major properties of the mask's parameters (see "Dialog Parameters Panel" on page 10-18).

- The **Options for selected parameter** panel allows you to set additional options for the parameter selected in the **Dialog parameters** panel.

- The buttons on the left side of the **Parameters** pane allow you to add, delete, and change the order of appearance of parameters on the mask's parameter dialog box (see "Dialog Parameters Panel" on page 10-18).

Dialog Parameters Panel

Lists the mask's parameters in tabular form. Each row displays the major attributes of one of the mask's parameters.

Prompt. Text that identifies the parameter on a masked subsystem's dialog box.

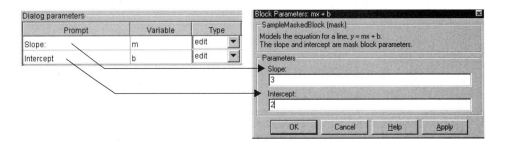

Variable. Name of the variable that stores the parameter's value in the mask's workspace (see "Mask Workspace" on page 10-4). You can use this variable as the value of parameters of blocks inside the masked subsystem, thereby allowing the user to set the parameters via the mask dialog box.

Note Simulink does not distinguish between uppercase and lowercase letters in mask variable names. For example, Simulink treats gain, GAIN, and Gain as the same name.

Type. Type of control used to edit the value of this parameter. The control appears on the mask's parameter dialog box following the parameter prompt. The button that follows the type name in the **Parameters** pane pops up a list of the controls supported by Simulink (see "Control Types" on page 10-20). To change the current control type, select another type from the list.

Evaluate. If checked, this option causes Simulink to evaluates the expression entered by the user before it is assigned to the variable. Otherwise, Simulink treats the expression itself as a string value and assigns it to the variable. For example, if the user enters the expression gain in an edit field and the **Evaluate** option is checked, Simulink evaluates gain and assigns the result to the variable. Otherwise, Simulink assigns the string 'gain' to the variable.

See "Check Box Control" on page 10-21 and "Pop-Up Control" on page 10-22 for information on how this option affects evaluation of the parameters.

If you need both the string entered and the evaluated value, clear the **Evaluate** option. Then use the MATLAB `eval` command in the initialization commands. For example, if `LitVal` is the string `'gain'`, then to obtain the evaluated value, use the command

```
value = eval(LitVal)
```

Tunable. Selecting this option allows a user to change the value of the mask parameter while a simulation is running.

Options for Selected Parameter Panel

This panel allows you to set additional options for the parameter selected in the **Dialog parameters** table.

Show parameter. The selected parameter appears on the masked block's parameter dialog box only if this option is checked (the default).

Enable parameter. Clearing this option grays the selected parameter's prompt and disables its edit control. This means that the user cannot set the value of the parameter.

Popups. This field is enabled only if the edit control for the selected parameter is a pop-up. Enter the values of the pop-up control in this field, each on a separate line.

Callback. Enter MATLAB code that you want Simulink to execute when a user edits the selected parameter. The callback can create and reference variables only in the block's base workspace. If the callback needs the value of a mask parameter, it can use `get_param` to obtain the value, e.g.,

```
if str2num(get_param(gcb, 'g'))<0
    error('Gain is negative.')
end
```

Parameter Buttons

The following sections explain the purpose of the buttons that appear on the **Parameters** pane in the order of their appearance from the top of the pane.

Add Button. Adds a parameter to the mask's parameter list. The newly created parameter appears in the adjacent **Dialog parameters** table.

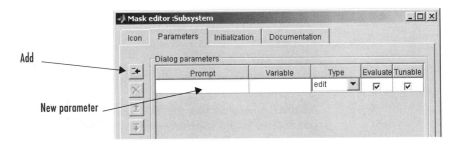

Delete Button. Deletes the parameter currently selected in the **Dialog parameters** table.

Up Button. Moves the currently selected parameter up one row in the **Dialog parameters** table. Dialog parameters appear in the mask's parameter dialog box (see "Mask Parameter Dialog Box" on page 10-3) in the same order in which they appear in the **Dialog parameters** table. This button (and the next) thus allows you to determine the order in which parameters appear on the dialog box.

Down Button. Moves the currently selected parameter down one row in the **Dialog parameters** table and hence down one position on the mask's parameter dialog box.

Control Types

Simulink enables you to choose how parameter values are entered or selected. You can create three styles of controls: edit fields, check boxes, and pop-up controls. For example, this figure shows the parameter area of a mask dialog box that uses all three styles of controls (with the pop-up control open).

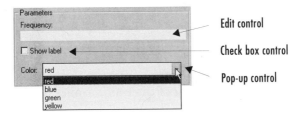

Edit Control

An *edit field* enables the user to enter a parameter value by typing it into a field. This figure shows how the prompt for the sample edit control was defined.

The value of the variable associated with the parameter is determined by the **Evaluate** option.

Evaluate	Value
On	The result of evaluating the expression entered in the field
Off	The actual string entered in the field

Check Box Control

A *check box* enables the user to choose between two alternatives by selecting or deselecting a check box. This figure shows how the sample check box control is defined.

The value of the variable associated with the parameter depends on whether the **Evaluate** option is selected.

Control State	Evaluated Value	Literal Value
Selected	1	'on'
Unselected	0	'off'

Pop-Up Control

A *pop-up* enables the user to choose a parameter value from a list of possible values. Specify the values in the **Popups** field on the **Parameters** pane (see "Popups" on page 10-19). The following example shows a pop-up parameter.

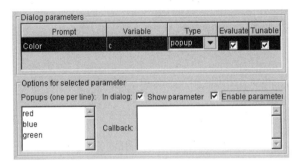

The value of the variable associated with the parameter (Color) depends on the item selected from the pop-up list and whether the **Evaluate** option is checked (on).

Evaluate	Value
On	Index of the value selected from the list, starting with 1. For example, if the third item is selected, the parameter value is 3.
Off	String that is the value selected. If the third item is selected, the parameter value is 'green'.

Changing Default Values for Mask Parameters in a Library

To change default parameter values in a masked library block, follow these steps:

1 Unlock the library.

2 Open the block to access its dialog box, fill in the desired default values, and close the dialog box.

3 Save the library.

When the block is copied into a model and opened, the default values appear on the block's dialog box.

For more information, see "Working with Block Libraries" on page 6-18.

The Initialization Pane

The **Initialization** pane allows you to enter MATLAB commands that initialize the masked subsystem.

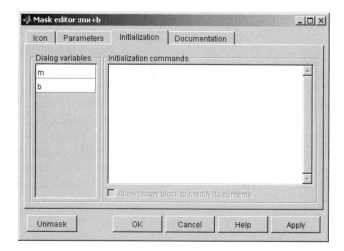

Simulink executes the initialization commands when it

- Loads the model
- Starts the simulation or updates the block diagram
- Rotates the masked block
- Redraws the block's icon (if the mask's icon creation code depends on variables defined in the initialization code)

The **Initialization** pane includes the following controls.

Dialog variables

The **Dialog variables** list displays the names of the variables associated with the subsystem's mask parameters, i.e., the parameters defined in the **Parameters** pane. You can copy the name of a parameter from this list and paste it into the adjacent **Initialization commands** field, using the Simulink keyboard copy and paste commands. You can also use the list to change the names of mask parameter variables. To change a name, double-click the name in the list. An edit field containing the existing name appears. Edit the existing name and press **Enter** or click outside the edit field to confirm your changes.

Initialization commands

Enter the initialization commands in this field. You can enter any valid MATLAB expression, consisting of MATLAB functions, operators, and variables defined in the mask workspace. Initialization commands cannot access base workspace variables. Terminate initialization commands with a semicolon to avoid echoing results to the Command Window.

Allow library block to modify its contents

This check box is enabled only if the masked subsystem resides in a library. Checking this block allows the block's initialization code to modify the contents of the masked subsystem, i.e., it lets the code add or delete blocks and set the parameters of those blocks. Otherwise, Simulink generates an error when a masked library block tries to modify its contents in any way. To set this option at the MATLAB prompt, select the self-modifying block and enter the following command.

```
set_param(gcb, 'MaskSelfModifiable', 'on');
```

Then save the block.

Debugging Initialization Commands

You can debug initialization commands in these ways:

- Specify an initialization command without a terminating semicolon to echo its results to the Command Window.

- Place a keyboard command in the initialization commands to stop execution and give control to the keyboard. For more information, see the help text for the keyboard command.

- Enter either of these commands in the MATLAB Command Window:

```
dbstop if error
```

```
dbstop if warning
```

If an error occurs in the initialization commands, execution stops and you can examine the mask workspace. For more information, see the help text for the dbstop command.

The Documentation Pane

The **Documentation** pane enables you to define or modify the type, description, and help text for a masked block. This figure shows how fields on the **Documentation** pane correspond to the mx + b sample mask block's dialog box.

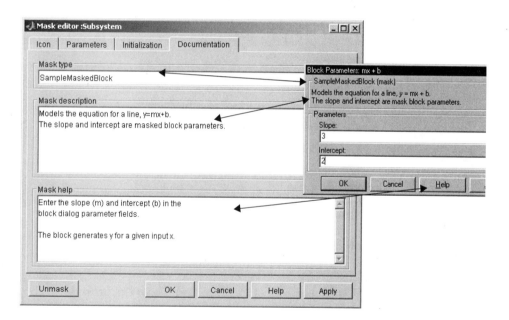

Mask Type Field

The mask type is a block classification used only for purposes of documentation. It appears in the block's dialog box and on all Mask Editor panes for the block. You can choose any name you want for the mask type. When Simulink creates the block's dialog box, it adds "(mask)" after the mask type to differentiate masked blocks from built-in blocks.

Mask Description Field

The block description is informative text that appears in the block's dialog box in the frame under the mask type. If you are designing a system for others to use, this is a good place to describe the block's purpose or function.

Simulink automatically wraps long lines of text. You can force line breaks by using the **Enter** or **Return** key.

Block Help Field

You can provide help text that is displayed when the **Help** button is clicked on the masked block's dialog box. If you create models for others to use, this is a good place to explain how the block works and how to enter its parameters.

You can include user-written documentation for a masked block's help. You can specify any of the following for the masked block help text:

- URL specification (a string starting with `http:`, `www`, `file:`, `ftp:`, or `mailto:`)
- `web` command (launches a browser)
- `eval` command (evaluates a MATLAB string)
- HTML-tagged text to be displayed in a Web browser

Simulink examines the first line of the masked block help text. If Simulink detects a URL specification, for example,

```
http://www.mathworks.com
```

or

```
file:///c:/mydir/helpdoc.html
```

Simulink displays the specified file in the browser. If Simulink detects a `web` command, for example,

```
web([docroot '/My Blockset Doc/' get_param(gcb,'MaskType')...
'.html'])
```

or an `eval` command, for example,

```
eval('!Word My_Spec.doc')
```

Simulink executes the specified command. Otherwise, Simulink displays the contents of the **Block Help** field, which can include HTML tags, in the browser.

Linking Mask Parameters to Block Parameters

The variables associated with mask parameters allow you to link mask parameters with block parameters. This in turn allows a user to use the mask to set the values of parameters of blocks inside the masked subsystem.

To link the parameters, open the block's parameter dialog box and enter an expression in the block parameter's value field that uses the mask parameter. The mx + b masked subsystem, described earlier in this chapter, uses this approach to link the Slope and Intercept mask parameters to corresponding parameters of a Gain and Constant block, respectively, that reside in the subsystem.

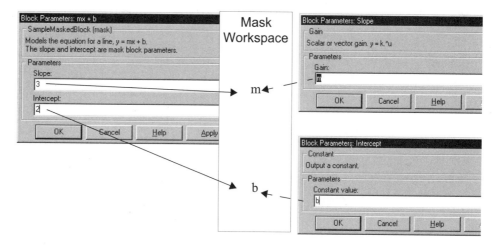

You can use a masked block's initialization code to link mask parameters indirectly to block parameters. In this approach, the initialization code creates variables in the mask workspace whose values are functions of the mask parameters and that appear in expressions that set the values of parameters of blocks concealed by the mask.

Simulink Debugger

The following sections tell you how to use the Simulink debugger to pinpoint bugs in a model.

Introduction

The Simulink debugger allows you to run a simulation method by method, stopping the simulation after each method, to examine the results of executing that method. This allows you to pinpoint problems in your model to specific blocks, parameters, or interconnections.

Note Methods are functions that Simulink uses to solve a model at each time step during the simulation. Blocks are made up of multiple methods. "Block execution" in this documentation is shorthand notation for "block methods execution." Block diagram execution is a multi-step operation that requires execution of the different block methods in all the blocks in a diagram at various points during the process of solving a model at each time step during simulation, as specified by the simulation loop.

The Simulink debugger has both a graphical and a command-line user interface. The graphical interface allows you to access the debugger's most commonly used features. The command-line interface gives you access to all the debugger's capabilities. If both interfaces enable you to perform a task, the documentation shows you first how to use the graphical interface, then the command-line interface, to perform the task.

Using the Debugger's Graphical User Interface

Select **Debug** from a model window's **Tools** menu to display the Simulink debugger's graphical interface.

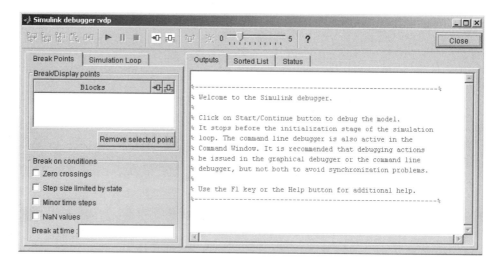

The following topics describe the major components of the debugger's graphical user interface:

Toolbar

The debugger toolbar appears at the top of the debugger window.

Toolboar

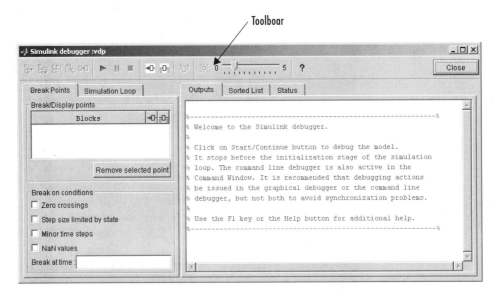

From left to right, the toolbar contains the following command buttons:

Button	Purpose
	Step into next method (see "Stepping Commands" on page 11-17 for more information on this and the following stepping commands).
	Step over next method.
	Step out of current method.
	Step to first method at start of next time step.
	Step to next block method.

Button	Purpose
▷	Start or continue the simulation.
‖	Pause the simulation.
▮	Stop the simulation.
◂▯	Break before the selected block.
▯	Display inputs and outputs of the selected block when executed.
▯	Display current inputs and outputs of selected block.
☀	Toggle animation mode on or off (see "Animation Mode" on page 11-18). The slider next to this button controls the animation rate.
?	Display help for the debugger.
Close	Close the debugger.

Breakpoints Pane

To display the **Breakpoints** pane, select the **Break Points** tab on the debugger window.

Breakpoints pane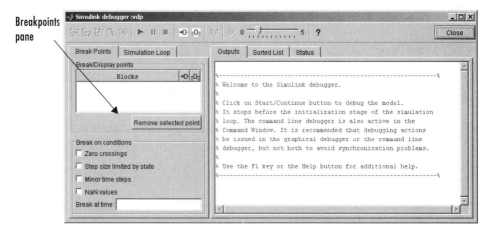

The **Breakpoints** pane allows you to specify block methods or conditions at which to stop a simulation. See "Setting Breakpoints" on page 11–22 for more information.

Note The debugger grays out and disables the **Breakpoints** pane when its animation mode is selected (see "Animation Mode" on page 11-18). This prevents you from setting breakpoints and indicates that animation mode ignores existing breakpoints.

Simulation Loop Pane

To display the **Simulation Loop** pane, select the **Simulation Loop** tab on the debugger window.

Simulation Loop pane

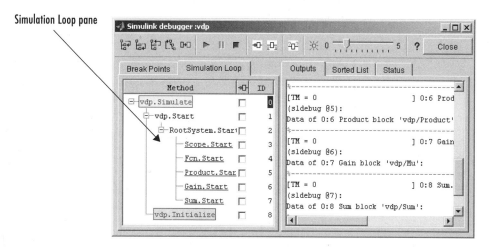

The Simulation Loop pane contains three columns:

- Method
- Breakpoints
- ID

Method Column

The **Method** column lists the methods that have been called thus far in the simulation as a method tree with expandable/collapsible nodes. Each node of the tree represents a method that calls other methods. Expanding a node shows the methods that the block method calls. Block method names are hyperlinks. Clicking a block method name highlights the corresponding block in the model diagram. Block method names are underlined to indicate that they are hyperlinks.

Whenever the simulation stops, the debugger highlights the name of the method where the simulation has stopped as well as the methods that directly or indirectly invoked it. The highlighted method names visually indicate the current state of the simulator's method call stack.

Breakpoints Column

The breakpoints column consists of check boxes. Selecting a check box sets a breakpoint at the method whose name appears to the left of the check box. See "Setting Breakpoints from the Simulation Loop Pane" on page 11-24 for more information.

Note The debugger grays out and disables this column when its animation mode is selected (see "Animation Mode" on page 11-18). This prevents you from setting breakpoints and indicates that animation mode ignores existing breakpoints.

ID Column

The ID column lists the IDs of the methods listed in the **Methods** column. See "Method ID" on page 11–11 for more information.

Outputs Pane

To display the **Outputs** pane, select the **Outputs** tab on the debugger window.

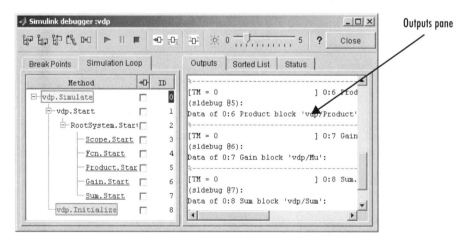

The Outputs pane displays the same debugger output that would appear in the MATLAB Command Window, if the debugger were running in command-line mode. The output includes the debugger command prompt and the inputs, outputs, and states of the block at whose method the simulation is currently paused (see "Block Data Output" on page 11-16). The command prompt displays current simulation time and the name and index of the method in which the debugger is currently stopped (see "Block ID" on page 11-11).

Sorted List Pane

To display the **Sorted List** pane, select the **Sorted List** tab on the debugger window.

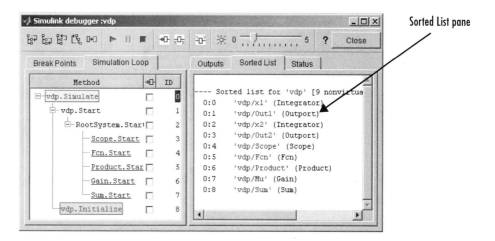

Sorted List pane

The **Sorted List** pane displays the sorted lists for the model being debugged. See "Displaying a Model's Sorted Lists" on page 11-32 for more information.

Status Pane

To display the **Status** pane, select the **Status** tab on the debugger window.

Status pane

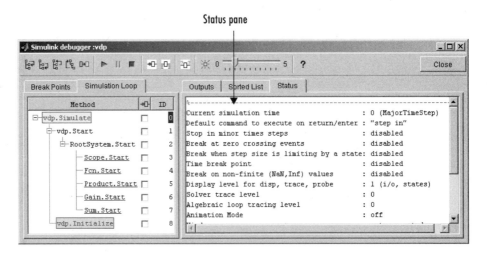

The **Status** pane displays the values of various debugger options and other status information.

Using the Debugger's Command-Line Interface

In command-line mode, you control the debugger by entering commands at the debugger command line in the MATLAB Command Window. The debugger accepts abbreviations for debugger commands. See "Debugger Command Reference" in the online Simulink Help for a list of command abbreviations and repeatable commands. You can repeat some commands by entering an empty command (i.e., by pressing the **Enter** key) at the MATLAB command line.

Method ID

Some Simulink commands and messages use method IDs to refer to methods. A method ID is an integer assigned to a method the first time it is invoked in a simulation. The debugger assigns method indexes sequentially, starting with 0 for the first method invoked in a debugger session.

Block ID

Some Simulink debugger commands and messages use block IDs to refer to blocks. Simulink assigns block IDs to blocks while generating the model's sorted lists during the compilation phase of the simulation. A block ID has the form sid:bid where sid is an integer identifying the system that contains the block (either the root system or a nonvirtual subsystem) and bid is the position of the block in the system's sorted list. For example, the block index 0:1 refers to the first block in the model's root system. The slist command shows the block ID for each block in the model being debugged (see slist in the "Debugger Command Reference" in the online Simulink Help).

Accessing the MATLAB Workspace

You can enter any MATLAB expression at the sldebug prompt. For example, suppose you are at a breakpoint and you are logging time and output of your model as tout and yout. Then the following command

```
(sldebug ...) plot(tout, yout)
```

creates a plot. You cannot display the value of a workspace variable whose name is partially or entirely the same as that of a debugger command by entering it at the debugger command prompt. You can, however, use the MATLAB eval command to work around this problem. For example, use eval('s') to determine the value of s rather then s(tep) the simulation.

Getting Online Help

You can get online help on using the debugger by clicking the **Help** button on the debugger's toolbar or by pressing the **F1** key when the text cursor is in a debugger panel or text field. Clicking the Help button displays help for the debugger in the MATLAB Help browser.

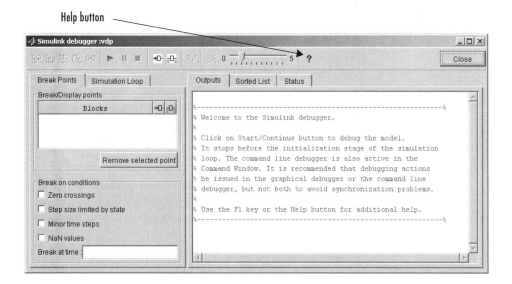

Pressing the **F1** key displays help for the debugger panel or text field that currently has the keyboard input focus. In command-line mode, you can get a brief description of the debugger commands by typing help at the debug prompt.

Starting the Debugger

You can start the debugger either from a model window or from the MATLAB command line. To start the debugger from a model window, select **Debugger** from the model window's **Tools** menu. The debugger's graphical user interface appears (see "Using the Debugger's Graphical User Interface" on page 11–3).

To start the debugger from the MATLAB Command Window, enter either the sldebug command or a sim command. For example, either the command

```
sim('vdp',[0,10],simset('debug','on'))
```

or the command

```
sldebug 'vdp'
```

loads the Simulink demo model vdp into memory, starts the simulation, and stops the simulation at the first block in the model's execution list.

Note When running the debugger in graphical user interface (GUI) mode, you must explicitly start the simulation. See "Starting the Debugger" on page 11-13 for more information.

Starting a Simulation

To start the simulation, click the Start/Continue button on the debugger's toolbar.

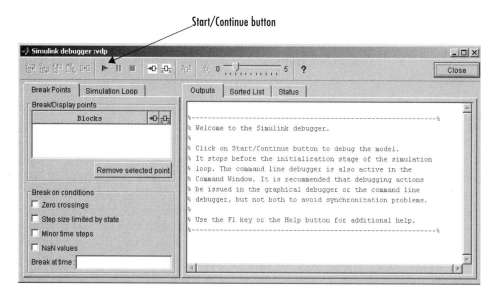

Start/Continue button

The simulation starts and stops at the first simulation method to be executed. It displays the name of the method in its **Simulation Loop** pane and in the current method annotation on the Simulink block diagram. At this point, you can set breakpoints, run the simulation step by step, continue the simulation to the next breakpoint or end, examine data, or perform other debugging tasks. The following sections explain how to use the debugger's graphical controls to perform these debugging tasks.

Note When you start the debugger in GUI mode, the debugger's command-line interface is also active in the MATLAB Command Window. However, you should avoid using the command-line interface, to prevent synchronization errors between the graphical and command-line interfaces.

Running a Simulation Step by Step

The Simulink debugger provides various commands that let you advance a simulation from the method where it is currently suspended (the next method) by various increments (see "Stepping Commands" on page 11-17). For example, you can advance the simulation into or over the next method, or out of the current method, or to the top of the simulation loop. After each advance, the debugger displays information that enables you to determine the point to which the simulation has advanced and the results of advancing the simulation to that point.

For example, in GUI mode, after each step command, the debugger highlights the current method call stack in the **Simulation Loop** pane. The call stack comprises the next method and the methods that invoked the next method either directly or indirectly. The debugger highlights the call stack by highlighting the names of the methods that make up the call stack in the **Simulation Loop** pane.

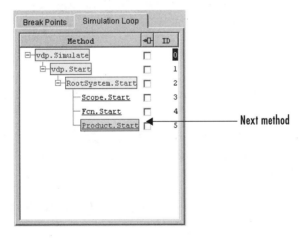

In command-line mode, you can use the where command to display the method call stack. If the next method is a block method, the debugger points the debug pointer at the block corresponding to the method (see "Debug Pointer" on page 11-20 for more information). If the block of the next method to be executed resides in a subsystem, the debugger opens the subsystem and points to the block in the subsystem's block diagram.

Block Data Output

After executing a block method, the debugger prints any or all of the following block data in the debugger Output panel (in GUI mode) or in the MATLAB Command Window (in command-line mode):

- Un = v

  where v is the current value of the block's nth input.

- Yn = v

  where v is the current value of the block's nth output.

- CSTATE = v

  where v is the value of the block's continuous state vector.

- DSTATE = v

  where v is the value of the blocks discrete state vector.

The debugger also displays the current time, the ID and name of the next method to be executed, and the name of the block to which the method applies in the MATLAB Command Window. The following example illustrates typical debugger outputs after a step command.

Current time   Next method

```
%---------------------------------------------------------------%
[Tm = 2.009509145207664e-005 ] 0:2 Integrator.Outputs 'vdp/x2'
(sldebug @44):
Data of 0:2 Integrator block 'vdp/x2':
U1    = [-2]
Y1    = [-4.0190182904153282e-005]
CSTATE = [-4.0190182904153282e-005]
%---------------------------------------------------------------%
[Tm = 2.009509145207664e-005 ] 0:3 Outport.Outputs 'vdp/Out2'
```

Stepping Commands

Command-line mode provides the following commands for advancing a simulation incrementally:

Command	Advances the simulation...
step [in into]	Into the next method, stopping at the first method in the next method or, if the next method does not contain any methods, at the end of the next method
step over	To the method that follows the next method, executing all methods invoked directly or indirectly by the next method
step out	To the end of the current method, executing any remaining methods invoked by the current method
step top	To the first method of the next time step (i.e., the top of the simulation loop)
step blockmth	To the next block method to be executed, executing all intervening model- and system-level methods
next	Same as step over

Buttons in the debugger toolbar allow you to access these commands in GUI mode.

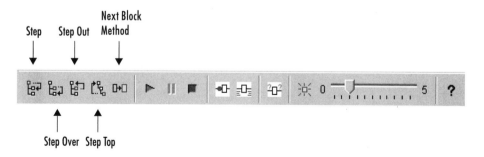

Clicking a button has the same effect as entering the corresponding command at the debugger command line.

11-17

Continuing a Simulation

In GUI mode, the Stop button turns red when the debugger suspends the simulation for any reason. To continue the simulation, click the Start/Continue button. In command-line mode, enter continue to continue the simulation. By default, the debugger runs the simulation to the next breakpoint (see "Setting Breakpoints" on page 11-22) or to the end of the simulation, whichever comes first.

Animation Mode

In *animation mode*, the Start/Continue button or the continue command advances the simulation method by method, pausing after each method, to the first method of the next major time step. While running the simulation in animation mode, the debugger uses its debug pointer (see "Debug Pointer" on page 11-20) to indicate on the block diagram which block method is being executed at each step. The moving pointer providing a visual indication of the progress of the simulation.

Note When animation mode is enabled, the debugger does not allow you to set breakpoints and ignores any breakpoints that you set when animating the simulation.

To enable animation when running the debugger in GUI mode, click the Animation Mode toggle button on the debugger's toolbar.

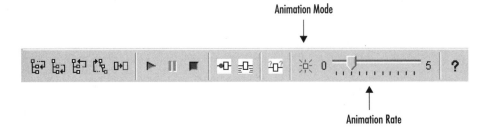

The slider on the debugger toolbar allows you to increase or decrease the delay between method invocations and hence to slow down or speed up the animation rate. To disable animation mode when running the debugger in GUI mode, toggle the Animation Mode button on the toolbar.

To enable animation when running the debugger in command-line mode, enter the animate command at the MATLAB command line. The animate command's optional delay parameter allows you to specify the length of the pause between method invocations (1 second by default) and thereby accelerate or slow down the animation. For example, the command

```
animate 0.5
```

causes the animation to run at twice its default rate. To disable animation mode when running the debugger in command-line mode, enter

```
animate stop
```

at the MATLAB command line.

Running a Simulation Nonstop

The run command lets you run a simulation to the end of the simulation, skipping any intervening breakpoints. At the end of the simulation, the debugger returns you to the MATLAB command line. To continue debugging a model, you must restart the debugger.

Note The GUI mode does not provide a graphical version of the run command. To run the simulation to the end, you must first clear all breakpoints and then click the Start/Continue button.

Debug Pointer

Whenever the debugger stops the simulation at a method, it displays a debug pointer on the block diagram of the model being debugged.

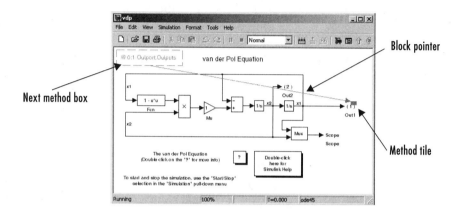

The debug pointer is an annotation that indicates the next method to be executed when simulation resumes. It consists of the following elements:

- Next method box
- Block pointer
- Method tile

Next Method Box

The next method box appears in the upper left corner of the block diagram. It specifies the name and ID of the next method to be executed.

Block Pointer

The block pointer appears when the next method is a block method. It indicates the block on which the next method operates.

Method Tile

The method tile is a rectangular patch of color that appears when the next method is a block method. The tile overlays a portion of the block on which the next method executes. The color and position of the tile on the block indicate the type of the next block method as follows.

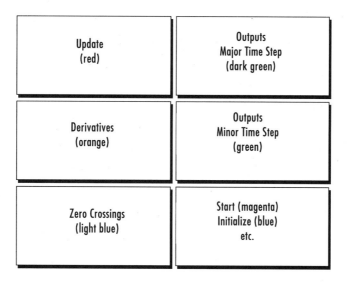

In animation mode, the tiles persist for the length of the current major time step and a number appears in each tile. The number specifies the number of times that the corresponding method has been invoked for the block thus far in the time step.

Setting Breakpoints

The Simulink debugger allows you to define stopping points in a simulation called breakpoints. You can then run a simulation from breakpoint to breakpoint, using the debugger's continue command. The debugger lets you define two types of breakpoints: unconditional and conditional. An unconditional breakpoint occurs whenever a simulation reaches a method that you specified previously. A conditional breakpoint occurs when a condition that you specified in advance arises in the simulation.

Breakpoints are useful when you know that a problem occurs at a certain point in your program or when a certain condition occurs. By defining an appropriate breakpoint and running the simulation via the continue command, you can skip immediately to the point in the simulation where the problem occurs.

Setting Unconditional Breakpoints

You can set unconditional breakpoints from the

- Debugger toolbar
- **Simulation Loop** pane
- MATLAB Command Window (command-line mode only)

Setting Breakpoints from the Debugger Toolbar

To set a breakpoint on a block's methods, select the block and then click the Breakpoint button on the debugger toolbar.

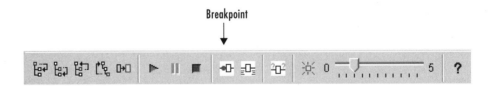

The debugger displays the name of the selected block in the **Break/Display points** panel of its **Breakpoints** pane.

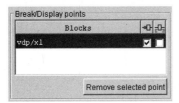

Note Clicking the Breakpoint button on the toolbar sets breakpoints on the invocations of a block's methods in major time steps. To enable breakpoints in minor time steps, you must select the debugger's **Minor time steps** option (see "Breaking in Minor Time Steps" on page 11-27).

You can temporarily disable the breakpoints on a block by deselecting the check box in the breakpoints column of the panel. To clear the breakpoints on a block and remove its entry from the panel, select the entry and then click the **Remove selected point** button on the panel.

Note You cannot set a breakpoint on a virtual block. A virtual block is a block whose function is purely graphical: it indicates a grouping or relationship among a model's computational blocks. The debugger warns you if you attempt to set a breakpoint on a virtual block. You can obtain a listing of a model's nonvirtual blocks, using the slist command (see "Displaying a Model's Nonvirtual Blocks" on page 11-33).

Setting Breakpoints from the Simulation Loop Pane

To set a breakpoint at a particular invocation of a method displayed in the Simulation Loop pane, select the check box next to the method's name in the breakpoint column of the pane.

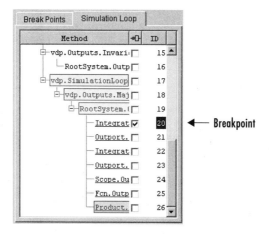

To clear the breakpoint, deselect the check box.

Setting Breakpoints from the MATLAB Command Window

In command-line mode, use the break and bafter commands to set breakpoints before or after a specified method, respectively. Use the clear command to clear breakpoints.

Setting Conditional Breakpoints

You can use either the **Break on conditions** panel of the debugger's **Breakpoints** pane

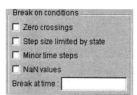

or the following commands (in command-line mode) to set conditional breakpoints.

Command	Causes Simulation to Stop
`tbreak [t]`	At a simulation time step
`minor`	At methods invoked in minor time steps
`nanbreak`	At the occurrence of an underflow or overflow (NaN) or infinite (Inf) value
`xbreak`	When the simulation reaches the state that determines the simulation step size
`zcbreak`	When a zero crossing occurs between simulation time steps

Setting Breakpoints at Time Steps

To set a breakpoint at a time step, enter a time in the debugger's **Break at time** field (GUI mode) or enter the time using the `tbreak` command. This causes the debugger to stop the simulation at the Outputs.Major method of the model at the first time step that follows the specified time. For example, starting `vdp` in debug mode and entering the commands

```
tbreak 2
continue
```

causes the debugger to halt the simulation at the `vdp.Outputs.Major` method of time step 2.078 as indicated by the output of the `continue` command.

```
%------------------------------------------------------------%
[TM = 2.078784598291364     ] vdp.Outputs.Major

(sldebug @18):
```

Breaking on Nonfinite Values

Selecting the debugger's **NaN values** option or entering the `nanbreak` command causes the simulation to stop when a computed value is infinite or outside the range of values that can be represented by the machine running the simulation. This option is useful for pinpointing computational errors in a Simulink model.

Breaking on Step-Size Limiting Steps

Selecting the **Step size limited by state** option or entering the xbreak command causes the debugger to stop the simulation when the model uses a variable-step solver and the solver encounters a state that limits the size of the steps that it can take. This command is useful in debugging models that appear to require an excessive number of simulation time steps to solve.

Breaking at Zero Crossings

Selecting the **Zero crossings** option or entering the zcbreak command causes the simulation to halt when Simulink detects a nonsampled zero crossing in a model that includes blocks where zero crossings can arise. After halting, Simulink displays the location in the model, the time, and the type (rising or falling) of the zero crossing. For example, setting a zero-crossing break at the start of execution of the zeroxing demo model,

```
sldebug zeroxing
%-----------------------------------------------------------------%
[TM = 0                        ] zeroxing.Simulate
(sldebug @0): zcbreak
Break at zero crossing events             : enabled
```

and continuing the simulation

```
(sldebug @0): continue
```

results in a rising zero-crossing break at

```
[Tz = 0.2                      ] [Hz = 0                        ]
Detected 2 Zero Crossing Events 0:5:1R, 0:5:2R
%-----------------------------------------------------------------%
[Tm = 0.4                      ] zeroxing.ZeroCrossingDetectionLoop
(sldebug @45):
```

If a model does not include blocks capable of producing nonsampled zero crossings, the command prints a message advising you of this fact.

Breaking in Minor Time Steps

To break at invocations of a block's methods in minor time steps, select the **Minor time steps** option on the debugger's **Break on conditions** panel or enter minor at the debugger command prompt.

Note For this option to take effect, you must previously or subsequently set breakpoints on all the block's methods, using either the Breakpoint button on the debugger's toolbar or the break gcb or bafter gcb command. This option has no effect on breakpoints set on specific invocations of a block's methods set in either the **Simulation Loop** pane or via the break/bafter m:id commands.

Displaying Information About the Simulation

The Simulink debugger provides a set of commands that allow you to display block states, block inputs and outputs, and other information while running a model.

Displaying Block I/O

The debugger allows you to display block I/O by clicking the appropriate buttons on the debugger toolbar

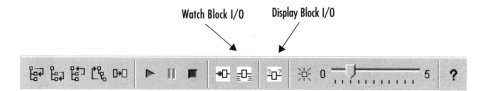

Watch Block I/O   Display Block I/O

or by entering the appropriate debugger command.

Command	Displays a Block's I/O
probe	Immediately
disp	At every breakpoint
trace	Whenever the block executes

Displaying I/O of Selected Block

To display the I/O of a block, select the block and click ⊞ in GUI mode or enter the probe command in command-line mode.

Command	Description
probe	Enter or exit probe mode. In probe mode, the debugger displays the current inputs and outputs of any block that you select in the model's block diagram. Typing any command causes the debugger to exit probe mode.
probe gcb	Display I/O of selected block.
probe s:b	Print the I/O of the block specified by system number s and block number b.

The debugger prints the current inputs, outputs, and states of the selected block in the debugger **Outputs** pane (GUI mode) or the MATLAB Command Window.

The probe command is useful when you need to examine the I/O of a block whose I/O is not otherwise displayed. For example, suppose you are using the step command to run a model method by method. Each time you step the simulation, the debugger displays the inputs and outputs of the current block. The probe command lets you examine the I/O of other blocks as well.

Displaying Block I/O Automatically at Breakpoints

The disp command causes the debugger to display a specified block's inputs and outputs whenever it halts the simulation. You can specify a block either by entering its block index or by selecting it in the block diagram and entering gcb as the disp command argument. You can remove any block from the debugger's list of display points, using the undisp command. For example, to remove block 0:0, either select the block in the model diagram and enter undisp gcb or simply enter undisp 0:0.

Note Automatic display of block I/O at breakpoints is not available in the debugger's GUI mode.

The disp command is useful when you need to monitor the I/O of a specific block or set of blocks as you step through a simulation. Using the disp command, you can specify the blocks you want to monitor and the debugger will then redisplay the I/O of those blocks on every step. Note that the debugger always displays the I/O of the current block when you step through a model block by block, using the step command. You do not need to use the disp command if you are interested in watching only the I/O of the current block.

Watching Block I/O

To watch a block, select the block and click ▤ in the debugger toolbar or enter the trace command. In GUI mode, if a breakpoint exists on the block, you can set a watch on it as well by selecting the check box for the block in the watch column ▤ of the **Break/Display points** pane. In command-line mode, you can also specify the block by specifying its block index in the trace command. You can remove a block from the debugger's list of trace points using the untrace command.

The debugger displays a watched block's I/O whenever the block executes. Watching a block allows you obtain a complete record of the block's I/O without having to stop the simulation.

Displaying Algebraic Loop Information

The atrace command causes the debugger to display information about a model's algebraic loops (see "Algebraic Loops" on page 2-23) each time they are solved. The command takes a single argument that specifies the amount of information to display.

Command	Displays for Each Algebraic Loop
atrace 0	No information
atrace 1	The loop variable solution, the number of iterations required to solve the loop, and the estimated solution error
atrace 2	Same as level 1
atrace 3	Level 2 plus the Jacobian matrix used to solve the loop
atrace 4	Level 3 plus intermediate solutions of the loop variable

Displaying System States

The states debug command lists the current values of the system's states in the MATLAB Command Window. For example, the following sequence of commands shows the states of the Simulink bouncing ball demo (bounce) after its first and second time steps.

```
sldebug bounce
[Tm=0                        ] **Start** of system 'bounce' outputs
(sldebug @0:0 'bounce/Position'): states
Continuous state vector (value,index,name):
  10                         0 (0:0 'bounce/Position')
  15                         1 (0:5 'bounce/Velocity')
(sldebug @0:0 'bounce/Position'): next
[Tm=0.01                     ] **Start** of system 'bounce' outputs
(sldebug @0:0 'bounce/Position'): states
Continuous state vector (value,index,name):
  10.1495095                 0 (0:0 'bounce/Position')
  14.9019                    1 (0:5 'bounce/Velocity')
```

Displaying Integration Information

The ishow command toggles display of integration information. When enabled, this option causes the debugger to display a message each time the simulation takes a time step or encounters a state that limits the size of a time step. In the first case, the debugger displays the size of the time step, for example,

```
[Tm=9.996264188473381    ] Step of 0.01 was taken by integrator
```

In the second case, the debugger displays the state that currently determines the size of time steps, for example,

```
[Ts=9.676264188473388    ] Integration limited by 1st state of
block 0:0 'bounce/Position'
```

Displaying Information About the Model

In addition to providing information about a simulation, the debugger can provide you with information about the model that underlies the simulation.

Displaying a Model's Sorted Lists

In GUI mode, the debugger's **Sorted List** pane displays lists of blocks for a model's root system and each nonvirtual subsystem. Each list lists the blocks that the subsystems contains sorted according to their computational dependencies, alphabetical order, and other block sorting rules. In command-line mode, you can use the slist command to display a model's sorted lists.

```
---- Sorted list for 'vdp' [12 blocks, 9 nonvirtual blocks,
directFeed=0]
  0:0    'vdp/Integrator1' (Integrator)
  0:1    'vdp/Out1' (Outport)
  0:2    'vdp/Integrator2' (Integrator)
  0:3    'vdp/Out2' (Outport)
  0:4    'vdp/Fcn' (Fcn)
  0:5    'vdp/Product' (Product)
  0:6    'vdp/Mu' (Gain)
  0:7    'vdp/Scope' (Scope)
  0:8    'vdp/Sum' (Sum)
```

These displays include the block index for each command. You can thus use them to determine the block IDs of the model's blocks. Some debugger commands accept block IDs as arguments.

Identifying Blocks in Algebraic Loops

If a block belongs to an algebraic list, the slist command displays an algebraic loop identifier in the entry for the block in the sorted list. The identifier has the form

```
algId=s#n
```

where s is the index of the subsystem containing the algebraic loop and n is the index of the algebraic loop in the subsystem. For example, the following entry for an Integrator block indicates that it participates in the first algebraic loop at the root level of the model.

```
0:1 'test/ss/I1' (Integrator, tid=0) [algId=0#1, discontinuity]
```

You can use the debugger's ashow command to highlight the blocks and lines that make up an algebraic loop. See "Displaying Algebraic Loops" on page 11-35 for more information.

Displaying a Block

To determine the block in a model's diagram that corresponds to a particular index, enter bshow s:b at the command prompt, where s:b is the block index. The bshow command opens the system containing the block (if necessary) and selects the block in the system's window.

Displaying a Model's Nonvirtual Systems

The systems command displays a list of the nonvirtual systems in the model being debugged. For example, the Simulink clutch demo (clutch) contains the following systems:

```
sldebug clutch
[Tm=0                          ] **Start** of system 'clutch' outputs
(sldebug @0:0 'clutch/Clutch Pedal'): systems
  0    'clutch'
  1    'clutch/Locked'
  2    'clutch/Unlocked'
```

Note The systems command does not list subsystems that are purely graphical in nature, that is, subsystems that the model diagram represents as Subsystem blocks but that Simulink solves as part of a parent system. In Simulink models, the root system and triggered or enabled subsystems are true systems. All other subsystems are virtual (that is, graphical) and hence do not appear in the listing produced by the systems command.

Displaying a Model's Nonvirtual Blocks

The slist command displays a list of the nonvirtual blocks in a model. The listing groups the blocks by system. For example, the following sequence of commands produces a list of the nonvirtual blocks in the Van der Pol (vdp) demo model.

```
sldebug vdp
[Tm=0                            ] **Start** of system 'vdp' outputs
(sldebug @0:0 'vdp/Integrator1'): slist
---- Sorted list for 'vdp' [12 blocks, 9 nonvirtual blocks,
directFeed=0]
  0:0      'vdp/Integrator1' (Integrator)
  0:1      'vdp/Out1' (Outport)
  0:2      'vdp/Integrator2' (Integrator)
  0:3      'vdp/Out2' (Outport)
  0:4      'vdp/Fcn' (Fcn)
  0:5      'vdp/Product' (Product)
  0:6      'vdp/Mu' (Gain)
  0:7      'vdp/Scope' (Scope)
  0:8      'vdp/Sum' (Sum)
```

Note The slist command does not list blocks that are purely graphical in nature, that is, blocks that indicate relationships or groupings among computational blocks.

Displaying Blocks with Potential Zero Crossings

The zclist command displays a list of blocks in which nonsampled zero crossings can occur during a simulation. For example, zclist displays the following list for the clutch sample model:

```
(sldebug @0:0 'clutch/Clutch Pedal'): zclist
  2:3     'clutch/Unlocked/Sign' (Signum)
  0:4     'clutch/Lockup Detection/Velocities Match' (HitCross)
  0:10    'clutch/Lockup Detection/Required Friction
            for Lockup/Abs' (Abs)
  0:11    'clutch/Lockup Detection/Required Friction for
            Lockup/ Relational Operator' (RelationalOperator)
  0:18    'clutch/Break Apart Detection/Abs' (Abs)
  0:20    'clutch/Break Apart Detection/Relational Operator'
            (RelationalOperator)
```

```
0:24   'clutch/Unlocked' (SubSystem)
0:27   'clutch/Locked' (SubSystem)
```

Displaying Algebraic Loops

The ashow command highlights a specified algebraic loop or the algebraic loop that contains a specified block. To highlight a specified algebraic loop, enter ashow s#n, where s is the index of the system (see "Identifying Blocks in Algebraic Loops" on page 11-32) that contains the loop and n is the index of the loop in the system. To display the loop that contains the currently selected block, enter ashow gcb. To show a loop that contains a specified block, enter ashow s:b, where s:b is the block's index. To clear algebraic-loop highlighting from the model diagram, enter ashow clear.

Displaying Debugger Status

In GUI mode, the debugger displays the settings of various debug options, such as conditional breakpoints, in its **Status** panel. In command-line mode, the status command displays debugger settings. For example, the following sequence of commands displays the initial debug settings for the vdp model:

```
sim('vdp',[0,10],simset('debug','on'))
[Tm=0                          ] **Start** of system 'vdp' outputs
(sldebug @0:0 'vdp/Integrator1'): status
  Current simulation time: 0 (MajorTimeStep)
  Last command: ""
  Stop in minor times steps is disabled.
  Break at zero crossing events is disabled.
  Break when step size is limiting by a state is disabled.
  Break on non-finite (NaN,Inf) values is disabled.
  Display of integration information is disabled.
  Algebraic loop tracing level is at 0.
```

Block Libraries

The following sections describe the usage and contents of the Simulink block libraries. You can use either the Simulink Library Browser on Windows or the MATLAB command `simulink` on UNIX to display and browse the libraries.

Commonly Used (p. A-2)	Blocks from other libraries that most models use.
Continuous (p. A-4)	Blocks that model linear functions.
Discontinuities (p. A-5)	Blocks whose outputs are discontinuous functions of their inputs.
Discrete (p. A-6)	Blocks that represent discrete-time functions.
Logic and Bit Operations (p. A-8)	Blocks that represent discrete-time functions.
Lookup Tables (p. A-10)	Blocks that use lookup tables to determine outputs from inputs.
Math Operations (p. A-11)	Blocks that model general mathematical functions.
Model Verification (p. A-13)	Blocks that enable you to create self-validating models.
Model-Wide Utilities (p. A-15)	Various utility blocks.
Ports & Subsystems (p. A-16)	Blocks for creating various types of subsystems.
Signal Attributes (p. A-18)	Blocks that modify or output attributes of signals.
Signal Routing (p. A-19)	Blocks that route signals from one point in a block diagram to another.
Sinks (p. A-21)	Blocks that display or write block output.
Sources (p. A-22)	Blocks that generate signals.
User-Defined Functions (p. A-24)	Blocks that allow you to define the function that relates inputs to outputs.
Simulink Extras (p. A-25)	Blocks that perform specialized operations.

Commonly Used

The Commonly Used library contains blocks from other libraries that most models use.

Block Name	Purpose
Bus Creator	Create a signal bus.
Bus Selector	Select signals from an incoming bus.
Constant	Generate a constant value.
Data Type Conversion	Convert an input signal to a specified data type.
Discrete Time Integrator	Perform discrete-time integration or accumulation of a signal.
Gain	Multiply the input by a constant.
Ground	Ground an unconnected input port.
Inport	Create an input port for a subsystem or an external input.
Integrator	Integrate a signal.
Logical Operator	Perform the specified logical operation on the input.
Mux	Combine several input signals into a vector or bus output signal.
Outport	Create an output port for a subsystem or an external output.
Product	Multiply or divide inputs.
Relational Operator	Perform the specified relational operation on the inputs.
Saturation	Limit the range of a signal.

Block Name	Purpose
Scope	Display signals generated during a simulation.
Subsystem	Represent a system within another system.
Sum	Add or subtract inputs.
Switch	Switch output between the first input and the third input based on the value of the second input.
Terminator	Terminate an unconnected output port.
Unit Delay	Delay a signal one sample period.

Continuous

The Continuous library contains blocks that model linear functions.

Block Name	Purpose
Derivative	Output the time derivative of the input.
Integrator	Integrate a signal.
State-Space	Implement a linear state-space system.
Transfer Fcn	Implement a linear transfer function.
Transport Delay	Delay the input by a given amount of time.
Variable Transport Delay	Delay the input by a variable amount of time.
Zero-Pole	Implement a transfer function specified in terms of poles and zeros.

Discontinuities

The Discontinuities library contains blocks whose outputs are discontinuous functions of their inputs.

Block Name	Purpose
Backlash	Model the behavior of a system with play.
Coulomb and Viscous Friction	Model discontinuity at zero, with linear gain elsewhere.
Dead Zone	Provide a region of zero output.
Dead Zone Dynamic	Set inputs within dynamically determined bounds to zero.
Hit Crossing	Detect crossing point.
Quantizer	Discretize input at a specified interval.
Rate Limiter	Limit the rate of change of a signal.
Rate Limiter Dynamic	Limit the rising and falling rates of the signal.
Relay	Switch output between two constants.
Saturation	Limit the range of a signal.
Saturation Dynamic	Bound the range of the input to limits that can change with time.

Discrete

The Discrete library contains blocks that represent discrete-time functions.

Block Name	Purpose
Difference	Calculate the change in a signal over one time step.
Discrete Derivative	Compute a discrete time derivative.
Discrete Filter	Implement IIR and FIR filters.
Discrete State-Space	Implement a discrete state-space system.
Discrete Transfer Fcn	Implement a discrete transfer function.
Discrete Zero-Pole	Implement a discrete transfer function specified in terms of poles and zeros.
Discrete-Time Integrator	Perform discrete-time integration of a signal.
First-Order Hold	Implement a first-order sample-and-hold.
Memory	Output the block input from the previous time step.
Tapped Delay	Delay a scalar signal for multiple sample periods and output all the delayed versions.
Transfer Fcn First Order	Implement a discrete-time first-order transfer function.
Transfer Fcn Lead or Lag	Implement a discrete-time lead or lag compensator.
Transfer Fcn Real Zero	Implement a discrete-time transfer function that has a real zero and no pole.
Unit Delay	Delay a signal one sample period.

Block Name	Purpose
Weighted Moving Average	Implement a weighted moving average.
Zero-Order Hold	Implement zero-order hold of one sample period.

Logic and Bit Operations

The Logic and Bit Operations library contains blocks that apply logic and bit operations to their inputs.

Block Name	Purpose
Bit Clear	Set the specified bit of the stored integer to zero.
Bitwise Operator	Perform the specified bitwise operation on the inputs.
Combinatorial Logic	Implement a truth table.
Compare To Constant	Determine how a signal compares to the specified constant.
Compare To Zero	Determine how a signal compares to zero.
Detect Change	Detect a change in a signal's value.
Detect Decrease	Detect a decrease in a signal's value.
Detect Fall Negative	Detect a falling edge when the signal's value decreases to a strictly negative value, and its previous value was nonnegative.
Detect Fall Nonpositive	Detect a falling edge when the signal's value decreases to a nonpositive value, and its previous value was strictly positive.
Detect Increase	Detect an increase in a signal's value.
Detect Rise Nonnegative	Detect a rising edge when a signal's value increases to a nonnegative value, and its previous value was strictly negative.
Detect Rise Positive	Detect a rising edge when a signal's value increases to a strictly positive value, and its previous value was nonpositive.

Block Name	Purpose
Extract Bits	Output a selection of contiguous bits from the input signal.
Interval Test	Determine if a signal is in a specified interval.
Interval Test Dynamic	Determine if a signal is in a specified interval whose limits can change.
Logical Operator	Perform the specified logical operation on the input.
Relational Operator	Perform the specified relational operation on the inputs.
Shift Arithmetic	Shift the bits and/or binary point of a signal.

Lookup Tables

The Lookup Tables library contains blocks that use lookup tables to determine outputs from inputs.

Block Name	Purpose
Cosine	Implement a cosine function in fixed point using a lookup table approach that exploits quarter wave symmetry.
Direct Lookup Table (n-D)	Index into an N-dimensional table to retrieve a scalar, vector, or 2-D matrix.
Interpolation (n-D) Using PreLookup	Perform high-performance constant or linear interpolation.
Lookup Table	Perform piecewise linear mapping of the input.
Lookup Table (2-D)	Perform piecewise linear mapping of two inputs.
Lookup Table (n-D)	Perform piecewise linear or spline mapping of two or more inputs.
PreLookup Index Search	Perform index search and interval fraction calculation for input on a breakpoint set.
Sine	Implement a sine wave in fixed point using a lookup table approach that exploits quarter wave symmetry.

Math Operations

The Math Operations library contains blocks that model general mathematical functions.

Block Name	Purpose
Abs	Output the absolute value of the input.
Add	Add or subtract inputs.
Algebraic Constraint	Constrain the input signal to zero.
Assignment	Assign values to specified elements of a signal.
Bias	Add a bias to the input.
Complex to Magnitude-Angle	Output the phase and magnitude of a complex input signal.
Complex to Real-Imag	Output the real and imaginary parts of a complex input signal.
Divide	Multiply or divide inputs.
Dot Product	Generate the dot product.
Gain, Matrix Gain	Multiply block input by a specified value.
Magnitude-Angle to Complex	Output a complex signal from magnitude and phase inputs.
Math Function	Perform a mathematical function.
Matrix Concatenation	Concatenate inputs horizontally or vertically.
MinMax	Output the minimum or maximum input value.
MinMax Running Resettable	Determine the minimum or maximum of a signal over time.

Block Name	Purpose (Continued)
Polynomial	Perform evaluation of polynomial coefficients on input values.
Product	Generate the product or quotient of block inputs.
Real-Imag to Complex	Output a complex signal from real and imaginary inputs.
Reshape	Change the dimensionality of a signal.
Rounding Function	Perform a rounding function.
Sign	Indicate the sign of the input.
Sine Wave Function	Output a sine wave.
Slider Gain	Vary a scalar gain using a slider.
Subtract	Add or subtract inputs.
Sum	Generate the sum of inputs.
Sum of Elements	Add or subtract inputs.
Trigonometric Function	Perform a trigonometric function.
Unary Minus	Negate the input.
Weighted Sample Time Math	Support calculations involving sample time.

Model Verification

Acknowledgment. The Model Verification blocks were developed in conjunction with the Control System Design team of the Advanced Chassis System Development group of DaimlerChrysler AG, Stuttgart, Germany.

The Model Verification library contains blocks that enable you to create self-validating models.

Block Name	Purpose
Assertion	Assert that the input signal is nonzero.
Check Discrete Gradient	Check that the absolute value of the difference between successive samples of a discrete signal is less than an upper bound.
Check Dynamic Gap	Check that a gap of varying width occurs in the range of a signal's amplitudes.
Check Dynamic Lower Bound	Check that a signal is always greater than a value that can vary at each time step.
Check Dynamic Range	Check that a signal always lies in a varying range of amplitudes.
Check Dynamic Upper Bound	Check that a signal is always less than a value that can vary at each time step.
Check Input Resolution	Check that a signal has a specified resolution.
Check Static Gap	Check that a fixed-width gap occurs in the range of a signal's amplitudes
Check Static Lower Bound	Check that a signal is greater than (or optionally equal to) a lower bound that does not vary with time.
Check Static Range	Check that the input signal falls in a fixed range of amplitudes.

Block Name	Purpose (Continued)
Check Static Upper Bound	Check that a signal is less than (or optionally equal to) an upper bound that does not vary with time.

Model-Wide Utilities

The Model-Wide Utilities library contains various utility blocks.

Block Name	Purpose
DocBlock	Create text that documents the model and save the text with the model.
Model Info	Display revision control information in a model.
Time-Based Linearization	Generate linear models in the base workspace at specific times.
Trigger-Based Linearization	Generate linear models in the base workspace when triggered.

Ports & Subsystems

The Ports & Subsystems library contains blocks for creating various types of subsystems.

Block Name	Purpose
Configurable Subsystem	Represent any block selected from a specified library.
Enable	Add an enabling port to a subsystem. Note that this block resides inside the Enabled Subsystem and the Enabled and Triggered Subsystem in the Subsystems library.
Enabled and Triggered Subsystem	Represent an enabled and triggered subsystem.
Enabled Subsystem	Represent an enabled subsystem.
For Iterator Subsystem	Implement a C-like `for` loop.
Function-Call Generator	Execute a function-call subsystem a specified number of times at a specified rate
Function-Call Subsystem	Represent a function-call subsystem.
If	Implement C-like `if-else` statement logic.
If Action Subsystem	Represent a subsystem whose execution is triggered by an If block.
Inport	Create an input port for a subsystem or an external input. Note that this block resides inside the Subsystem block and inside other subsystem blocks in the Subsystems library.
Model	Include a model as a block in another model.

Block Name	Purpose (Continued)
Outport	Create an output port for a subsystem or an external output. Note that this block resides inside the Subsystem block and inside other subsystem blocks in the Subsystems library.
Subsystem, Atomic Subsystem	Represent a system within another system.
Switch Case	Implement C-like `switch` statement logic.
Switch Case Action Subsystem	Represent a subsystem whose execution is triggered by a Switch Case block.
Trigger	Add a trigger port to a subsystem. Note that this block resides inside the Triggered Subsystem and the Enabled and Triggered Subsystem in the Subsystems library.
Triggered Subsystem	Represent a triggered subsystem.
While Iterator Subsystem	Represent a subsystem that executes repeatedly while a condition is satisfied during a simulation time step.

Signal Attributes

The Signal Attributes library contains blocks that modify or output attributes of signals.

Block Name	Purpose
Data Type Conversion	Convert a signal to another data type.
Data Type Conversion Inherited	Convert from one data type to another using inherited data type and scaling.
Data Type Duplicate	Force all inputs to the same data type.
Data Type Scaling Strip	Remove scaling and map to a built-in integer.
IC	Set the initial value of a signal.
Probe	Output a signal's attributes, including width, sample time, and/or signal type.
Rate Transition	Specify the data transfer mechanism between the data rates of a multirate system.
Signal Conversion	Convert a signal to a new type without altering signal values.
Signal Specification	Specify attributes of a signal.
Weighted Sample Time	Support calculations involving sample time.
Width	Output the width of the input vector.

Signal Routing

The Signal Routing library contains blocks that route signals from one point in a block diagram to another.

Block Name	Purpose
Bus Creator	Create a signal bus.
Bus Selector	Output signals selected from an input bus.
Data Store Memory	Define a shared data store.
Data Store Read	Read data from a shared data store.
Data Store Write	Write data to a shared data store.
Demux	Separate a vector signal into output signals.
Environment Controller	Create branches of a block diagram that apply only to simulation or only to code generation.
From	Accept input from a Goto block.
Goto	Pass block input to From blocks.
Goto Tag Visibility	Define the scope of a Goto block tag.
Index Vector	Switch output between different inputs based on the value of the first input.
Manual Switch	Switch between two inputs.
Merge	Combine several input lines into a scalar line.
Multiport Switch	Choose between block inputs.
Mux	Combine several input lines into a vector line.

Block Name	Purpose
Selector	Select or reorder the elements of the input vector.
Switch	Switch between two inputs.

Sinks

The Sinks library contains blocks that display or write block output.

Block Name	Purpose
Display	Show the value of the input.
Outport	Create an output port for a subsystem or an external output.
Scope	Display signals generated during a simulation.
Stop Simulation	Stop the simulation when the input is nonzero.
Terminator	Terminate an unconnected output port.
To File	Write data to a file.
To Workspace	Write data to a variable in the workspace.
XY Graph	Display an X-Y plot of signals using a MATLAB figure window.

Sources

The Sources library contains blocks that generate signals.

Block Name	Purpose
Band-Limited White Noise	Introduce white noise into a continuous system.
Chirp Signal	Generate a sine wave with increasing frequency.
Clock	Display and provide the simulation time.
Constant	Generate a constant value.
Counter Free-Running	Count up and overflow back to zero after the maximum value possible is reached for the specified number of bits.
Counter Limited	Count up and wrap back to zero after outputting the specified upper limit.
Digital Clock	Generate simulation time at the specified sampling interval.
From File	Read data from a file.
From Workspace	Read data from a variable defined in the workspace.
Ground	Ground an unconnected input port.
Inport	Create an input port for a subsystem or an external input.
Pulse Generator	Generate pulses at regular intervals.
Ramp	Generate a constantly increasing or decreasing signal.
Random Number	Generate normally distributed random numbers.

Block Name	Purpose (Continued)
Repeating Sequence	Generate a repeatable arbitrary signal.
Repeating Sequence Interpolated	Output discrete-time sequence and repeat, interpolating between data points.
Repeating Sequence Stair	Output and repeat the discrete time sequence.
Signal Builder	Generate an arbitrary piecewise linear signal.
Signal Generator	Generate various waveforms.
Sine Wave	Generate a sine wave.
Step	Generate a step function.
Uniform Random Number	Generate uniformly distributed random numbers.

User-Defined Functions

The User-Defined Functions library contains blocks that allow you to define the function that relates inputs to outputs.

Block Name	Purpose
Embedded MATLAB Function	Include MATLAB code in models that generate embeddable C code.
Fcn	Apply a specified expression to the input.
MATLAB Fcn	Apply a MATLAB function or expression to the input.
M-File S-Function	Use a Level-2 M-file S-function in a model.
S-Function	Access an S-function.
S-Function Builder	Build a C MEX S-function from specifications and code that you supply.

Simulink Extras

The Extras block library c ontains specialized blocks.

Index